THE EDUCATION OF WADHURST

THE EDUCATION OF WADHURST

Kenneth F. Ascott

The Book Guild Ltd
Sussex, England

The Book Guild Ltd.
25 High Street,
Lewes, Sussex

First published 1998
© Kenneth F. Ascott 1998

Set in Times

Typesetting by
Acorn Bookwork, Salisbury, Wiltshire

Printed in Great Britain by
Antony Rowe Ltd, Chippenham, Wiltshire

A catalogue record for this book is
available from the British Library

ISBN 1 85776 209 6

CONTENTS

PREFACE

This is an account of the education of Wadhurst parish, East Sussex, by church and school, community and state, as expressed through village records, school log-books, parish magazines, the memories of old inhabitants and the history of state intervention.

The material, with more than local implication, for the most part speaks for itself, to tell not only of the slow and the uncertain pace of educational advancement, dependent only too often on the goodwill of too few people, but also of the social conditions and attitudes against which it progressed.

Although this account ends shortly after the outbreak of the 1914–18 war, past and present are linked by a short postscript and educational pronouncements made towards the end of the twentieth century.

1

The Education of Wadhurst

Introduction

Wadhurst is a large Wealden village on the Kent–Sussex border. Six miles from Tunbridge Wells and about an hour's train journey from London, it is set in the midst of still beautiful, unspoilt countryside.

In spite of a plane crash on the village in 1956, which led to a pathetic rebuilding of the southern side of the High Street, and with the presence of overmuch traffic and street parking, the village is worth visiting.

Back from the village, but gently grasped by it, is the spired church of St Peter and St Paul, with its floor paved in many places with iron ledgers, relics of the Wealden iron industry.

Further down the road is the old church school, now used for other purposes. Opposite, hidden among the trees, is the secondary school, now the Uplands Community College. Back up the village street, past the Old Vicarage, Hill House and the fire station, in the adjoining hamlet of Sparrows Green, is the present primary school, still a church school.

Wadhurst College, a private school for girls, is a little apart from the hamlet, in Mayfield Lane, and has near it the Roman Catholic Church with its own primary school.

Wadhurst is a growing area, but back in the thirteenth century it was already a chartered town, with a fair, market, pillory and tumbrel, as well as its own vicar. The church was the community's centre, but if it had a school attached, no record remains.[1]

Whether William Wyly, Godfrey of Combe, Petronilla of

1

Buckhurst, Richard Carpenter or any of the other inhabitants who at this time held land of the Archbishop, for service, rent, or Hen-rent, could read or write, is lost in time. Long dark nights, the pinch of cold and hard work on the land prevented, for most, anything but education by the environment, the church[2] and for some, there was contact with the world outside, for Wadhurst, although remote, was not inaccessible. Archbishops, with their retinues, passed through its boundaries, to visit their manor of Malling, in which Wadhurst was situated, and to stay at their palace in Mayfield. King Edward I[3] and other processions of the great, came this way. Carrier and other services for the Archbishop, took Wadhurst men to Lewes and to Croydon and some conducted the Archbishop, or his men, through the Weald.

Although during the thirteenth century ten men from the neighbouring village of Lamberhurst received their first tonsures, three more became subdeacons, and another the Abbot of Robertsbridge, no inhabitant of Wadhurst appears to have been so inspired, encouraged, or enabled to seek the education that would make such things possible.

Wills

It was not until 1568 that the first known direct mention of education occurred in Wadhurst. This was in the will of Nicholas Turke, whose family had held land in Wadhurst since the fourteenth century. He directed that, in default of issue by his cousin John, all his lands in Wadhurst, free and copyhold, should be left to the poor children of the Greyfriars,[4] in Newgate market, London, for ever, on condition that the 'masters and governors for the tyme beinge shall take and kepe in the said house to learninge tooe poore children of the pish of Wadhurst...' However, it appears that cousin John did have issue, for there is no record of any children from Wadhurst being so educated.

Seventy years later, in 1638, Gregory Markwicke of Mayfield, yeoman, whose father had held property in Wadhurst, left £6 to the poor of Wadhurst, together with 10s for a sermon on the day of distribution, 'That the poor should be instructed as well of the good of their souls as relieved for the supportacion of their bodies', and William Kitchenham of Wadhurst, who died in 1676, provided 10s to the minister for the time being for preaching a sermon on Ascension Day, as well as the yearly sum of 10s for the 'ancientist poore', and further, The Society for the Promotion of Christian Knowledge, established in 1698, made efforts to set up charity schools[5] countrywide. However, it was not until 1716 that the next direct mention of education was made. This was in the will of Lucy Barham,[6] wife of John Barham of Shoesmiths,[7] ironmaster and onetime Sheriff of Sussex.

Lucy made her will in July 1716, two months before she died. She directed that £5 a year, chargeable on Shoesmiths, should be given for the teaching of 'Such poor children to read whose parents are not of ability to have them taught'. She also 'relieved' the bodies of 12 Wadhurst poor, not receiving relief, by leaving a further £5 4s a year to buy 12 twopenny loaves, to be distributed after evening service.

It is not known who taught, or who did benefit from the terms of Lucy's will at this time, or what educational opportunities existed for those who could pay, but over the country, private schools of the 'dame' variety abounded and, doubtless, they were to be found in Wadhurst.

It is, perhaps, significant that in an account book kept between 1760 and 1783 by Wadhurst's vicar, Samuel Bush, out of 107 people – tradesmen, farmers and servants – only six needed to receipt his payments with a cross.

A poor, sick, old lady, living away from the parish, was able to write to its overseer, Thomas Patey:

I am verey bad of the Destemper ... and Have nothing to help myself ... Dokter will Dou nothing exsept you will sen to him to se him payed if not you moust send for me ... my life is a burden to me so from you fren Marey Whit ... I bound to Cut(?) the Ropemaker for I fare I shall never be well no more.

3

(From 1662, various Acts of Settlement ordered that incomers to a parish who fell on hard times should be returned to their parish of origin. The system sometimes caused the break-up of families – some members retained, others sent back.)

It is, perhaps, also of significance that Samuel Bush said of his parishioners: 'There is no other difference or distinction amongst the inhabitants than that of rich and poor, they being in every other respect upon a perfect equality.'

Interlude: The Rev. Samuel Bush, Vicar of Wadhurst 1743–83

Samuel Bush, an Oxford MA, endured nearly 40 years of strife with his parishioners. They underpaid their tithes – in his first year in Wadhurst, Bush received £195 instead of the £300 due to him – unfairly charged him for rates, distrained on his goods for nonpayment, tampered with his mail and, for absence from his parish, reported him to the Archbishop.

During these years, there was no vicarage and Bush lodged with John Legas, ironmaster of the Lamberhurst Works, at what is now known as the Old Vicarage.

When, in 1745, Legas moved to his newly built Hill House, Bush remained as a tenant and later, in his memoirs, claimed that Legas offered him both house and niece, Anne. (Bush also claimed that, shortly after his removal to Hill House, Legas was fined £2,000 for supplying guns to the French.) Anne, however, in 1751, married Richard Tapsell, who, on John Legas's death the following year, inherited the Lamberhurst Works and Anne, the house. Bush had to find other accommodation. In 1759 Anne died and in 1765 Richard Tapsell went bankrupt. Bush bought Tapsell's life interest in the house and returned to it. In order that no future Vicar of Wadhurst should be homeless, as he had been, Samuel Bush left money to buy a house suitable as a vicarage, which proved to be the one in which he had lived.

From 1750, he suffered from a stone in his bladder. Twenty-five years later, he wrote that it was: 'Still remaining there ... attended with the most accute pain of body as well as anguish of mind.'

Although Bush recorded the purchase of books, including four volumes of Erskine's *Sermons*, Buchart's *Geography Folio*, seven volumes of Yoking's *Works*, a subscription to a circulating library and, in 1770, spent more on such items – £14 11s 10½d – than on a year's wages for his three servants, Ann Mandy, Harry Wickham and Mary Manser, which together came to £12, there is no evidence that, beset as he was by tribulations, Bush was able to take any real interest in his parishioners' education, let alone their spiritual and material well-being.

Bush's curate received £10 a quarter for serving the cure. Bush's other expenses included: Mr Blackman's bill for medicine: 11s, a year's powdering and buckling of his wig: 12s, John Eldrige for weaving 44 yards of diaper table linen: £3 13s 4d, five pairs of worsted knit hose: £1 8s, waistcoat, breeches and trimming and making: £7 2s.

Samuel Bush died in 1783 and was buried in the chancel of his church.

Teenager, Eighteenth Century

'After having been at public devotions with the ordinary near an hour, Roberts and Taplin had their irons knocked off and were put in a cart and conveyed to Bow St., the place destined for their execution – Roberts was a child of fourteen years and seven months, apprentice, ... (he) was decently dressed in brown clothes and a hearse waiting to receive his body. ... The gallows were fixed close to the end of Bow St. so that both prisoners saw the houses for which they suffered. ... They were stood in a cart which was then moved away'. *Universal Magazine*, July 1770.

During riots, Richard Roberts had destroyed a house in Bow Street. Taplin had obtained 2s 6d by threats from an apothecary of Bow Street.

The First Sunday School – The Rev. A. Litchfield, Vicar of Wadhurst 1783–1804

Bush was succeeded by the Rev. A. Litchfield, who was also an Oxford MA, married, with two daughters and had witnessed Bush's will. Litchfield retained his living at Noke, Oxfordshire, at which he was to spend six months of every year. Like Bush, he appeared preoccupied with tithes, taxes and other expenses and receipts of the living. When considering his acceptance of the living he wrote: 'Tythes, £270, Surplice Fees, £10, Land Tax, £45, Curate, £60, Tythe Feast, £10.'

When he arrived in Wadhurst, Mr Litchfield recorded an account of Mr Bush's Tithe Treat. It lasted two days and included:

About 30 stone of Beef, but sometimes less – 2 rounds and 1 Rump each day.

Near a Bushel of Flour used in Puddings for the two days and about 11 pounds of Currants and Raisins both together.

Near a Bushel of Flour used for Bread.

About 6 or 7 of the Principal People used to dine each day with Mr. Bush.

Generally dined about 2 o'clock.

Sometimes a little common Beer before Dinner.

Fifty people sit down each Day at the 2nd Table – Nothing but Beer at the 2nd Table.

Strong Beer and Wine in the Parlour.

Mr. Bush used to mix with the Strong Beer about 24 Gallons of Mild Ale made out of 3 Bushels of Malt.

No Cheese at the 2nd Table.

Common Small Beer with Dinner and Ale and Strong Beer mixed after Dinner.

The 3 Bushels of Malt brew'd in Sept. – A gallon of salt for the Beef.

Two holes made in the Casks and never draw'd below the 1st Hole on the First Day.

In spite of the distractions, Mr Litchfield managed to note that the workhouse, which was by the south-eastern entrance to the churchyard, had its own school of 20 workhouse children. He used Mr Bush's old account book to write of it: 'The difficulty is not having a proper room – spinners in the room and in the kitchen too much company.'

Mr Litchfield also recorded that the school's equipment consisted of: 'One Spelling Book, One Bible, (Imperfect). Two Testaments and two old Prayer Books.'

He made no mention of a teacher, nor did he say if he took any action to help the situation, but the school was not forgotten, for on 8 January 1793, from a Communion service collection,[8] £1 6s was spent on 12 Common Prayer Books 'for the use of the Poor House Children in church'.

> *The Workhouse*: Referred to as 'The Old Vine', was bought by the parish in 1778 for £280. By the Gilbert Act of 1783, it was restricted to the aged, impotent and the young: others received out-relief. At the time of Litchfield's death in 1804, there were 55 adults together with 220 children, on out-relief. In the workhouse, there were 46 people, together with 13 over 60, or disabled.

The eighteenth century had seen widespread establishment of Sunday schools, as a means of educating poor children through the teaching of Christian principles. At first, reading only was taught, for which the Bible, service books and other allied material were used. This was the better to observe religious duties, as attendance at church services, for both teacher and taught, was considered obligatory.

The establishment of Sunday schools is usually associated with Robert Raikes, who set up a Sunday school in Gloucester in 1780, but they had existed from earlier in the century through the work of such as John Wesley and others. By 1795, nearly 250,000 children throughout the country attended, for on Sundays, children were wanted by neither parent nor employer.

Hannah More, authoress and educationalist, was influenced by the idea and set up schools in the Mendip area. She wrote:

I allow of no writing for the poor. My object is not to make fanatics but to train the lower classes in habits of industry and piety. I know of no way of teaching morals but by teaching principles: or by inculcating Christian principles without imparting a knowledge of Scripture.

During the week, coarse work, 'to fit them for servants', was also taught, and instruction in reading was given to adults, particularly women.

In 1788, Mr Litchfield set up a Sunday school in Wadhurst, financed by public subscription. In its first year, 35 people subscribed, together with eight benefactors. Several people, including Mr Litchfield, Mr Benge, of Cousely Wood (whose family had been involved in the iron industry), Mr Paul Legas (nephew of Mr John Legas), and Mr John Newington, of High Town, Tidebrook, gave a guinea; Mr Blackman, the surgeon (whose name still appears on a High Street knocker), gave 10s 6d; Mr Hammond (a dealer in malt and wood), gave 5s, as did Mr Bull (a shopkeeper); and Mr Moren (a farmer), gave 2s 6d. In all, £13 8s was donated. No wage earner appears to have contributed, either in this, or in any other year.[9]

Wadhurst Sunday School followed the practice of teaching only reading[10] and used for the purpose the Book of Common Prayer and the metrical Psalms. Very little elementary reading material was bought – just seven primers when the school first opened and three more ten years later, when two spelling books were also bought. That so few elementary books were bought suggests that either many of the children could read reasonably well already, or, as perhaps happened in many Sunday schools, reading was taught solely by repetition.

Later in 1794–5, when some of the children were old enough to be confirmed, *Commentaries on the Catechism* by Lewis and Mann were bought, so that the instruction contained in the Prayer Book could be followed more easily: 'A Catechism, that is to say, an instruction to be learned by every person before he be brought to be confirmed by the Bishop.'

The children were taught by Mr Richard Jeffery (who, earlier, had borrowed from Mr Litchfield Watt's *Scripture History*) and Mr Samuel Hunt. They were assisted by two children, a boy and a girl. The teachers received 1s each a Sunday, later increased to 1s 6d and the children 2d. Mr Jeffery taught the children in his own room, for which he received an extra shilling a Sunday, plus an occasional coal allowance of 5s. Mr Hunt taught in a room hired from a Mr Thomas Wickham.

In 1771, Mr Bush employed a Richard Jeffery as a servant. At the turn of the century and beyond, a Richard Jeffery, of Cously Wood, held property there.

How long the lessons lasted each Sunday, or how many children attended, is not known, but from the number of books bought, it would seem that the school opened in 1788, with towards 30 children.

In 1788, the *Sussex Weekly Advertiser* reported that, on 9 June, 'a most most excellent game of Cricket was played in the Church Field at Wadhurst between the Great Packham Club and the parishes of Lamberhurst, Wadhurst and Mayfield, which ended the same day, won by the latter by four notches only'. (Reprinted in the *Sussex County Magazine* in 1940.)

In 1790, except for child help and for the occasional return of Mr Jeffery, Mr Hunt was left to run the school single-handed, which he did for another five years. Mr E. Mabb, a dealer in flour, pollard, oats and wood and the Assistant Land Tax Collector, then took over. No payments to him for a room, or coal, are recorded, so it is possible that classes were now being held in the church. If this is so, in winter at least, teacher and children worked in difficult conditions, for it was not until 1848 that the erection of two stoves was recorded and the church lit for the first time, possibly with tallow candles, fixed in clay on the pew ends.

Little is known of the school's children, save that, on St Thomas's Day, 3 July 1798, they were given 10s from the

Poor Fund, to share between them, and that the names of three of the assisting children were George Pratt, Baldwyn and Samuel Wallis. The Wallis family continued long in the service of the church and parish, as stone-masons, parish clerks and, sometimes, sextons. The last Wallis, also a Samuel, whose 'singing was an inspiration', died in 1934.

Mr Legas and Mr Newington were among the earlier auditors of the school accounts, but by 1800, they were sloppily kept and no longer audited. By the end of the next year, there were but 11 subscribers, who gave between them £6 18s, and of this Mr Litchfield gave £2 2s. Expenditure amounted to £9 14s and Mr Litchfield advanced the difference. The accounts finally petered out on 14 February 1802, when John Dann, who had succeeded Mr Mabb the previous year, 'Received for 8 Sundays and Christmas Day 13/6d'.[11]

Perhaps by now, the vicar's health and drive were failing, for two years later, he died at his Oxfordshire parish of Noke.

In 1801, the first Census gave the population of Wadhurst as 1,677. For the previous years, 1796–1800, there had been an average of 56 births, 11 marriages and 27 deaths per year.

Education by the State

Five years after Mr Litchfield's little school had failed, the first attempt was made to involve the state in the provision of education for the poor. This was through the efforts of Mr Whitbread, a Member of Parliament, who had realised that, by itself, voluntary effort was not enough to satisfy the need. Mr Whitbread, fired by the cheap and seemingly successful monitorial system, where teacher taught monitor, and monitor other children, introduced a Bill to the House of Commons which would provide parochial schools in England and Wales. The Bill was opposed by both affluent and church and it, too, failed.

10

Interlude: The Rev. William Salmon, Vicar of Wadhurst 1804–18

Mr Litchfield was succeeded by the Rev. William Salmon, a bachelor, whose mother lived with him at the vicarage. That Mr Salmon, with a tithe income of £350 a year, had no educational aspirations for his parishioners is not surprising, for he was described as 'a man of very frugle and inexpensive habits and not spending a sixth part of his income', and thus a person unlikely to incur the expense of setting up a school for the education of Wadhurst's poor.

Some children, however, did receive a form of instruction, for the work and services of the church still went on. In 1817, it was recorded that: 'six hundred was confirmed in this Parish by the Bishop of Chichester.' The Bishop was then eighty-three years of age. The candidates were all, presumably, instructed as laid down in the Book of Common Prayer to 'Say the Creed, the Lord's Prayer and the Ten Commandments, and can also answer to such questions as in the short Catechism are contained...'

And in the services, the children heard the sermons, the constant repetition of the liturgy, lessons from the King James's Bible and joined in the singing of the metrical psalms, accompanied by the violin, cello, flute and clarinet, which were used in Wadhurst Parish Church at this time.

Mr Salmon died in 1818, aged 53.

The Second Sunday School – The Rev. Robert Barlow Gardiner, Vicar of Wadhurst 1818–45

Mr Salmon was followed by the Rev. R.B. Gardiner. Born in 1771 at Yardley Hastings, Northamptonshire, where his father was rector, Robert Barlow Gardiner was educated at Rugby and at Wadham College, Oxford, of which he later became a fellow. He was ordained in 1794 and became a priest in the following year. After serving various curacies, he held posts at this college and university from 1804 to 1817. On three occasions he was also appointed Whitehall preacher. He died a bachelor in 1845.

He was inducted in the summer of 1818 and, by the end of the year, had 'instituted' another Sunday school.

Education by the State

In the same year, 1818, the state also made another attempt to involve itself in the provision of education for the poor. At the instigation of Mr Broughan, another Member of Parliament, a 'Select Committee on the Education of the Lower Orders' was set up. A comprehensive Education Bill followed two years later, the provisions of which were to be paid for by the levy of special rates and taxes, supplemented by pence from the parents who could afford it. Both master and instruction were to be Anglican-parson approved, but, to gain Nonconformist support, religious instruction was to be restricted to Bible study, and worship to the Lord's Prayer. On Sundays, the child was to attend church or chapel with its parents.

Neither church nor chapel supported the Bill, which failed.

Children at Work, Nineteenth Century

Naked to the waist, an iron chain fastened to a belt of leather runs between their legs clad in canvas trousers, while on hands and feet, an English girl, for twelve, sometimes for sixteen hours a-day, hauls and hurries tubs of coals up subterranean roads, dark, precipitous and plashy...

See too these emerge from the bowels of the earth, Infants of four and five years of age ... the earliest to enter the mine and the latest to leave it ... labour ... passed in darkness and in Solitude.

From Disraeli's *Sybil*, 1845

The Second Sunday School, continued

Mr Gardiner's 'Instruction for the Lower Orders' of Wadhurst was of more modest dimensions, but was supported by 25 voluntary subscriptions, ranging from a guinea downwards, given by the vicar, local gentry, farmers and shopkeepers. In all, £24 14s was collected. In addition, the vicar and Mrs Fookes each gave a 'benefaction' of a further guinea. Mrs Fookes, the widow of an admiral, was a niece of John Legas, the ironmaster, who had died in 1752. She now lived at Hill House, with her niece, Miss Mallin, who also subscribed a guinea. At this time, the vicar's tithe income was £750, partly accounted for by the increased hop-growing. Other subscribers included Alfred Player, a member of an old Wadhurst family, who lived at the present Institute, and John Newington, of Towngate, Tidebrook, whose uncle, John Newington, had subscribed to Mr Litchfield's Sunday school. Subscribers of 10s, included Edward Avard, a butcher, and Thomas Barton, a mercer and grocer.

The Sunday school's first teacher was John Cooper, who, in 1793, had succeeded his father Thomas as parish clerk.

To use the parish clerk as a teacher was no new thing, for as early as 1734 a book on parish law recommended that: 'The Clerk would do much to the service of God and the Benefit of the people, if he were employed to instruct the children in Reading, Writing and rehearsing the Church Catechism, that they might be bred to a sense of Christianity and good Manners.'

This work was, of course, extra to the clerk's duties in the church, which, primarily, were to assist the minister in the preparation and performance of the services, particularly by leading the singing and saying of the congregation. The parish clerk was expected to have a competent singing voice and to be at least 20 years of age.

For his work as parish clerk, John Cooper received £11 a year, to which was now added £2 2s a quarter for his new teaching duties. He also received 12s a year for collecting the subscriptions.

Twenty-four copies each of the Book of Common Prayer and the New Testament were bought for the school, as well as 12 Trimmer's spelling books. A box to keep the books in and benches for the children to sit on completed the equipment. Within a month or so, new benches were obtained and the number of books doubled. Later, 48 'Church Catechisms broken into Short Questions' were introduced. It would appear that there were at least that number of children attending the school. In the first year, £22 8s 8d was spent, which left £2 6s 2d owing to the vicar.

> Mrs Trimmer, a well-to-do philanthropist and educationalist, wrote several books for the use of children and others. She instructed children: 'Do not fight or quarrel, call nick-names or tell tales. Bow to gentlemen and ladies when you meet them. Do not take birds' nests ... or do anything to torment dumb animals.'

John Cooper died in 1821 at the age of 62. His son Thomas, born in 1781, succeeded him, both as clerk and teacher, at the same remuneration, to include paying his own, unnamed, assistants.[12]

Thomas Cooper lived at the far end of a three-cottaged terrace in Washwell Lane, where he also plied the trade of shoemaker. He had seven children, only one of whom lived to adulthood. William Ashby, who was born in 1809, later to become the miller at Riverhall and also to play the cello in the church band, told his nephew Charles Ashby, who was born in 1849, that Thomas Cooper had one of the best and most powerful voices in England, with a very strong, deep tone. Thomas was parish clerk until 1855 and died three years later, at the age of 77.[13]

His cottage and those adjoining were pulled down in 1961, in order to widen the road.

Thomas Cooper's appointment seems to have provided some impetus to the work of the school. Writing was introduced, for which 25 manuscript books were bought from the depository at Uckfield. Study books on the Christian religion were also bought, to include 25 copies each of Lewis's *Exposition of the Catechism*, *Chief Truths of the Christian Religion*, *Our Saviour's Miracles*, *The Sermon on the Mount* and *Discourses*. Either the school had some very capable pupils at this time, or the vicar and Thomas Cooper had been over-optimistic, for except for the *Expositions*, no more such books were bought.

By the number of books bought by the end of 1823, it would appear that the number of pupils had considerably increased, with perhaps over 130 children on the roll.

Between Christmas 1818 and Christmas 1823, these books were:

```
Bibles 74   Testaments 36   Book of Common Prayer 120
Prayer Books 25
Trimmer's Spelling Book    Part 1.  87
                           Part 2.  74
Catechism broken into
   Short Questions              284
   Lewis's "Exposition"         125
   Lewis's On Paste Board        25
```

In the following year, 1824, a gallery was built across the tower arch to accommodate the children and also the church band and singers.

To teach anything like 130 children would have presented a formidable task for Thomas Cooper and his, possibly two, child assistants. No indication of the hours worked or the premises used for the school are given. As no payments are shown for room hire, heating or other expenses, it is possible that the church itself was again used, where teacher and taught would have worked still in difficult conditions of light, heat and disposition. Benches and rush matting were bought for the use of the school, but whether they were placed in the parvise, vestry, church, or gallery is not known.

In this year, 1824, when 21 people subscribed £16 4s to the school funds and Thomas Cooper's salary was the only expense, in its existing form, the school came to an end.

2

The National Day and Sunday School 1825–54

In 1825, the school was re-established as a National Day and Sunday School, under the auspices of the National Society, a Society which had been founded in 1811 for 'Promoting the Education of the Poor in the Principles of the Established Church throughout England and Wales'.

The first Annual Report of the society, published in 1812, made its intentions and attitudes abundantly clear – if its title had not already done so.

Its 'sole object' was:

> to communicate to the poor generally, by means of a summary mode of education, lately brought into practice, such knowledge and habits as are sufficient to guide them through life, in their proper stations, especially to teach the doctrines of Religion, according to the principles of the Established Church, and to train them to the performance of their religious duties by early discipline.

The 'summary mode of education' refers to the monitorial system, which had been advocated by Mr Whitbread (see Page 10). Independently, it had been 'brought into practice' by Andrew Bell, an Anglican clergyman, and also Joseph Lancaster, a Quaker; the master taught the more advanced pupils, who, in turn, taught the other children. In 1811, the Free Churches set up a body, The British and Foreign School Society, to build schools to make greater use of the system. Much ill will was generated between the Anglican and Free Churches, each of whom claimed prior right to the system.

By 1830, countrywide, there were 3,670 National Schools, with 346,000 children attending them.

Thomas Cooper could not, or would not, accept the change, for on Lady Day 1825, he received a last quarterly payment of £2 2s, plus a gratuity of £1 1s.

Samuel Baldwin, publican at the Greyhound, later to succeed his father as churchwarden and overseer, took over at £3 10s a quarter, very soon increased to £6. He was assisted by Hannah Baldwin, who received £2 10s, increased later to £3.

A change of teacher may have led to a change of method, but the material used continued as before, with Bibles, Testaments, Catechisms and Trimmer's spelling books.

There is still no indication of the days or hours worked, nor is there any indication of what writing materials, if any, were used. Just one item in the accounts suggests changing attitudes: '1828 Nov 11 Paid Mr. Barton for a Green Riband for a Boy's Medal 1½d.'

Boys and girls were now taught separately, in white-washed rooms, for which stoves, coal and hop poles for heating were supplied. If Samuel Baldwin provided a room, he did not get paid for it, but the girls were taught in a room supplied by Mrs F. Cooper, who received £1 6s for two quarters' rent.

Samuel Baldwin gave up in 1831. He was succeeded by Miles Bull and then by Miles's brother, Henry. Each was paid £5 a quarter, but, before long, Henry also supplied a schoolroom. Henry Bull lived in the High Street, and around 1840 was described as a newspaper agent, vestry clerk and rate-collector. By then, he also ran his own, private, school.

For three years, Hannah Baldwin continued to teach the girls, but on Christmas Day 1833 she received her last payment. She also received 2s to spend on cakes for the children. Perhaps this was meant as a little 'leaving' party for Hannah, or to celebrate Christmas Day, which was also always a school day.

Hannah was followed, first by Philadelphia Hammond and then, in January 1835, by Harriet Wisdom, each of whom received £2 10s a quarter, together with £1 for the use of a room. For teaching on Sundays at the Christmas she left, Philadelphia received another 2s 6d. She was perhaps related to Thomas Hammond, who kept a beer shop at Church House, near the south-eastern corner of the churchyard.

Harriet was the wife of Gideon Wisdom, who kept a butcher's shop in the High Street, on the corner of Washwell Lane. The Parish Magazine for June 1914 reported that Mrs Brooks, who lived in the High Street, had shown the vicar (the Rev. L.S. Stevenson)

> 'an old-fashioned, diamond-shaped pane of glass which had to be removed some years ago from a back bedroom window in her house – on it is written: "Gideon Wisdom is my name and england is my nation Wadhurst is my Dewling Place and Christ is my Salvation. Sep. 3rd. 1825 W."'

In 1825, to support the new National School, the vicar, Mr Gardiner, now sought and obtained financial help from a wider circle of people. It included Mr Courthope of Whiligh and Lord Camden of Bayham, both of whom owned much land in and around Wadhurst; Thomas Wace, a London merchant who had recently bought Hill House, and Henry Talbot of Maplehurst, the present Castle. (Until 1818, Maplehurst was a farmhouse, but was rebuilt, castle-like, by a Mr West in that year. He was the natural father of Henry Talbot and died in 1819 before the building was completed. It became known as 'Wadhurst Castle'.) Thomas Cooper gave 5s, but later it was returned to him.[14]

From a population of 2,106, consisting of 328 families, 270 of which were engaged in agriculture, 28 people contributed £34 7s 3d. The poor had nothing to give and the well-to-do had their difficulties, for agriculture recession in the 1830s caused landowners to reduce their farm rents and hence their income. In 1828, Thomas Blackman worked 5½ days in the churchyard for 9s 2d. William Courthope, a few years later, commented: 'Few parishes can boast less of the advantages enjoyed through a resident gentry than Wadhurst.'

To this contribution of £34 7s 3d was added Lucy Barham's bequest of £5, now mentioned in the accounts for the first time. The bequest was doubled by a contribution from the Church Rate.[15]

At this time, local affairs were still controlled by the Vestry. The Church Rate was among those imposed by it.[16]

By 1835, the subscriptions received by the school had risen to £45 6s, of which £8 8s was given by the vicar, £5 received from the Barham Charity and doubled, for the last time, by the church.

Of this sum, £36 19s 9d was spent, mainly on the salaries of Henry Bull and Harriet Wisdom; £2 12s on unspecified books and 12s on the 'repairing of the School window' by Joseph Stunt, all of which left a balance of £8 6s 3d.

In the March of 1835, according to a Governmental Inquiry which had commenced work in 1833, there were at the Wadhurst National School 30 males and 25 female pupils, with a master who received £20 a year, and a mistress £10. To these amounts was added penny weekly payments made by the children.

In addition, there were recorded in Wadhurst parish: A free Wesleyan Methodist Sunday school which was attended by 75 males and 75 females. (That it was free and restricted to Sundays helps to explain the fall in number at the National Schools.) And 'Eleven Daily schools, wherein 73 males and 105 females are receiving instruction at the expense of their parents.'

At this time, over the country as a whole, out of every ten children of school age, four went to no school at all, three to Sunday school only, two to inefficient dame or private school and but one received a satisfactory education.

On 6 August 1836 a short but very significant entry appeared in the school accounts: 'Paid for carriage of Parcel containing plan of school. 1.0.' Wadhurst, at last, was to have its own permanent school building, a happening which resulted from a joint local and national effort.

Education by the State

In 1832, influenced by revolution in France and agitation in England, a Reform Bill was passed, which extended the vote to the middle-class male, who, it was hoped, would elect a parliament sympathetic to further reform.

In the following year, 1833, at least one of its members, John Arthur Roebuck, lived up to expectations by making sweeping proposals for education, far in advance of the times. 'Education means ... training and fashioning the intellectual and moral qualities of the individual, that he may be able and willing to acquire knowledge and turn it to its right use,' he told Parliament. His proposals included: compulsory education for all children between the ages of six and twelve; evening classes in towns; a normal school for teacher-training; school districts superintended by an elected school committee and all to be supervised by a member of the Cabinet. Costs were to be met, where possible, by pence-fees, rates and taxes and the redistribution of existing endowments.

A counter-proposal was made: that £20,000 be allocated through the two School Societies, to aid private subscription to erect school houses. Even this modest proposal was opposed, for, it was claimed, charitable giving would be discouraged, crime increased, and a new race of idlers, in the form of schoolmasters and schoolchildren, would be encouraged. The counter-proposal, however, was passed by 50 to 26 votes from the 638 members of this new, reforming Parliament. An allocation of £50,000 to improve the Royal Stables was also approved.

> *Protection of the Young, Factory Act, 1833 (Textiles).*
>
> Children under Nine : Not to be employed.
> Children between Nine
> and Thirteen : 48 hours a week, maximum
> Children between
> Thirteen and Eighteen : 69 hours a week, maximum.
> *School*: Children between Nine and Thirteen were to attend
> school, provided by the employer, for at least two hours a
> week, after work.
> Four salaried Inspectors were to be appointed.

First National School Building, Pell Hill 1837.

Wadhurst applied for a grant from the £20,000 and received
£100. Local effort raised another £241, given by 111
subscribers, and George Campion Courthope of Whiligh gave
land for the school, on Pell Hill. It was so sited as to be
available, not only to the children of Wadhurst, but also to
the children of Sparrows Green and Cousely Wood.

The new school appears to have been built by July, 1837,
when two new teachers, Frederic and Elizabeth Fennell, from
outside the area, took up their duties, at £7 10s a quarter,
together with the children's pence-money, accommodation
and heating.

In the following year, 1838, further, unspecified, work was
carried out and two stoves, at the cost of £3, were installed.
The cost of fuel ranged from hop poles at 9s and faggots at
4s 6d, to coal at £3 15s for three tons. (Over £400 at present
prices.)

Education by the State

The new teachers were untrained, as, at that time, were most
teachers throughout the country, a situation which concerned
the government to the extent that another £10,000 was
allocated to help establish training colleges.

The only training institutions then available in England were the model schools of the National Society and of the British and Foreign School Society. The National Society opened its first college – St Mark's, Chelsea – in 1841. The nonconformist British and Foreign School Society opened a college in Borough Road, London, a little later.

By 1845, the National Society had established 22 colleges with 540 students. Attempts by the Council of Education to set up training colleges on non-denominational lines had failed through the resulting religious squabbles between the churches concerned.

> St Mark's College 'began operations in Stanley-grove, an old Chelsea home dating from the Stuart period ... Eight or nine years later, Blower, a well-known architect, was employed to design large additions to the mansion. These additions, under the influence of Derwent Coleridge, (son of the poet, S.T. Coleridge), the first Principal of the College, was built in a scholastic and, indeed, almost monastic style. The rooms and numerous corridors are a little cold and gloomy, yet their general effect is impressive, and youths fresh from country cottages and city back streets, could not fail to be influenced by the quiet dignity that pervades the building ... The College stands in nine acres of ground and attached to it are a chapel, a practising school, a gymnasium, a swimming bath and fives court.'
> From *Schoolmasters at School* – an unsigned press commentary on the Annual 'Elementary Teachers of England and Wales' Conference at Norwich in 1885.[17]

The First National School Building, continued.

The Fennells appear to have given far more attention to written work, for copy books and an amount of stationery were bought from the village shops of Mr Thomas Barton, mercer and grocer, and Mr MacDonald, draper and grocer.[18]

Slates were in use in the school, but go unmentioned in the

accounts. Bell's *Manual*, 50 Alphabets and 24 Bibles were bought and the newsman was paid 1s 6d for the carriage of further, unspecified books.[19]

But now, the government was to take decisions of consequence, for the Fennells and all teachers since.

Education by the State

In 1839, a Select Committee of the Privy Council, the first administrative authority for national education, was established to 'superintend the application of any sum of money voted by Parliament for the purpose of promoting Public Education'.

Dr Kay, later to be known as Sir James Kay-Shuttleworth, was its first Secretary and proved to be 'an able administrator' as well as 'an understanding and far-seeing educationalist'. (History of Education in G.B. S.J. Curtis).

In June, 1839, the new committee began its superintendency by issuing a Minute which instructed that, in future, all building grants would involve the right of inspection:

> The right of inspection will be required by the Committee in all cases; inspectors, authorised by Her Majesty in Council, will be appointed from time to time to visit schools to be henceforth aided by public money.

Most of the Minutes were passed by placing them in the House for one month, without recourse to Parliament.

The inspectors were required to gain accurate information about the school, but, although they were not to interfere with the conduct, management or discipline of it, they were, if so asked, to give advice and encouragement to those inspected.

The Church of England, still claiming a traditional right to dominate public education, resented the government interference which was suggested by this Minute. However in 1840, through the work of Kay-Shuttleworth, agreement

23

between church and government was reached by which the two Archbishops appointed their own supervisory inspectors, to be answerable to them on religious teaching, but to the Select Committee on secular teaching.[20]

> *Independent Inspectors*: 'A new, independent organisation now monitors standards in our schools. The Office for Standards in Education (OFSTED) is led by Her Majesty's Chief Inspector. OFSTED is in charge of the new inspection arrangements ... schools are inspected at least every four years ... the inspectors must publish the report. The school must act on the report ... the school's strengths and weaknesses. You will also receive the governing body's plans to develop the school and solve any problems which the inspection brought to light...'
> (*Our Children's Education*, DFE, 1994.)

The First National School Building continued.

Frederic and Elizabeth Fennell stayed for five years, and then, at the end of March 1842, were succeeded by Mr Preist, at £10 a quarter. No mention was made of any assistance, but necessity and the amount of his salary would presume a female assistant, either his wife or some other female relative. The *Infant Teachers' Assistant*, which ran into its tenth edition in 1846, said of staffing: 'We are bold to affirm that few females, if any, are competent to the charge and instruction of more than sixty or eighty children. Above that number will require a master and mistress.

At this time, there were towards 200 children on the roll of Wadhurst School, from a population of 2,482, of which 1,291 were males and 1,191 females.[21]

Mr Preist stayed but a year and on 25 March 1843, before the coming of his successors, Mrs Luck was paid 5s for cleaning the school house and rooms.

Although bills for brooms were frequent – from 6d for a birch broom to 2s 6d for a hair brush – bills for cleaning and privy-emptying were rare, which might suggest that those occupations lay within the scope of the teachers' duties.

The new teachers, William and Mary Ann Stiles, also came from outside the area, and, too, received a salary of £10 a quarter – later to rise to £12 10s a quarter.

Just over a year after their arrival, the Stiles received the inspection, which was the condition of all government grants.

On Inspection Day in 1844, there were 60 boys and 80 girls present – 36 boys and 11 girls absent. At this time, boys and girls were taught separately, each in their own three classes. Reading, writing, arithmetic and the Catechism only were examined and, perhaps, the only subjects taught.

Of them the inspector reported:

The first and second classes of boys and the first of girls, wrote on paper.

In Class 2, all the girls wrote on slates, but only some of the boys.

In Class 3, the boys wrote on slates. (The girls went unmentioned: presumably, they were unable to write.)

All three classes of boys had a knowledge of the Catechism, but only the first two of girls.

Of a knowledge of arithmetic, 'The First Class of Boys and Girls, well.' The other classes were unmentioned.

Nine boys and 17 girls could read with ease, 20 boys and 25 girls with difficulty.

At neighbouring Ticehurst, with 103 children present at the inspection, 26 could read with ease, 22 with difficulty.

In this year of inspection, 25 people (18 households) subscribed £47 2s 6d to school funds. A deficit of £17 4s 1½d was made up by the vicar, who had already subscribed £10, together with other donations from members of his family. Lord Camden gave £5 5s, and Mr Wace of Hill House, £3 3s, Mr Harding of Wadhurst Castle £5 5s, Mr Courthope, £10, Mr Penkivil, the surgeon, £1 1s, the Rev. C.B. Reid, the curate, £1 1s, and Mr Standen, the butcher, 5s.

In spite of the money problems, the tenure of William and Mary Stiles saw several innovations: two Sussex stoves and a water-cask were installed, a wash-house was built at a cost of £10, and a chain-clock was bought to hang on the white-washed walls. Knitting was introduced into the school, for which worsted knitting needles were purchased from Mr MacDonald for 7s 11d. In the year following the inspector's visit, an atlas was obtained by Mr Reid which, together with some books and stationery, cost £4 15s 8½d. For the first time, a bottle of ink was bought, which cost 1s 6d.

The Stiles left in the middle of the term; on 2 February 1846 the post was advertised in the *Sussex Advertiser* and on 18 February they served their last day. On the following day, at a salary of £10 a quarter, Mr Cogger took over.

The vicar, the Rev. R.B. Gardiner, died in 1845 and in the summer of 1846, was succeeded by the Rev. John Foley, aged 40 and recently married. The new vicar came to Wadhurst from Pershore, where he had been a curate for 17 years, following four years as proctor and don at Oxford.[22]

Mr Foley quickly showed an interest in the school[23] and brought to it a new enthusiasm by which more subscribers to the school fund were found. Out of the 37 subscribers, 15, Mr Foley claimed, were new. In his account book, all were designated by title: 17 were 'Mr', which included farmers and tradesmen; 12 were 'Esq.', including E. Hussey of Scotney Castle, who held 120 acres of land in Wadhurst; one was described as 'Honourable', the Hon. R. Ashburnham, and one Marquess, The Marquess Camden of Bayham. The Rev. John Foley was also included. (The use of 'Esq,' and 'Mr.' to denote status was used on the cover of the Parish Magazine from its commencement in 1893 until 1908, the year in which the Rev. L. Stevenson became vicar.)

Subscriptions ranged from Mr Courthope's £10 to the 1s of William Reid, the blacksmith. Altogether, £55 was raised, which still left a deficit over the year of 11s 10d.

Mr Cogger stayed but one year and was followed in quick succession by Mr Egglestone and Mr Thomas Holder, during whose tenure a map was bought by 'Order of the Committee'.

This management committee was chaired by the vicar, who nominated its members.

Education by the State

In 1847, a Minute of the Committee of Council required that all Church of England schools should be managed and controlled by a committee set up by the incumbent and chosen and chaired by him. The appointment and dismissal of teachers was in its hands. The incumbent was also responsible for the religious instruction. In the same year, the Committee of Council also offered grants for the purchase of school books and maps – on condition that two-thirds of their cost was met by subscription, which meant that poorer schools received smaller grants.

The First National School Building, concluded.

Mr Preece, the next master, came to the school in October 1848 and stayed until March 1854.

During this period, the subscription income rarely reached £60 a year, which had to cover Mr Preece's salary of £40 p.a., and such necessary expenses as heating and insurance. Around four tons of coal were bought each year, at £1 5s to £1 10s a ton, plus 10s 6d a ton for haulage. A water-cask was obtained, at a cost of 16s, and on two occasions in 1849, Mr Preece's travelling expenses were paid, at a total cost of £2. He probably travelled by stage-coach, for although the railway through Wadhurst was begun in 1847 and completed by 1849, it was not available for passenger traffic until 1851.

Over the whole period, less than £13 was spent on books and equipment, which included 25 testaments, sundry books, slates and stationery. Even so, the accounts only just balanced.

With Mr Preece's departure on 18 March 1854 came the end of an era, for he was the last of Wadhurst's uncertificated head teachers.

Education by the State

In 1846, through the efforts of James Kay-Shuttleworth, the Committee of Education introduced a system by which suitable children, at the age of 13, could be apprenticed to the master for a five-year period as a pupil-teacher. When successfully completed, admission to a training college, by the Queen's Scholarship Examination, could be sought. Candidates for the scholarship were required to pass in practical teaching, reading, recitation, arithmetic, music, English grammar (with a little literature), geography and history. Boys offered mathematics, and girls needlework. Certain additional subjects also could be added.

The pupil-teacher was to receive a stipend of £10 per annum rising to £20 by the end of the fifth year. In consideration of his giving the pupil-teacher instruction in prescribed subjects, before and after school for at least one and a half hours a week, the master was to receive a gratuity of £5. The pupil-teacher was subject to annual examination by the inspector.

By the same Minute, monitors were encouraged to stay in the schools by the payment of a stipend starting at £5 per annum. These children were not apprenticed but subject to a formal agreement between school and parent. Extra daily instruction was given by the master, who received £2 10s a year for his services. Many of the monitors remained to become unqualified teachers.

In the same year, Minutes of the Committee of Council of Education had established that a student who had completed two years' training should, on his appointment to a teaching post, receive a grant of £20–£25 p.a., on condition that he was provided with a rent-free house by the school and that his salary should be equal to at least twice the grant. A pension was to be paid to a person completing at least 15 years' service.

James Kay-Shuttleworth, later knighted, was Secretary to the Select Committee of the Privy Council from 1839 to 1849, when he retired through ill health. He is credited with laying the ground plan of English elementary education, and doing so without creating a breach between church and state. He described the monitorial system as 'humbug' and in advocating the use of pupil-teachers instead, his aim was to improve the supply and quality of teachers.

3

The Second National School Building,
Lower High Street
Boys, Girls and Infants, 1854–61

On 20 March 1854, Wadhurst had its first trained teacher, Mr Charles Booking, aged 28, who had taught previously at Lindfield, Sussex. He was married and had one daughter, Jane, who later became a teacher at Tidebrook School.[24]

Mr Bocking had been a chorister at St Mark's Church, Clerkenwell, London, educated at the City of London Grammar School and trained at St Mark's College, Chelsea.

At Wadhurst, Charles Bocking received a salary of £45 per annum, plus a government grant of £20 to £25. His salary was paid quarterly, but even from his first days at the school, he was constantly needing, and receiving, payment in advance. Mr Bocking was provided with a rent-free house and possibly received the children's pence-money, but of this there is no record.

Mr Bocking also took over the training of the church choir and, in 1870, at a salary of £12 a year, was appointed organist.[25]

It is possible that Charles Bocking was assisted at the school by his wife, for there is no mention in the accounts of either monitor or mistress until December 1855, when a mistress was paid £17 10s for six months' teaching.

Following Mr Bocking's appointment, a new school was built in the Lower High Street. The foundation stone was laid in May 1854 and the work completed in the following December. Until then, Mr Bocking was, of course, teaching in the school on Pell Hill. There he had spent £1 10s on stationery, £24 5s 6d on books and £2 10s on incidentals.

Mr George Courthope gave the new site in the Lower High Street in exchange for the old one on Pell Hill. He also bought back the old school buildings for £130, which still exist and continue as a private house. In addition, he gave a donation of £200. Mrs Courthope, the Rev. John Foley, Mr E. Watson Smyth of the Castle and Mr Dixon of Frankham each gave £50.

At the same time, a separate girls' and infants' department was formed and Miss Boulden, at an annual salary of £35, together with the girls' pence-money (£8 12s 10d in 1856), was appointed to take charge of it. She was assisted by a monitor, Ruth Pattenden, at £1 16s a year, who helped with the infants.

Miss Boulden stayed until July 1857, when Miss McNess succeeded her, at the same salary. Apart from the cash book entry 'Work done by girls 6.3d.' there is little evidence of the life and activity of the school at this time.

It is not known how long Miss McNess stayed, but in 1866, Miss Watson was appointed headmistress, to remain for 42 years, in which time she also became a member of the church choir.

Miss Watson came from Burwash, Sussex, where she was a pupil-teacher for five years. After serving as an assistant teacher at Framfield, Sussex, she entered the Normal Training College at Brighton.

To support the work of the schools, a great deal of extra money was required, which John Foley continued to seek.

In 1858 he wrote:

Dear Mrs. Courthope,

Let me acknowledge with sincere thanks, your sister's kind donation to the Funds of Wadhurst Schools. We have now a larger number of children in attendance with the certificated master and mistress, so that our expenses are increased and increasing. Every additional subscription is a help to our ways and means, as well as an encouragement to others to do as you have done...

In his letter, John Foley went on to ask for a 'trifle' towards the repair and restoration of the parish church which was then being carried out.

By 1860, over 60 people were subscribing to the school fund, still drawn largely from the local gentry, farmers, shopkeepers and tradesmen, but including as well, relatives of past clergy and residents, friends of friends and others. One of these included Mrs William Courthope, wife of the Somerset Herald and niece of the Rev. R.B. Gardiner.

The subscription income was still augmented by the £5 Barham legacy, the girls' pence-money, around £10 a year from special church collections, a collecting box in the vicarage and, from 1858, a Government Capitation Allowance, which was £18 in 1860. In that year, income totalled £117 2s 9d, but was over-spent by £4 6s 3d. As in previous years, the major expenses were salaries and heating. Only 9s was spent on books, 3s 6d on pens – mentioned in the accounts for the first time – and £3 16s on incidentals.

The vicar's account ended in 1861, too soon to show the effects of the Newcastle Commission deliberations, the report of which was published that year.

> ### Young People, 1866
> The disobedience of children is another pronounced evil of the day. The fastness and forwardness of youth is a subject of universal remark ... Parental authority is thus despised and set at nought ... Our streets are crowded with them at unseemly hours of the night.
>
> The Rev. J. Hutton, Rector of Stilton, writing in the *Sunday Reader*, 22 September 1866.
>
> ### Girls at Work, Nineteenth Century
> The girls nowadays don't know naun about work. When I was sixteen years old I was had out, like a cow to the market and any farmer who wanted a servant came and choosed one. I first went as a nurse girl and I got 1/3d. a week. Then I went to Early Farm in Wadhurst Parish, and there I was to have 1/6d. a week: but then I'd more work to do. I'd churning to do twice a week and cheesing twice a week and brewing twice a week, besides washing and baking and six cows to milk every night and morning and sometimes a dozen pigs to feed. There were four men lived in the house and I'd all the bilin to do – the cabbage and the peas and pork for their dinners – besides all the beds to make ... One morning, I mind, I got up at four and worked till twelve at night and then the missus wanted me to pick a couple of ducks. "No, Missus," says I, "I really can't: I be quite tired." "Tired," says she, "If I was a young woman like you I should be ashamed of myself."
> Ah! it was just a treat to get an hour or two to myself on a Sunday...
>
> An old lady writing in 1888. *Sussex County Magazine*. Vol. IX. 1935.

Education by the State

In 1856, two years after the Wadhurst schools had entered their new buildings, the Privy Council's Committee of Education was upgraded to become a Department of

Education. The Lord President of the Privy Council was still its head, but was represented in Parliament by a Vice-President, appointed by the Prime Minister.

Concern that the Crimean War had cost nearly £7 million and that the Education Grants in the past eight years had risen from £541,233 to £663,435, with, perhaps, the idea that value for money was not being obtained, a Royal Commission, under the chairmanship of the Duke of Newcastle, was set up in 1858 'To enquire into the present state of Popular Education in England and to consider and report what Measures, if any, are required for the extension of sound and cheap elementary instructions to all classes of people.'

The Newcastle Commission defined elementary education in terms of:

1. The ability to read 'a common narrative'.
2. Writing 'a letter which shall be both legible and intelligible'.
3. Knowing 'enough of ciphering to make out, or to test the correctness of a common shop bill'.
4. A little geography.
5. The ability 'to follow the allusions and the arguments of a plain Saxon sermon'.

In its report, issued in 1861, the Royal Commission considered that universal education was neither possible nor desirable and expressed its satisfaction in the system by which schools, provided by voluntary effort, were assisted by government grant.

The commission, however, was unhappy with the school attendance, for, even in the grant-aided, inspected schools, it was of such short duration that 'not more than one fourth of the children receive a good education'. Only 40 per cent attended at all regularly and only a minority stayed on beyond the age of ten. For all that, some members, including the Rev. James Frazer, who later became the Bishop of Newcastle, felt:

...it is quite possible to teach a child soundly and thoroughly ... all that is necessary for him to possess in the shape of intellectual attainment by the time that he is ten years old.

It was the teachers, however, who gave the commissioners the cause for their greatest concern:

...the trained teaches are conceited and dissatisfied ... their emoluments, though not too low, rise too soon to their highest levels...

So great a failure in the teaching demands the closest investigation ... the instruction [is] ... both too ambitious and too superfluous in its character [and] ... often omits to secure a grounding in the simplest but more essential parts of instruction...

(A Mr T. Ward, writing in *The Educational Guardian* of January 1861, commented: 'The opinions and habits of thought of many have never altered: they think as lightly of the modern teacher as of the one they knew in their youthful days. They think him a man to be patronised and snubbed like the one of old and if he resents such treatment their surprise is unbounded.')

The Commissioners decided that:

There is only one way of securing [increased efficiency], which is to introduce a searching examination by competent authority of every child in every school to which grants are paid ... to make the prospects and position of the teacher dependent to a considerable extent on the result of the examination.

Robert Lowe, a politician and administrator, had become Vice President of the Education Department in 1859. He was a great believer in the examination system, market forces and in obtaining value for money. He seized on this last recommendation to introduce it into his Code of 1862: future grants would now depend on examination results, to which regular attendance was added.[26] (Codes of Instruction were laid on the table of the House of Commons for one month, after which they became law.)

Of this new Code, Lowe told the House of Commons:

I cannot promise the House that this system will be an economical one and I cannot promise that it will be an efficient one, but I can promise...
if it is not cheap it shall be efficient;
if it is not efficient it shall be cheap.

By this Code, an attendance grant of 4s a scholar was to be paid on the average attendance at morning and afternoon school, throughout the year.

A further grant of 8s was to be paid for each child who passed an examination in reading, writing and arithmetic, dependent on attendance at 200 sessions of morning and afternoon schools. For each subject which was failed, 2s 8d was to be deducted.

For children under six, a grant of 6s 6d was to be made, subject to satisfactory inspector report. First thoughts subjected children aged three to seven to examination: second thoughts considered this absurd.

From a Department of Education pamphlet, 1992:

Seven year olds' progress will be measured this Spring and Summer against the National target in:

English; Mathematics; Science; and Technology.

In practice children may be six or eight years old when they are assessed.

Evening class grants, for those over 12, were now to be made.

Grants could be withheld completely for such reasons as bad lighting, drains or offices; defective registers; non-teaching of plain needlework. Grants could be reduced by one-tenth to one-half for faults in instruction, discipline, building defects, faulty provision of furniture, books and apparatus.

Altogether, the grant still depended 'upon the School's whole character and work...' Deductions, therefore, could be made for poor instruction in other subjects, but, in practice, this rarely occurred.

Under the same Code, a lower class of teaching certificate was accepted; the teachers' pension scheme, grants for apparatus, pupil-teachers' stipends were withdrawn; grants to training colleges were cut down and teachers' proficiency grants were no longer paid to the individual, but included in the grant paid to the managers.

The Code also required that a school log-book should be kept by the head teacher, to record the day-to-day running of the school.

An examination was devised which ranged as follows:

Reading
Standard	1.	A Narrative in mono-syllables.
	4.	A short Paragraph from a more advanced Reader.

Writing
Standard	1	Capitals and Small Manuscript, from Dictation on blackboard or slate.
	4.	A Sentence slowly dictated once, by a few words at a time, from the same book, but not from the paragraph read.

Arithmetic
Standard	1	The formation of figures up to twenty, from Dictation, on blackboard or slate, and the Addition and Subtraction of figures up to ten, orally, from the blackboard.
	4.	Working a sum in Compound Rules (money).

Many educationalists, writers and others commented on these provisions. Of the examination, Matthew Arnold, poet, writer and school inspector, wrote:

> ...it fosters teaching by rote ... certain minimum expressly laid down beforehand, must inevitably concentrate the teacher's attention on the means of producing the minimum.

He considered that, under the old system, the inspector's visit tested and questioned the intellectual life of a school, but with the introduction of the examination, this was no more. He went on to say that, in a country where everyone was prone to rely too much on mechanical processes and too little on intelligence, it was to be expected that by making two-thirds of the government grant depend on mechanical processes, mechanical examination and inspection would follow.

> '...I find in them, [the schools] if I compare them with their former selves, a deadness, a slackness and a discouragement ... I find in them a lack of intellectual life...'

Matthew Arnold claimed that the managers judged the teachers' standing by the grades given by the inspector, who thus, in the eyes of the teachers, became an enemy rather than a friend, and so a natural mistrust grew up between them.

In a letter to the politician Lord Granville, quoted in *The School Inspector*, by E.L. Edmonds, Kay-Shuttleworth wrote:

> All inspectors are not perfect either in manner, utterance, choice of words for poor children, method of examining them: nor in skill, kindness and patience required to bring out the true state of the children's knowledge.

Of the children inspected, one inspector, Mr Sneyd-Kynnersley, wrote:

Most of the children were in the two lowest standards. They were supplied with slates, pencils and a reading book and were drawn up in two long lines down the middle of the room. They stood back to back to prevent copying and did dictation and arithmetic, sometimes dropping their slates, sometimes their pencils, sometimes their books, not infrequently all three, with a crash on the floor.

Of the revised Code, Matthew Arnold said:

[it] has constructed nothing ... It has not succeeded in being efficient, but it is not even cheap; for it wastes the public money without producing the results which were declared to be its main object.

Matthew Arnold was distressed, too, by the damage done to the pupil-teacher and schoolmaster system erected in 1846. He wrote:

The present slack, languid condition of our elementary schools is the inevitable consequence ... The performance of the reduced number of candidates is weaker and more inaccurate.[27]

Mr Foley's account book ended too soon to show the financial effects of the new Code on the Wadhurst schools and further account books and the new, obligatory log-books appear not to have survived.

Fortunately, the Diocesan Inspectors for Chichester were both active and concerned, so that their reports from 1872 to 1892, which have survived, throw light, not only on the life and work of these schools, but also on inspectoral attitudes. Fortunately, too, a school to serve Cousely Wood was opened in 1868 and its log-books show, only too clearly, the impact of the Code, both on the school and on the morale of its staff.

4

The School at Cousely Wood
1868–1870

Soon after George Campion Courthope, in 1837, helped to set up a centrally placed school at Pell Hill, he bought a piece of land in Cousely Wood, on which he determined to build a separate school in order to save the hamlet's little children a very long walk each day.

Thirty years later, the school was built, to be opened on 3 January 1868.

On the eve of her twenty-first birthday, Miss Charlotte Page, its first mistress, wrote in the school's log-book: 'Commenced duties as the Mistress of the Cousely Wood Infant School. Weather very bad, School small in consequence.'

Charlotte had been two-year trained at Brighton College, after serving a five-year period as a pupil-teacher at St Peter's Infant School, Hammersmith.

On the first afternoon of the school's opening, Mrs Foley, the vicar's wife, came down to greet the new mistress. On the day following, the vicar, who had met her already when he picked her up in his horse and trap at the railway station, came down to greet Charlotte at the school. Later, on 29 January, Mrs Foley visited again, with several ladies including Miss Lucy Wace, the daughter of the Rev. R.H. Wace, who kept a small preparatory school at Hill House, which had been left to him by an uncle, Thomas Wace.[28]

Charlotte Page, assisted by monitor Esther Rose, had around 30 children in her school. (The Waces had 10 or 11.) Within two years, the number had risen to over 60, so that a second monitor, Hester Fuller, was appointed.

Much of the teaching was carried out with the children sitting in a 'gallery', which, according to Bilby and Ridgeway's Primer *The Infant Teachers' Assistant*, was a 'real necessity':[29]

> At one end of the school-room, or in a recess at the side, a gallery ... should be fitted up with steps and seats rising one above the other for the purpose of instructing the children with greater facility in some particular subject.

Miss Page's gallery lessons dealt with a remarkably wide range of subjects: form, including the triangle, pentagon and rhombus; general subjects, such as the manufacture of paper and its properties; rice and its cultivation and growth; water, the island, trains; natural life, with the wolf, mole, bat, ostrich, birds and their beaks, together with daffodils, roots and edible roots; colour, including shades of red, and, too, the 'general uses of the map'.

Miss Page made great use of the moment for her lesson subjects: Garland Day and Guy Fawkes Day – each had its appropriate lesson and when, on 14 May 1868, a boy was punished for stealing money, she gave a lesson on the Eighth Commandment. Later in the year, when Lucy Wace presented the six best babies with dolls to dress and one had been completed, a lesson on 'the doll' followed.

Scripture lessons, based on the Old and New Testaments, were of daily, or almost daily occurrence. They included the story of the Creation, Pharaoh's dream, Jacob gaining his father's blessing, the passage through the Red Sea, Elijah fed by the ravens, Daniel in the lion's den, David slaying Goliath, the Saviour walking on the sea, Christ healing the blind man and the Last Supper.

On 29 July 1869, Charlotte Page gave a lesson on 'Patience' taking Job as an example, and on the following day, she heard three elder children repeat the Parable of the Ten Virgins.

Miss Page also 'gave a lesson on the Catechism', and dealt

with such questions as: 'What did your godfathers and godmothers then promise for you?' and: 'What desirest thou then of God in this Prayer?' (The Lord's Prayer).

Visitors, too, helped with the Scripture lessons. Miss Lucy Wace presented the school with some Scripture prints, which also served as lesson subjects, including a gallery lesson on 'Christ announced to the Jewish Shepherds'.

Mr Charles Brissenden, a local farmer, and Mr Daniels, the Scripture reader from the parish church, sometimes visited and asked questions on the Scriptures. On one occasion Mr Ballard came in and spoke to the children about the Ten Commandments and then, on 28 January 1869, Miss Page examined the children in Old Testament history.

Needlework was an obligatory subject and one to which Miss Page referred quite frequently, particularly when it concerned the help which was given by the various ladies in the area. Not only were dolls brought in to be dressed, but also handkerchiefs to be hemmed. Mrs Bone brought some in and Mrs Watson Smyth and her friend praised the children for their work.

The music and poetry taught was slight, but it appears to have been of some significance in the life of the school. The children learnt hymns and songs, which Charlotte Page accompanied on the American organ. In her log-book, she refers to the teaching of such hymns as: 'Lord, I would own Thy tender care', 'Christ is merciful and mild', and the songs, 'Once there was a little kitten' and 'The North Wind doth blow'.

Over the course of the year, the words of poems, parables, songs and hymns were committed to memory by the children. On one occasion, on 6 May 1869, Charlotte recorded that she had given the children a conversational lesson, based on a piece of poetry, for our Queen and Country, called 'Hurrah for England'.

The children had drawing lessons and sometimes, when it was too wet for them to go out to play, they were 'allowed' to stay in to draw. The children not only drew, but were also shown pictures – one day by Miss Foley, who called in to show them illustrations which she had taken from the *Animal Friends Almanac.*

Arithmetic was of sufficient importance to receive little mention in the log-book, although, on one occasion, Miss Page did mention subtraction as the subject for a gallery lesson, and on another, after the installation of a ball-frame, 'parts and use of a ball-frame'.

Charlotte Page, it seems, had the personality to draw people to her to help her in the work. During the three years she was headmistress of the little Cousely Wood School, and persisting to the end of her career, 40 years later, she continued to receive many visitors and much support.

Mrs Caroline Foley, the vicar's wife, continued a constant visitor, at one time bringing with her 'dark curtains' for the use of the school; on another, a new clock, and sometimes she brought sweets for the children. On occasions, she brought with her Caroline Augusta (born 1857) and Mary Celia (born 1859) her two daughters. Sometimes their governess was with them, but sometimes 'they looked to the babies', or helped with their reading. Mrs Foley had nine children, one of whom died in 1852 and five around the Christmas of 1855. They are remembered in some chancel windows of Wadhurst Church. Caroline, Mary and Charles survived.

Miss Anstruther called in with her friend, Captain Stewart, and stayed to take some classes. Mr Courthope visited with a friend, who gave the children a 'brief address'. The Rev. F. Rawes, the curate, spoke to the children about the Provident Club, and Miss Watson, other teachers from the Wadhurst Schools, Mr Daniels, the Scripture reader at the parish church and Mr Watson Smyth, of the Castle, all looked in on various occasions to see how the children and staff were getting on.

One day, the clock stopped and Mr Bone, who had put up the dark curtains brought by Mrs Foley, came to wind it up. Mrs Bone also came to help, 'amusing the children with pictures and simple recitations'. Charlotte's friend also visited and gave a shilling's worth of sweets to the children, who scrambled for them in playtime.

At Christmas time, Miss Brissenden helped to put the

decorations up and Mr Courthope sent a quantity of evergreens. On other occasions, Miss Brissenden brought biscuits for the children and also took the first class for the dictation of letters, figures and other such things. The Brissendens, of Little Butts, gave constant help to the school, and Miss Page said of them that when there were any cases of distress among the children, the Brissendens were 'my staunch friends'. On 6 December 1869 she noted: 'Mrs. Brissenden sent a loaf and preserves to those children whose fathers were out of work.'

Weather was another source of distress and worry and received almost constant mention in Caroline's log-book:

April 20, 1868.
A very wet and dirty day only 25 children here in the morning.

August 11, 1868.
Only 12 children present in the morning owing to a thunderstorm which lasted from 8 o'clock to 11am.

Some children had a long journey to school, across fields and along ways which, in bad weather, were 'very dirty', so that, when they did arrive, they were 'troubled to get home'.

Charlotte Page had reason to fear a low attendance, for, by the new Revised Code of 1862, grants were paid by results: small attendance, small grant; small grant, small salary.

On 28 May 1869, after a very wet day, with only 12 children present in the morning and 13 in the afternoon, Charlotte commented: 'Such frequent wet days pull the average down greatly', and sometimes the weather was so severe that even the mistress, who lived in apartments some distance from the school, was unable to attend.

On 20 July 1868, however, Miss Page was called by the workmen to lay a corner brick for the new school house, of which, on 8 February 1869, she was able to write: 'Took possession of the new school house.'

When those who could, did come, their troubles were not

yet over, for several times Charlotte Page recorded that smoke from the fire was filling the room and hindering the work of the school. On one miserable, cold and snowy morning in March 1869, when only five children managed to reach the school, so great was the smoke from the fire that the mistress had to put it out.

Even when all was well with the fire, the room was sometimes so cold that the children were 'marched' to keep them warm and, on one occasion, so intense was the cold, the clock stopped. Then there was the time, so bad was the weather, that Charlotte was moved to provide the children who stayed at the school during dinnertime with hot soup, to have with their sandwiches.

Miss Page – and the children – had endured these conditions for two years, when, on 21 January 1870, George Campion Courthope presented the school with a new stove. The children were given a short holiday during its installation and three days later, the teacher recorded that she had: 'Found that the School had been thoroughly cleaned and supplied with a new stove and door-mat.'

Summertime, too, sometimes presented problems, for the classroom became unbearably hot and the babies, very tired and sleepy. Then, to get the benefit of any breeze, the children were allowed to sit outside in the playground.

With the heat came the summer's storms and, one day in 1870, so severe was the storm that Charlotte Page read a story to the children 'to calm them'.

Weather conditions were not the only hindrance to good attendance, for although Cousely Wood was quite remote, it was not entirely isolated and the children had access to many and varied occupations which kept them from school.

Just up the road was, and is, a cricket ground, which on the day of a match brought a considerable drop in attendance at school. On 16 July 1868, Charlotte wrote: 'Only 43 children present in the afternoon many having been away at a cricket match held in a field at a short distance from the school.'

Education by the Hamlet of Cousely Wood

Countrywide, new school buildings were helping to stimulate and encourage the growth of village activities, and Cousely Wood School was also used for church services and other organised activities. A Sunday school was provided for the children. Evening lectures were given, including one in 1869, which a few of the children were allowed to attend, and at the beginning of the same year, provision for a public library was made and books to the value of £5 placed in it.

The School at Cousely Wood, 1868–70, continued.

Teas and outings, supplied by local churches and gentry, also removed many children. On 9 July 1868, the school was closed in consequences of a treat given to both the Sunday and day schools in Mr Wace's grounds and, on the following day, 'a treat and scramble were given to the babies who were absent from the previous day'.

A tea, or some celebration, also marked the paying out days of the various benefit clubs[30] which existed in the area at this time and Miss Page frequently records the absence of children to attend them.

> 7 May 1868. 'Only 39 children in the afternoon owing to a club being held in Wadhurst'.
>
> 14 May 1869. 'A Street Club held in the neighbourhood several children absent in consequence'.
>
> 4 November 1869. 'Several children absent through their mothers being at Wadhurst for the clothing club benefit'.

Mutual benefit clubs, some very small, abounded in the villages. Members subscribed to them against such things as sickness, old age, death and the mundane need to buy clothes. An annual cash share-out would take place, accompanied, perhaps, by a church parade, a tea and other celebrations.

Miss Page recorded, too, that children were absent on 1 November, in order to attend a fair in Wadhurst and then, on 5 November, she again reported the absence of children, for they had gone 'Remembering'.

On 19 August 1869, Miss Page recorded that 10 children under six years of age went to a treat at Mrs Anstruther's as they attended Sunday School there. Earlier in the year, several girls were late for school because they had 'been down to Mrs Anstruther to receive their Sunday School prizes.'

In these early days at Cousely Wood Infant School, illness was not a frequent reason for absence and rarely does Miss Page say:

29 April 1870. 'Average for the week only 16.7 owing to sickness in the village.'

More frequently does she report isolated cases which, in later years, were often the prelude to epidemics and school closures:

21 April 1868. 'Sent two children home having heard that their father was suffering from Typhus Fever.'

10 January, 1870. 'A case of scarlet fever...'

Two children were also sent home because of a skin eruption, 'perhaps infectious'.

Charlotte, from 23 to 27 March, had to close the school completely, for she herself, through sickness, was unable to attend.

Absence through truancy was sometimes recorded by Miss Page, for which she described the culprits as having been 'punished'. A variety of other misdemeanours were also recorded: theft of money and property, biting, disorderly and noisy conduct, as well as idleness, for which the boys concerned were kept from play and made to learn the Fourth Commandment – presumably with the emphasis on 'Six days shalt thou labour'. Detention during playtime appears to have

47

been the most favoured form of punishment. On one, rare, occasion, two policemen visited the school to question a boy about the damage done to the lock of a house window.

Wages were low and poverty abounded, so that, in order to augment the family income, children were frequently absent to help their parents in the fields, according to the season, with such occupations as wheat bond-making, leasing, acorn gathering, hop-pole shaving and hop preparation. The actual hop-picking took place in the summer holidays, which were fixed to coincide with it. If necessary, the holiday was prolonged until the completion of the picking.

Under the requirements of the Revised Code of 1862 (see Appendix[31]), Miss Page and her newly opened Cousely Wood Infant School received its first yearly inspection on 29 January 1869. Her Majesty's Inspector was N.L. Roe, Esq., who reported:

Miss C. Page was appointed to this school in January last and is conducting it with much tact and judgement. The general condition of the school does her much credit.

The second inspection took place a year later, again conducted by Mr Roe. This time, it was in the presence of the Rev. John Foley, his daughter, Mrs Anstruther and her daughter and also Miss Wace. There were 38 children present, including 26 who were under six and 12 who were in Standard 1. Mr Roe reported that: 'The school is in creditable condition considering the time it has been in operation. Miss Page will shortly receive her certificate.'

On 10 October 1870, when the school resumed after the hop-picking holidays, Miss Page reported that she had found 'the school cleaned and varnished and the class room being built'.

Ten days later, she wrote: 'Arranged the children in a group outside the school and had them photographed with the teacher and myself.'

Then, in the following month, the children were given a holiday, 'to enable the men to fix the sliding doors'.

Encouraged by an Act which had been passed that year, which promised grant-assistance, the managers had decided to enlarge the school for the admittance of both junior and infant children. Miss Page declined the headship of it, for she wished to teach but infants. The Wadhurst school, however, was also being enlarged at this time, to form a separate infant school, and Mr Courthope now offered her the headship. Miss Page accepted the post and on 22 December 1870, wrote her last entry in the Cousely Wood log-book: 'School visited by G. Courthope, Esq. Gave up duties as the Mistress of Cousely Wood Infant School.'

Education by the State

During the years following the introduction of the Revised Code of 1862, it was realised that voluntary effort, even when government-supported, was not sufficient to provide enough schools or places for the growing child population. It was estimated that but 40 per cent of the country's children were receiving any form of education, and even that was frequently of a poor quality.

In 1870, to deal with this situation, an Elementary Education Bill was introduced by Mr W.E. Forster, the vice president in charge of the Education Department and Member of Parliament for Bradford.

Mr Forster proposed to create a dual system of voluntary and state schools, the object of which, as he said in his introductory speech to Parliament, was

to complete the present voluntary system, to fill up the gaps ... to bring elementary education within the reach of every English home ... even to those children who have no homes.

Public expense was to be spared by calling on the compulsory assistance of the parent and the charity of the affluent.

In support of his Bill, Mr Forster, brother-in-law of Matthew Arnold, said that the industrial prosperity of the nation depended upon 'the speedy provision of elementary education' and that, if the work force was left unskilled, it would become 'over-matched in the competition of the world'. Furthermore, since by the Reform Bill of 1867 many more men had received the vote and thus political power, 'we must not wait any longer to give them education'. The growing number of children who were neither at school or at work, provided further argument for compulsory education.

> 'Poor levels of literacy among large swathes of the population cost Britain around £10 billion a year...' The *Sunday Telegraph*, 23 February 1997.

In order 'to fill up the gaps', the country was to be divided into school districts, based on municipal boroughs and civil parishes, in which, if voluntary effort had failed to provide sufficient, or any, local elementary education, school boards, elected by the ratepayer and open to female members, were to be set up to do so.

The Board Schools were to be financed by government grant and the imposition of a local rate. This rate assistance tended to help the board schools to pay higher salaries, which perhaps drew in better teachers. The voluntary, denominational sector was to be aided by a 50 per cent government grant and given six months in which to provide satisfactory school accommodation. Mr Forster welcomed 'as much as we rightly can the co-operation and aid of those benevolent men who desire to assist their neighbours'.

In Wadhurst, two such 'benevolent men' who desired 'to assist their neighbours' continued in the persons of the vicar and George Campion Courthope, both of whom already had done much to promote, provide and help the National Schools of Wadhurst and who were now to secure their enlargements, to meet any requirement of the new Act.

Under this new Act, education was still not free or

compulsory. Parents who could afford it paid up to ninepence a week: compulsion was left to the discretion of the local schools boards, which could, with Parliamentary assent – and with certain qualifications – decide on the school-leaving age and enforce attendance.

Inspection-dependent grants, based on attendance and examination in the 3Rs, together with optional geography and history, which were added in 1867, were still to be awarded and thus the 'payment by result' scheme of 1862 continued as before.

Inspection was now to be non-denominational, but Diocesan Inspectors were to examine religious education in the National Schools. In Board Schools, religious instruction, of a non-denominational nature, was at the discretion of the individual board, but in both Denominational and Board School, parents had the right of child withdrawal. Religious instruction in the Wadhurst schools consisted at this time of: The Old and New Testaments, the Catechism, Prayer Book Repetition and Hymn Singing, to which, later, the Ten Commandments and chanting (of the Psalms) were added.

5

The Second National School Building with the New Infant School, 1871–73

In 1871, the year following the acceptance of the Education Act, Mr Charles Bocking had been headmaster of the boys' school for 17 years, Miss Watson headmistress of the girls' and infant school for five years and Miss Charlotte Page, after three years as headmistress of the Cousely Wood School, had taken up her post as headmistress of the newly created Wadhurst Infant School.

By now, Mr Bocking was the father of nine children and, in the previous year, had become the organist of the parish church, as well as continuing as its choirmaster.

The nineteenth-century log-books of the Wadhurst schools have either been lost or destroyed, but, fortunately, the diocesan reports on the religious instruction for the years 1872–92 throw considerable light on the work of the schools for these years.

The wise and helpful remarks of the Diocesan Inspectors stand in stark contrast to those issued by Her Majesty's Inspectors on the work of the school at Cousely Wood, which, only too often, confirm the worst fears expressed by the opponents of 'payment by results'.

In this year, 1872, the church spire was struck by lightning.

When Diocesan Inspector the Rev. Robert Blight visited the schools on 20 April 1872, and graded two divisions of the boys' school from 'Fair' to 'Good' for its work on the Old Testament, New Testament, Catechism and Prayer Book

Repetition, he commented: 'On the whole, the school is doing good work in religious subjects in a satisfactory manner', but, although he did realise the teaching difficulties involved, he felt that 'The teaching in the Catechism should be more distinct and careful'.

In addition, he considered the Lower Division to be below the standard of the school and that attention should be given to the matter.

The hymn singing of the school, however was 'Good', as was its tone and discipline.

The two divisions of the girls' school were graded 'Very Fair' to 'Good' and Mr Blight considered: 'This school is working in a very satisfactory manner in Religious Subjects. The children answer with intelligence and correctness', and gave special praise to the Upper Division for its 'careful Reading'.

Unlike that in the boys' school, the teaching throughout the girls' school was very uniform, which showed a 'great power of supervision on the part of the Mistress'. The singing was 'Very Fair' and the tone and discipline of the school was 'Very Good'.

At this time, infant schools were not graded, but Mr Blight gave Charlotte Page's new school fulsome praise:

This department of Wadhurst School is very good indeed in Religious subjects. The Mistress deserves every praise for the confident way in which she is training the children and for the thoroughly happy tone and good discipline found in the school. The intelligent way in which the children answer, calls for special mention.

In the following year, 1873, Mr Blight's comments were rather more critical. The boys' work, although of a 'Fair Character', wanted 'more vigour'. He also gave the wise advice that: 'Every narrative should supply the basis of a living lesson. At present, facts seem to be regarded as the only thing necessary.' He suggested, too, that the boys should be divided into three divisions as: 'The elder boys who showed mostly very good ability, were held back by the younger boys.'

The girls' school was told: 'The fault of the religious teaching in this school is that it is too dry. The facts of The Bible are taught as something quite apart from human nature...'

Mr Blight considered that, although Miss Watson was a 'good teacher', she should remedy these failings on the part of her assistants.

The infants, under Miss Page, alone received high praise for they 'passed a remarkably good exam'.

The Wadhurst schools' singing frequently received praise from the Diocesan Inspector, which reflects the special interest of Mr Bocking and also that of Miss Watson, who was a member of the parish church choir.

This, in turn, perhaps reflects the considerable village interest in music-making at this time. The church choir had continued from at least the end of the previous century; the village orchestra perhaps stemmed from the church band of the same time, but which was supplanted by a barrel organ around 1848; and now, in 1871, a town band was formed.

In 1892, a Salvation Army Corps was founded, which then had its own band.

Concerts, consisting of vocal and instrumental music, penny readings and plays, fixed to coincide with the full moon, were frequent.

Around 1870, in neighbouring Tunbridge Wells, 27 'professors' of music advertised their music lessons in the local press and regular concerts, some by well-known artistes, were given.

In the eighteenth century, Handel took the waters there.

The School at Cousely Wood, now Infant and Lower Junior, 1871–73

On 2 January 1871, Miss Emma Brown succeeded Charlotte Page as Headmistress of Cousely Wood School. It was now intended for both infants and younger juniors, who previously had been sent up to Wadhurst. There were now four standards, with about 60 children on the roll. By the end of the year, this number had increased to about 100.

Emma Brown had been trained at Brighton College, from which she had come direct to Cousely Wood as a probationary teacher. She was assisted by pupil-teacher Hester Walters. (Under the 1862 Code, head teachers no longer received a grant for training their pupil-teachers, whose five-year contract could be terminated at any time. Fewer candidates now came forward.)

Life at the school, for a while, appears to have gone on as in the years before. There were still many visitors: the vicar and his wife, the curate, the Scripture reader, still frequently came; Mrs Bone still brought handkerchiefs for the children to sew, cakes and apples for them to eat and one of her friends brought Fodel-work for them to do. Mr and Mrs Watson Smyth, of the Castle, occasionally visited, and Mr Courthope, of Whiligh, brought hangers for the pictures and pegs for the clothes. But, overall, there appear far fewer visits from the ladies who at one time helped to teach the children. Perhaps they received no encouragement to do so.

There were still many absences – through illness, street, church and chapel treats, village clubs, and children still helped their parents on the land.

The work of the school went on. Standard 2 had a lesson on numeration and, on another occasion, was taught how to do long division; Standard 1 received some new books and, shortly after, was examined in reading. It was also examined in arithmetic, and was found to be 'progressing'. The children continued with their gallery lessons, which included Scriptural subjects, and they also learnt some new hymns – but fewer of these lesson are recorded in the log-book.

And here, in this little hamlet school, the Newcastle Report of 1861 and the subsequent Revised Code of 1862, which required

a searching examination by competent authority of every child in every school to which grants are paid ... with a view to ascertaining whether the indispensable elements of knowledge are thoroughly acquired and to make the prospects of the position of the teacher dependent to a considerable extent on the result of this examination...

gradually began to have its effects.

Inspection 1997.

A Church of England primary school was among the 18 schools publically named as failing by the Secretary of State for Education.

To meet the requirements of this 'searching examination', which was focused on the three Rs, 21-year-old Emma Brown, assisted by the teenage pupil-teacher and the even younger monitress, worked and constantly examined and re-examined the hundred children in their charge, at the expense of other subjects.

At last, on 22 January 1872, in the presence of the Rev. John Foley, his curate and Mr George Courthope, the children were examined by HMI F. Moncreiff.

In the report received the following March, the inspector considered that the discipline, reading and spelling of the school, were 'Fair', but that improvement was required in handwriting and in arithmetical tables in the lower part of the school. He deplored, furthermore, the habit of children whispering the answer to each other, which was destructive to teaching, but which no remonstration would stop.

In the following year, 1873, although the inspector made allowances for the fact that the school was still, in great measure, an infant school, that the proportion of older children was small, that the more advanced boys were drafted off to Wadhurst when sufficiently instructed, and was aware that there had been fever in the school, he was far less sympathetic than in the previous year.

Standard 1 was 'really weak', too much was left to the pupil-teacher, so that the results, particularly in arithmetic, were not 'creditable'. The pupil-teacher was a 'poor teacher', her examination result was indifferent and her grammar paper, a failure. 'If she fails to the same extent next year, the Grant will have to be reduced by £10. Thenceforth by £20 for every year.'

The deductions were empowered by Article 52 of the Revised Code of 1862 for, among other things, faults of instruction or discipline on the part of the teacher.

The mistress, however, had satisfactorily passed her two probationary years and would receive her certificate.

By this time, visitors were even fewer and help and gifts to the school rarely given.

On 10 April 1873, Emma gave up her duties as headmistress of the school.

Progress and standards, 1997

Mr. Major (Prime Minister), said '...The first pillar will be the tests ... at 7, 11 and 14. We'll publish the results ... tests (will be) marked so that children get scores out of 100. That's common sense.'

6

The Wadhurst National Schools – Boys, Girls and Infants. 1873–86

When Mr Blight, the Diocesan Inspector, visited the schools in April 1874, he was rather less pleased with the work than in the year before.

In the boys' school, he complained that there was 'Not much progress during the past year', and graded the work on the Old Testament, New Testament and the Ten Commandments as 'Moderate' in Division 1 and only 'Fair' in Division 2. The extra division which he had advocated in the previous year had not materialised, and did not for many a year to come. Even the hymn repetition was graded but 'Fair' in Division 1 and went unheard in Division 2.

The girls' school faired rather better, to receive 'Good' grades in Division 2 for the Old Testament and the new Testament, 'Very Fair' for the Creed and the Ten Commandments; but in Division 1, although a 'Very Fair' was given for the Old Testament, only a 'Fair' was given for the Creed, Ten Commandments and Prayer Book repetition.

There were some 'good features', said the inspector, but there was a lack of 'systematic teaching ... If only Miss Watson will devote some of her excellent teaching powers to this...'

Again, it was the infant school which received almost unreserved praise for its 'thorough good character and Miss Page deserves the greatest praise for the excellent way in which she trains the young children under her care...'

The inspector suggested, however, that there should be a

more 'systematic repetition of parts of the Catechism by the children, for when they get older'.

Good, steady, overall progress was maintained in the three schools over the next years, with, in 1878, the boys' school being graded 'Good' to 'Very Good', which gave 'great credit' to Mr Bocking and his assistant, Mr Larcombe, who had come to the school two years before.

In 1878, the girls' school was also graded 'Good' to 'Very Good' and Miss Watson praised for her 'careful and earnest work'. The senior girls, too, were praised, for answering 'very eagerly'.

Fulsome praise also continued for Miss Page and her infant school, with, in this year, the babies having a 'wide range of narrative' and answering 'very nicely'.

For some years, Mr Blight described the boys in such terms as 'eager and bright', which was reflected in their 'hearty hymn singing' – even although it was, perhaps, a 'little rough' – and gave grades of 'Good' to 'Very Good'. But in 1883 there was indication that all was not quite right with the school.

In that year, although the grades of 'Good' to 'Very Good' were still given, and the teachers praised for their 'careful and methodical work', Mr Blight added: 'I was present at prayers and was grieved to see so large a number of boys in late. They can surely remedy this.' Even worse: 'The order in Assembly might be greatly improved.'

Soon after, the school door was locked against 'late boys', who, when let in, were caned – perhaps as the result of Mr Blight's complaint.

In the years previous, the girls had also received satisfactory grades, together with such comments as: 'Nothing could be better than the careful way in which the girls answered ... reflecting the thoroughly good teaching.'

A comment which was made, in spite of the lower divisions not doing 'full justice' to its teacher. On another occasion, Mr Blight felt that the attention of the pupil-teacher should be drawn to the fact that her teaching of elementary doctrine to the lower group was 'deficient'. But, happily, the 'tone' of the school was 'Good' and the upper group gave 'accurate and careful answers'.

In 1883, the girls continued to receive the satisfactory grades of 'Very Fair' to 'Very Good', but, although the 'tone' of the school still did credit to Miss Watson, and in each group the girls were 'cheerful and fairly intelligent', the inspector felt that the elder girls should practise writing out the Lord's Prayer and that the younger ones should not only learn to speak more readily, but also have a 'few more lessons in Elementary Doctrine'.

Over these years, the infant school continued to receive much praise. Miss Page was described as an 'Excellent' teacher and even if, sometimes, the children were a 'little shy', they appeared thoroughly interested in their work and answered with 'intelligence, originality and accuracy'. The inspector hoped that Miss Page's 'kind and sympathetic influence' would bear 'lasting fruit', and expressed the 'great pleasure he had obtained from examining the children in their work'.

Mr Boys, who was born in the village in 1878, remembered Miss Page as a tall, thin lady. He remembered the large classes she taught and the visitors who came – but not the sweets they brought. He recalled, however, that the children's outdoor clothes were kept in the vestibule, from where, at 4 o'clock, she brought them in a large clothing basket. Item by item, she held up the clothes until each was claimed by its owner. Unfortunately, Mr Boys claimed the wrong article, for which he was reproved. Very severely, it would seem, for he felt himself so unjustly treated, that he threatened to kick her.[32]

In 1886, the year in which Mr Blight retired, Mr Foley died and the Cross Commission was set up to enquire into the workings of The Elementary School Act, the inspector's grade for the boys' school had dropped from 'Good' to 'Fair' and his adverse criticisms were reserved for that school only. The elements of church teaching were 'Unsatisfactory', the repetition of Scripture 'Below Average', the hymn singing but 'Fair' and, in addition, Mr Blight regretted having to call attention to the noisy conduct of the upper group, whilst he was talking to the lower.

Mr Bocking, too, retired from his post as parish organist in this year, a post which he had held for the past sixteen years.[33]

Overall, however, the girls' school managed to retain its momentum and, in 1886, Mr Blight gave it the grade of 'Very Good', after a 'very successful examination', with 'scholars bright and eager', and giving answers which showed 'great intelligence'. Singing and chanting, too, were 'Good' and the 'Tone' of the school 'Admirable'.

Of the infant school, Mr Blight wrote: 'I cannot speak too highly of Miss Page's work and influence.'[34]

The Rev. John Foley, MA, the father of nine children, three living and six dead, died in 1886, at the age of 80.

He was described as a tall, bearded man, learned, but kindly and genial. He visited around his parish by means of a pony and trap and frequently called in at the schools.

During his 40 years as Vicar of Wadhurst, John Foley had taken a constant interest in its education. He had re-established the Sunday school and then helped to set up and maintain the first National School in Wadhurst. With the help of George Campion Courthope, he initiated and energetically promoted the building of new schools and their subsequent enlargement, in both Wadhurst and Cousely Wood, to which he and his family gave enduring help and support.[35]

The School at Cousely Wood, Infant and Lower Junior, 1873–86

Miss Ellen Mary King succeeded Emma Brown and took up her duties on 21 April 1873. She recorded in her log-book: 'Weather very bad – School very small in consequence.'

On the very next day, in the presence of the curate (the Rev. Richards), George Courthope, Esq., and Mr Daniels (the Scripture reader), the new headmistress was faced with a school examination in Scripture by the Diocesan Inspector. For the next 20 years, examinations and inspectors continued a dominating and traumatic feature of school life for Ellen King, her staff and children.

For the most part, diocesan reports went unrecorded in the log-book, but the attitudes of the government inspectors which resulted from the payment by result scheme of 1862, stand out in stark contrast to the everyday life of the school and its around 90 children.

Children were still absent through sickness, weather, treats or work; they were still punished for their disobedience, swearing or truancy; they sang 'The North Wind doth Blow', 'The Fire Went Out', 'Alone at Night I Stand'; in the gallery, they learnt about the Tower of Babel, The formation of valleys, photography and cleanliness – and sometimes they were awarded buns for their good attendance.

But then Her Majesty's Inspector visited. Following his inspection of 5 January 1874, he reported:

My Lords [of the Privy Council] have felt great doubt whether they ought not with-hold a portion of the Grant for the failure in Arithmetic of the first standard.

Although the inspector could not speak highly of the infant lessons and could only hope that the pupil-teacher would show general improvement the next year, his threat of the previous year of grant deduction was not repeated. He realised that the school was intended mainly for infants and standards one and two, but as a third of the children were nine and over, he expected a good third standard in the next year. (See Appendix page 252 for comparative requirements, 1862 and 1992.)

During the ensuing year, monitress Mary Boorman was replaced by Nancy Manktelow, pupil-teacher Hester Walters was confirmed at the parish church, and attendance still suffered through illness, weather and treats.

In 1875, 'My Lords' did carry out their threat and the grant was reduced by one-tenth for 'defective instruction', especially in arithmetic. The inspector was scathing in his comments: The work did not even 'give promise'; the most ordinary words, such as 'free', 'nose', 'his', were misspelt and in arithmetic, there was 'a complete breakdown in every child ... through bad notation and inaccurate work'.

Hester Walters again passed an unsatisfactory examination and she, too, suffered a grant deduction of £10.

Ellen King's Teachers' Certificate was deferred.

In 1876, the inspector, H.G. Allington, saw no improvement in the work. He wrote: 'Very few children have reached a pass in any subject'.

'My Lords' hoped that 'the managers would see that strenuous efforts were made to improve the children's attainments'.

One-tenth was again deducted and for the third time, Hester failed her examination. Hester resigned and monitor Nancy Manktelow took her place as pupil-teacher. The headmistress suffered a breakdown.

When HMI Allington retired in 1901, the parish magazine described him as an 'able and thorough examiner ... who had always shown himself most kind and considerate'.

In spite of an epidemic of measles, the next inspection, in 1877, did show a very satisfactory improvement in reading and writing; no loss of grant was suffered and the teacher was granted her certificate. The inspector, however, did hope that it was not beyond the teacher's power to produce, in addition, good results in arithmetic.

During the course of the following year, two new monitresses, Sarah Ann Ross and Mary Parkhurst, were appointed, and Miss Ellen King became Mrs Ballard; but it still appeared beyond Ellen's power to produce good results in arithmetic.

In 1878, the inspector reported:

The results in Arithmetic are worse than I have ever found them before ... in and above the Second Standard eight sums only out of seventy-seven set have been carefully worked...

In addition, writing was 'very poor' and composition 'very weak'.

Countrywide, it was estimated that only 25 per cent of those examined managed to qualify for a grant in the three Rs.

For the first time, extra subjects, permitted from 1875, had been submitted for inspection. Of these, geography (for boys only) was considered 'Indifferent', grammar 'passably well-taught', and the needlework 'Satisfactory', with the 'cutting-out' done during the year being 'particularly good'.

But the defects in arithmetic outweighed all the rest and the grant, again, was reduced by one-tenth. The next year, when the school suffered a 'cold and draughty classroom' and 'damp and rather dirty offices', yet again the grant was reduced by one-tenth.

The year passed into 1880, when the inspector expressed his pleasure in 'a most satisfactory increase in numbers,' but the results had not, he was sorry to say, improved in proportion.

Pupil-teacher Nancy Manktelow passed an unsatisfactory exam and was threatened with a loss of grant, which the school itself did suffer.

Following the reception of the inspector's report, Mrs Ballard was, again, too ill to attend.

Education by the State

In 1880, the year which saw the 'most satisfactory increase in numbers' at Cousely Wood School, an Act of Parliament, the 'Mundella', ensured the compulsory education of children between the ages of five and ten, with local authorities empowered to increase the leaving age to 14, with exemptions based on proficiency or attendance.

With the introduction of compulsory education, school fees became hard to collect, so that, in 1891, a fee-grant of 10s per head was introduced. Fees in elementary schools were finally abolished in 1918.

A previous Act of 1876, the 'Sandon', had already authorised the establishment of attendance committees, in the absence of school boards, which through their attendance officer could enforce regular attendance.

The Act laid upon the parent the duty of seeing that his child received 'efficient elementary instruction in Reading, Writing and Arithmetic', but it implied rather than compelled and contained loopholes for avoidance. Necessary by-laws of compulsion, too, were often non-existent. In 1893, the school-leaving age was raised to 11 and in 1899 to 12.

The School at Cousely Wood, continued

The first attendance officer for the Wadhurst area was Mr Clark, who made his first recorded visit to Cousely Wood School on 31 January 1882, a year of many out-breaks of measles.

The appointment of Mr Clark did not appear to improve attendance and Mrs Ballard made repeated comments about his unhelpfulness.

There were few visitors to the school and the enthusiastic help and support which it had received in its early days had almost completely disappeared. Occasionally, the curate, Mr C.C. Allen, took a lesson, Mrs Bone brought sweets and Mary Foley 'looked in', but sometimes, months would pass without a single visitor and, by now, the vicar and George Courthope were both growing old.

There was, however, an exception, for, in 1883, a year of fever, Mrs Wilkin, whose husband had land in the area, visited the school for the first time. From then and for the next 30 years she and her husband continued their association with it, encouraging and helping the staff and the children with treats and prizes and parties and greeting cards at Christmas.

It is doubtful whether such treats compensated for the uncertain conditions contained in the school day. How much inspector pressures, directly, or indirectly through the teachers, weighed upon the children, goes unmeasured, but the payment by result system, with its yearly tests and carping criticism, was hardly conducive to a warm, happy and anxiety-free atmosphere.

In the 1880s, the school was not helped by an ever-changing junior staff. In 1882, Nancy Manktelow, the pupil-teacher, became an unqualified teacher, but, in the following year, resigned. Perhaps she was asked to resign, for the log-book records that the inspector had asked the managers 'to specify their dissatisfaction with N. Manktelow'. No enlightenment follows. Nancy was replaced by Miss Louisa Makepeace, who stayed two weeks, returned two months later, and received recognition as a teacher, only to resign by the end of the year.

In turn, she was replaced by Miss Kemsett, who became a member of the staff on 4 January 1886. The yearly inspection followed a fortnight later. A month later, Miss Kemsett was left in sole charge of the school, for again the report was unsatisfactory and again Mrs Ballard was too ill to attend. By the time of the hop-picking holidays, Miss Kemsett had resigned. After the holidays, Frances Stevenson joined the staff, caught the measles at the beginning of December, and was absent until the end of the year. The yearly inspection followed immediately after her return.

Education by the State

In 1886 – the year of Mr Foley's death, the retirement of Mr Blight and measles in the school – when, once again, the government had begun to realise that the cost of running an ever-increasing number of schools was never failing to rise and that there was discontent with the working of the voluntary system, a Royal Commission, under the chairmanship of Lord Cross, was set up. It was 'To enquire into the workings of the Elementary School Act, England and Wales'. Its findings were published two years later, in the form of a Major-Minor Report. In spite of this, agreement was found on a number of important points, including:

The modification and relaxation of the payment by result scheme.

The provision of a wider and more liberal curriculum, to include such subjects as science, technical instruction, drawing and cookery. (The commission considered that too much importance was attached to spelling, but that more should be paid to handwriting, practical arithmetic and the learning by heart of poetry.)

The provision of better school buildings, grounds and equipment.

A more liberal supply of school books and the introduction of school libraries.

The extension of Evening Education in a similar manner, but to include also, social and recreational activities and the admission of adults.

The provision of more and better-trained teachers.

The means for providing these better-trained teachers, however, proved divisive. (See Appendix 36 for teacher training.) A majority felt that the existing pupil-teacher system provided a valuable means of recruitment and training, and with an improved educational provision and a raising of the entry age, should be retained.

A minority felt that the training given by headmasters was frequently poor; that many pupil-teachers very soon gave up, did not enter college, left early when they did and that many continued only as uncertificated teachers. Some considered it unnecessary to have high entry qualification, lest it should exclude those 'with a natural aptitude and a love of learning', but, however, did consider that 'more women of superior social position and general culture' were needed.[37]

A minority also expressed the opinion that education should be decentralised and recognised as an important branch of local government.

Religious issues created the main divisions. The majority felt that the Voluntary Schools should have equal rights with the Board Schools and so be rate-assisted. Some felt that denominational teaching should be made available in Board Schools. A minority not only opposed rate-assistance for Voluntary Schools but considered that purely secular schools should be available and that students as well as children should be free to opt out of religious studies.

The commission recorded that 4.5 million children were in inspected schools, 64 per cent of which had been erected and supported by local, voluntary effort. In 1876, the average cost per scholar was £1 14s 8d, but by 1886 had risen to £1 19s 5d, with a government grant of £2,866,700.

Lord Linger, the Permanent Secretary to the Treasury from 1869 to 1885, considered that the cost per scholar was larger than need be; that the salaries of some teachers were unnecessarily high, the 'golden rule of making things do,' was overlooked and that efficiency was considered dependent on expenditure.

Over the next years, culminating in the Education Act of 1902, a number of the commission's recommendations were put into effect. In 1890, a Code abolished grants for the three

Rs and retained them only for class and specific subjects. The Secretary of the Education Department, Sir George Kekewich, said of this Code that its aim was 'to substitute for the bald teaching of facts and the cramming which was necessary ... the development of interest and intelligence and the acquirement of real, substantial knowledge'. Later Codes encouraged the addition of more subjects to the curriculum and also visits to museums, art galleries and historic buildings. The remnants of the payment by result system were removed finally in 1897.

An Enquiry of 1896–98 recommended that the qualifying age for pupil-teachers should be 15–16 and that pupil-teaching centres should approximate to secondary schools. In 1899, it became possible to substitute London Matriculation and the Senior Local Examination of Oxford and Cambridge for the Queen's Scholarship Examination, itself abolished in 1907.

Residential training colleges were improved and staffed by men and women of higher qualification and wider experience. An Education Regulation of 1890 enabled day colleges to be attached to universities and for university colleges to be recognised. Day students were permitted to attend residential colleges and three-year students were authorised, some of whom read for degrees.

7

The School at Cousely Wood, 1887–1902

The Diamond Jubilee of Queen Victoria in 1887, with which the Cross Commission deliberations coincided, was celebrated at Cousely Wood School with a whole-day's holiday.

There was little for Mrs Ballard to celebrate, however, for earlier, the school had received its annual inspection. The inspector was warned that there had been measles in the school, which the teacher, Miss Frances Stevenson, had caught, and he professed to understand and appreciate that good results could not be expected.

His report belied his words: 'The lamentably bad ones of today, however, do not appear to be altogether due to exceptional causes. Children do not suddenly become exceedingly bad writers.'

Of the infants' department, he complained: 'The Object lesson was profitless ... judged by the methods used ... poor needlework of the boys, lack of expression in the Recitation, want of uniformity in the Action Songs, but the great deficiency seems to be the lack of intelligence in the instruction.'

Frances Stevenson's reaction reflected, perhaps, the changing attitudes to be found in a younger generation, for, in reply, she wrote: 'Finding that I cannot give satisfaction in my duties at this school, I think it best to resign them and I therefore give three months notice from the above date.' (February 15.)

On 15 May, 1887, Frances gave up her duties and for a couple of weeks Miss Mary Bocking, the daughter of Wadhurst's headmaster, helped out.

During this year, Mr Foley's successor, Dr Codrington, was inducted, but of greater significance to Cousely Wood School, was, after an approval period, the appointment of a new assistant mistress, Miss Mayne, who not only helped to create more settled conditions in the school by staying 19 years, but, for the first time, provided in the infant class the presence of an experienced adult.

More satisfactory reports at last began to appear and in 1889, even with half the infants away with whooping cough, the inspector considered the children 'well taught' and in the upper school, which had now extended to a sixth standard, 126 were 'Creditable', even although Standards 3 and 4 were weak in all subjects.

Unfortunately, in the very next year, the school – or the inspector – returned to old ways, for grant loss, through deficiencies in the basic subjects, was again threatened.

It was for the last time, for the recommendations of the Cross Report were beginning to work through, and now the Code of 1890 abolished grants in respect of the three Rs, to retain them only for certain other subjects.

Illness was still an almost constant factor for poor attendance, with frequent epidemics of measles, whooping cough and influenza. Bad weather still resulted in an empty, or near-empty school. Children continued to help in the fields, attend treats and clubs, or to be kept at home by the needs or indifference of their parents.

In 1893, the inspector blamed the poor work above the second standard on the irregular attendance. He recommended that: 'If it were due to the slackness of the Attendance Committee, the Managers must make a definite complaint to the Education Department.'

The Attendance Committee appears to have taken some action, for a little later in the year, Mrs Ballard reported: 'Four children delayed until 5.00pm., according to a new rule by order of the Committee, for absence the previous day.'

At this time, Mrs Ballard began to record attendance averages, which, for the year 1893 was 60 per cent. On 14 June 1895, 15 years after education had become compulsory, Mrs

Ballard gave the week's average as 74.7 and commented that it was the highest since the previous August.

Mr Clark had now been Attendance Officer for 13 years, but during that time had neither attended regularly at the school nor acted on Mrs Ballard's absentee lists. A new Attendance Officer, Mr Foster, was appointed in 1897, but little improvement in the children's attendance followed.

In these circumstances, it is to be wondered at that, with around 100 boys and girls on the register, with an age range of under five to over ten and with a wide ability range, two teachers, Mrs Ballard and Miss Mayne, assisted by two teenage monitors, Eva F. Easter and Frances Funge, could achieve any progress whatsoever. It was a credit to the staff, perhaps, that to the extra subjects – geography and grammar – the additional subjects of music and drawing could be added for inspection.

Music, in the form of singing, had been noted in the school log-book since the school opened in 1868, but its first inspectoral acknowledgement did not occur until 1884, when it was remarked by the inspector: 'The children's voices should be better trained...'

Other remarks followed in subsequent years with such as: 'Weak singing', 'Action songs lacked uniformity'.

In 1888, there was a new musical development when a Mr Parnum came to take tonic sol-fa lessons, which took place on Wednesday mornings from 10.45 to 12 noon. Unfortunately, Mr Parnum's attendance was irregular, so that Mrs Ballard was caused to write: 'Mr. Parnum frequently away from his singing lessons even when expected.'[38]

For all that, 24 children attended the Singing Competition at Tunbridge Wells held in 1889. After the competition, Mr Parnum came no more, but Mr Pierson took over and stayed for at least a year.

Over the following years, inspector-comment ranged from the 'Ear-testing in Singing needs more Practise', of 1892, to the 'bright singing' of 1896, after which comment ceased.

Drawing began to receive special mention, so that, on 18 December 1891, Mrs Ballard was able to record: 'Drawing

Exam. today. Revd. A. Kirke, (curate), present.' Followed by: 'Received the Drawing Report. Have earned the "Good" Grade.' This was in 1897, the last year of 'payment by result' in any form.

Local effort, through the Annual Cottagers' Flower Show, also encouraged the children's efforts by promoting competitions in drawing, writing and needlework. In this same year, Mrs Ballard wrote in her log-book: 'Prize Money earned at the Flower Show distributed by Mrs. Wilkin.'

The diocese, too, encouraged the children's efforts in the Annual Scripture Examination, for which it awarded certificates to successful candidates.

Geography, restricted to the boys, was first inspected in 1878. Fifteen years later, it was extended to the girls, when cardinal points and England and Wales were studied.

In 1899, elementary science was added to the timetable.

In her log-book of 1901, Mrs Ballard gave an outline of her syllabus. It included:

Arithmetic

English:	Reading. Copy Books. Writing: formation of easy sentences, oral and written. Recitation. Upper Division also included: letter-writing, Descriptive writing, after previous discussion. Grammar, with a view to Composition. Recitation for the Upper Division included the poem, 'Evangeline'.
Geography:	Neighbourhood. England. Geographical terms. Upper Division – Australia.
Other Subjects:	included Object lessons, Needlework, Drawing. Varied Occupations. Singing. Drill.

By 1898, the inspector considered that;

> The Reading of the Upper Standard reaches a high level of proficiency ... the Manual Occupations of the boys are well selected and thoroughly carried out ... The Infants were very well taught.

In the year of the new Education Act (1902) in spite of much influenza, 'Composition and Arithmetic improved ... Infants creditably advanced and interest well secured.'

In anticipation of this Act, the school buildings had been receiving attention. In 1901, the parish magazine reported that the school playground had been 'greatly improved' and that there was a gain in 'light and cheerfulness' through the replacement of the semi-opaque glass by clear glass in the school windows.

In addition, the Inspector was able to comment: 'The writing on the walls of the Offices [of which he had complained previously] was no longer apparent.'

During the last years of the century, the school, again, began to receive more visitors, the impetus given, perhaps, by the Rev. W. Wace, when he acted as locum tenens for Dr Codrington. Dr Codrington himself seems to have had little time for the schools, but his successor, the Rev George MacLean, who became vicar in 1893, was greatly interested in them, particularly the infants school.

It sounds like a return to the earlier, happier days of the school that Mrs Ballard could write in her log-books on 6 May 1901, 'The Misses MacLean showed the children how to spin.'

8

The Wadhurst National Schools, Boys, Girls and Infants, 1887–1902

The Rev. John Foley, who died in 1886, was succeeded in the following year by the Rev. Dr Codrington, a missionary from the Melanesian Islands, but who returned to them for a long period. He was born in 1830 and educated at Charterhouse and Wadham College, Oxford. In later years he was a Canon of Chichester Cathedral and died in 1922. Although seemingly well-liked, he appears to have taken little part in the life of the parish and even less in the schools.

The new Diocesan Inspector, the Rev. Walter Walsh, made his first visit to Wadhurst in the year of Dr Codrington's induction and, like Mr Blight, spoke well of the three Wadhurst schools. The new inspector graded the boys' school from 'Fair' to 'Very Good', found the written work accurate, but considered that a 'little improvement' in spelling was possible. The singing was satisfactory and the discipline 'Good'. He felt that Mr Bocking and his assistants, Mr Larcombe and Mr Dengate (who had come to the school from Ticehurst in 1887), deserved commendation for their 'Excellent work'.

Miss Watson, in the girls' school, with the tone of the school 'excellent', also deserved 'high praise'. The written work was 'creditable', and although some girls had difficulty with their spelling, many did well. Overall, the school was graded from 'Good' to 'Excellent'.

The graded subjects continued as: the Old Testament, New Testament, Catechism, Liturgy and Repetition. With the coming of Mr Walsh, the infants, too, were graded.

As usual, the infants were 'a credit' to Miss Page, who taught them 'with intelligence'. The children behaved well, were attentive and sang 'very nicely'. The grades given ranged from 'Good' for the Old Testament, Catechism and Liturgy, to 'Very Good' for the New Testament and Repetition.

The next year, the boys' school excelled itself and grades from 'Very Good' to 'Excellent' were given. The boys sang well, their written work was 'extremely good', and the teaching was 'conscientious and intelligent'.

The girls, however, received rather less praise, but they sang well and had fewer spelling mistakes in their written work, which was 'Highly Satisfactory'. Mr Walsh considered the girls well taught and graded them from 'Good to Very Good'.

The infants continued to receive 'Very Good' grades and were, also praised for their behaviour.

Following an attack of apoplexy, Mr Bocking retired in 1890, after 38 years as Wadhurst's headmaster. He was given a leaving present of around £70 and received a teachers' pension of £25 a year, which, even at the time was described as 'not considerable'.

At the inspection in this year, Mr Walsh graded the school from 'Very Good' to 'Excellent'. He considered that the boys 'sang in harmony with taste', that the written work was 'commendable', and that 'excellent work was going on'.

The girls' school, as well, received high praise, with 'Very Good' to 'Excellent' grades. The singing was 'pleasing', the written work was 'Very Good', and Miss Watson was doing 'admirable work'. By now, she had a pupil-teacher and two monitors to help her.

The infants received 'Very Good' grades and continued to do Miss Page credit.

Mr Bocking was succeeded by his assistant, Mr Larcombe, who had joined the school in 1876, to receive his teaching certificate in 1880. Mr Larcombe came to Wadhurst a bachelor, but later married Mary Ann Wallis, the daughter of Mr H.G. Wallis, who had succeeded Mr G. Wallis as parish clerk in 1868.[39] She had been a pupil-teacher in the school, then trained at Brighton from 1882–83 and rejoined the school in 1899. They had three daughters, Gladys, Marjorie and Winnie, and one son, Reginald.

Mr Larcombe is said to have had a good voice, he sang in the church choir and also recruited for it from among the boys in the school. According to Mr Harry Watts, who was a pupil in the school at this time, Mr Larcombe heard him and his cousin, Maurice Watts, singing so well at assembly one day in 1888 that he bent over the better to hear them; then invited them to join the church choir.[40]

Mr Boys, by now in the boys' school, remembered Mr Larcombe as being a rather short-tempered man who would lash about him with the cane. On one occasion, when Mr Larcombe was about to cane a boy, two other boys rushed out to stop him, so he called out to Mr Goodall for help.

On Mr Bocking's retirement, Mr Williams joined the staff. He was described by Harry Watts as being a 'little bald-headed man, getting on a bit, but a nice chap who everybody liked'. Mr Dengate and Mr Williams were both, in turn, organist and choirmaster at the parish church.[41]

With the coming of Mr Williams, a third division, which had been suggested by the Diocesan Inspector, Mr Blight, nearly 18 years before, was, at last, formed. The new division appears to have made a good start, for at the Diocesan Inspection in 1891, its Old Testament, New Testament, Catechism and Liturgy were awarded 'Excellent' grades and for the Repetition, a 'Very Good'. The other two divisions were also well-graded. The inspector remarked that the boys sang exceedingly well, that their written work deserved praise and that the school was 'in a much better condition than last year'.

Since, in the previous year, according to the inspector, 'Excellent work' was going on, perhaps reference was being made to the physical state of the school. On the other hand, perhaps Mr Walsh had seen more than on what he had made comment, for Mr Boys said of Mr Bocking:

He was very easy minded and didn't lose control ... but, in these latter years ... he was beginning to tire, and sometimes in lessons he would doze and the boys would shoot peas at him and Mr Bocking would awake with a start and say, 'What's that? What's that?'

In this year of 1891, grades for the girls' school ranged from 'Fairly Good' to 'Very Good' and the inspector felt that the girls had sung very well, that their written work was 'Generally Good' and in a certain number of cases, it was 'Very Good'.

As usual, 'The Infants sung well, behaved well and acquitted themselves in such a manner as to do credit to Miss Page.'

In 1892, the year in which the diocesan reports end, the boys' school was again graded from 'Very Good' to 'Excellent'; the boys sang well, their written work was satisfactory and Mr Larcombe and his assistants had taught well.

The girls' singing was nicely done, the written work was 'Very Good', but Mr Walsh felt that 'more definite teaching of the Catechism was desirable', a sentiment which had been expressed in the three schools many times before. The girls, still in two divisions, were graded from 'Good' to 'Very Good'.

The infants, too, were graded, 'Good' to 'Very Good' and not only did they sing 'in a pleasing manner', but, also, they were 'very eager' to answer the questions proposed to them. All in all, it would appear, however, that Mr Walsh was a little less enthusiastic about Miss Page's work than had been his predecessor.

Mr Dengate and Mr Williams were the first of a succession of assistant teachers and organist-choirmasters who, in the last decade of the nineteenth century played a part both in the community and the school and were still to be remembered with affection 60 years and more later.

Mr Williams was followed by 27-year-old Allan Rigg, who had been a pupil-teacher in West Ham, East London, teacher-trained in Cheltenham and then had come to Wadhurst, at £70 a year. According to Harry Watts, Allan Rigg was a small, tubby, jokey man, who, although nice to the boys, kept them in their place. He liked a drink, which was, perhaps, why Authority didn't like him.

Mr Rigg had his church choir practices on Friday nights. They started at 8.00 p.m. and sometimes continued to 10.00 p.m., which, the choirmen considered, was far too late for the boys, particularly those who lived at Stonebridge and had to walk home in the dark. To solve the problem, the men encouraged the boys to walk out of practice, without permission, at 9.00 p.m. 'But,' said Harry Watts, 'they weren't thinking of the boys, but of themselves, for all they wanted to do was to get to the pub. for a drink, before it closed.'

Twenty-five-year-old James Worth succeeded Allan Rigg. James Worth had been a pupil-teacher at Bromborough Pool Works, Birkenhead, from 1886 to 1890; two years an assistant teacher at St James's School, Birkenhead and perhaps two years at Harbleden, Henley-on-Thames. With other teaching experience, but still uncertificated, James Worth came to Wadhurst in 1895, at a salary of £60 per annum.

Augustine Pearse came next. He had been a pupil-teacher at Weston-super-Mare and trained at Exeter. Mr Watts described him as a 'good chap who they all respected'. Mr Pearse conducted the newly formed and short-lived Choral Society and was the first organist on the Vowles organ, which was installed in 1896 and placed at the south-east corner of the church.[42]

Mr Pearse was succeeded by Mr Marsh Sanders Goodall, an Associate of the Tonic Sol-fa College, who had served as a pupil-teacher at Middleport Board School and trained at Bangor College, from where he came to Wadhurst. He conducted the Choral Society and as organist-choirmaster at the parish church received £25 a year. Organists prior to him had received £20.

Mr 'Wiggie' Knight, who came to the school in 1898, had trained at Chester from 1897 to 1898, after serving as a pupil-teacher. Mr Harry Watts said of him, 'He was a good chap, he was, and could play', although, it seems, he was a 'bit bald'. Mr Bond, who was born in 1883, remembered him as a 'jocular' person, who would, with feigned anger, pretend to hit them across the back of the head with a book.

Mr Knight, too, became organist and choirmaster and in 1899 played at Mr Bocking's funeral.

At Mr Bocking's funeral, Mr Knight played the *Marche Funebre* the *Dead March* and accompanied the choir, which was in 'surplices'.

A newspaper report of the funeral said of Mr Bocking: '...none was so universally known throughout the Parish ... former pupils and friends by their large attendance at the funeral showed the regard by which he was held by them.'

Mr Harry Watts said of him: 'He was a nice old fellow; taught me when I first went to school. He was a good master, really.'

Mr Bocking had 12 children, the first of whom, Jane, born in 1849, became a teacher at Tidebrook School. Another, Marie Eliza, who was born in 1866, was assistant organist at the church and the last, Henry Charles, born in 1871 (d. 1945), became the village hairdresser. He married the daughter of Mr G.W. Ashby, Marie Beatrice, who was also an assistant organist. Their son, Charles, became manager of Watson's, the estate agents, and, too, built up an important collection of Wadhurst memorabilia and photographs.

Except for Mr Knight, who resigned in 1916 on his appointment as headmaster of a Hampshire school, not one of the male assistant teachers stayed for more than a year or two. For the most part, they had come from towns and possibly found the stratified conditions of village life unacceptable. Although the Mundella Act of 1880 had enforced attendance for those between the age of five and ten, with exemptions for those between ten and fourteen, based on attendance or proficiency and the will of the local authority, it would appear that there was still a restless element of unwilling parents and children, which, no doubt, helped towards unsatisfactory teaching conditions. Salaries, too, were fixed locally, and frequently higher ones could be obtained elsewhere.

Local records give little or no information about the teachers who assisted Miss Watson or Miss Page during these last years of the nineteenth century and those they taught tended to be reticent with their recollections.

> According to a Harold Hodge in *The Fortnightly* Review, 1899: 'The elementary school teacher is not likely to be a person of superior type. He is, in truth, a small middle-class person – with all the usual intellectual restrictions of his class. He is, in other words, unintellectual, knowing hardly anything well ... vulgar in the accent and style of his talking, with a low standard of manner. He is, withall, respectable and correct morally, with a high sense of duty, as he understands it, competent in the technique of his calling ... What we want is educated ladies and gentlemen as teachers.'

Dr Codrington, who had succeeded Mr Foley in 1887, retired on health grounds in 1893 and was, in turn, succeeded by the Rev. G.G. MacLean, who came to Wadhurst from Southorpe, Gloucestershire, where he had been vicar from 1883 to 1893.[43]

The new vicar, the father of three grown children, was actively interested in education and although ageing and crippled, maintained this interest until his retirement in 1907. As well as serving as chairman and correspondent of the managers, he constantly went into the schools, particularly the Wadhurst Infant School, where he gave much practical help and a great deal of encouragement.

Within two years of his arrival, perhaps stimulated by the possibility of a new Education Bill (but which, in the face of much opposition, was not presented), efforts were made to improve and enlarge the school buildings, for which £670 was required.

The money was raised by direct donation, church collections and special efforts, which included a concert, organised by the school staffs, when 'very charming scenes from *A Midsummer Night's Dream* were performed', as well as the *Toy Symphony*, flute and piano solos.

In the parish magazine for June 1896, the vicar wrote:

From June 1 all new classrooms and cloakrooms will be in use ... rooms ... large and airy and well-lighted ... no expense has been spared in making perfect the sanitary arrangements and in ensuring as far as possible that there shall be a supply of pure water for drinking ... [There was no piped water into Wadhurst at this time] ... the best education under the most favourable circumstances and that absolutely free of cost.

For long, the vicar was preoccupied with the poor attendance. In a parish magazine of 1896 he wrote:

The managers would never willingly deal hardly with any one, but it cannot be too strongly impressed upon parents that they can no longer be allowed to keep children under 13 at home ... they [the parents] ought to feel that it is their duty to see that their children attend regularly and punctually ... instead of allowing them to remain at home for the most trifling causes.

Later in the same year, the vicar again drew attention to the poor attendance, but added: 'The want of punctuality, especially among the girls is also a serious evil...' And reminded the reader that: 'This excellent education ... is provided for in great measure by the efforts of voluntary subscribers.'

Three years later, in 1899, the vicar was even more outspoken about the poor attendance:

Irregularity of attendance in both schools [Wadhurst and Cousely Wood], is much to be deplored ... it will be necessary to take very stringent measures to compel parents to send their children regularly to school ... the loss of income to the schools through the reduction of average attendance is most serious.

In 1901, ten years after free and compulsory education had been established, the vicar was compelled to continue with his strictures. In spite of that, the Diocesan Inspector was able to report that the 'children had been carefully and conscientiously taught.'

The vicar added:

Great as is the importance of the excellent secular education which is given in our schools, it need hardly be said how infinitely more important it is that our children should have such a religious training as will prepare them, not only for this life, but for the life to come ... There are a great many Board schools [with] no religious instruction...

In the following year, with another Education Act pending, the vicar wrote:

Whatever may be the effect of the present Education Act in the case of the schools, there seems to be every reason to hope that Wadhurst Schools may receive substantial benefit, particularly as the accommodation is sufficient and buildings are in good condition.

1901, the death of Queen Victoria

By the wonderful means of communication we now possess, there flashed forth to every country the sad news of the illness of the oldest and greatest Sovereign and then ... the tidings that it had pleased God to take from us our beloved Queen...

The sombre hangings of the Parish Church on Sunday the 27th, were in keeping with the sad thoughts ... of every worshipper...

Parish magazine, February 1901

In the magazine for March, the editor records that, on the day of the Queen's funeral, there was a special service, for which the church was filled beyond standing room, so that people gathered outside the doors, in the churchyard.

83

9

Education by the State: Education Act of 1902

This new Education Act of which the vicar spoke was the first comprehensive Education Bill to become law. It resulted from the Cross Report of 1888 on elementary education, and the Bryce Report of 1895 on secondary education, each of which advocated a more systemised scheme of control. An Act of 1899 had already replaced the Education Department with a Board of Education, which now became the sole, central authority for primary, secondary and technical education, with its own permanent secretary, who was responsible to a minister in Parliament.

The new Act reorganised education on a municipal basis, by which the county and county boroughs set up in 1888 became responsible for both secondary and elementary education, with smaller authorities having control of elementary education only. The old school boards and attendance committees were terminated and education committees, consisting of councillors and other suitable men and women, were set up by the new, local education authorities.[44]

The new authorities had to supply elementary education in the old, now 'provided' schools; erect new ones where necessary; and to control, and to be responsible for, secular education in the voluntary, now 'non-provided', schools.

The non-provided, denominational schools were to be eligible for rate-support, but, except for fair wear and tear, were still responsible for capital expenditure on the buildings, together with structural repairs and alterations.

The managers of the non-provided schools retained the right of teacher appointment and dismissal, subject to the

84

approval of the LEA on educational grounds, but one-third of the staff had to be LEA appointed.

Religious instruction could be given in a provided school, but subject to the Cowper-Temple clause, introduced into the 1870 Act by an MP of that name, by which it was to be of an undenominational character, with children subject to parental withdrawal in both provided and non-provided schools.

In a non-provided school, it was to be given in accordance with the provisions, if any, of the school's trust deeds and under the control of the managers. The right of withdrawal remained.

Of the 1902 Education Act religious deliberations, Lloyd George said: 'For hours this House whirled round and round in a vortex of a mad frenzy of Theological controversy.'

The Coronation of Edward VII and Alexandra, 1902

Wadhurst celebrated with a special church service and a procession of decorated vehicles, with costumed people on foot and on horse.

For the old people and widows, there was a dinner at 1.00 p.m. in the Market Hall, with meals taken to those too old or infirm to attend. After dinner, all the schoolchildren, accompanied by the whole population, marched to the Castle grounds. The town band and that of the Salvation Army both played, and there were sports and games and tents for tea and at the end, as a gift from Mr Drew of Wadhurst Hall, there was a firework display, for which the rain held off until it was finished.

By this year of 1902, there were 5,030,219 children attending elementary schools, nationally. The output of trained teachers, annually, was 2,791.

Each local authority was also required to:

Consider the educational needs of their area and take such steps as seem to them desirable, after consultation with the board of Education, to supply or aid the supply of education other than elementary and to promote the general co-ordination of all forms of education. (Paragraph 7, Education Act)

The authority was to have regard to the existing supply of schools and colleges and to any other steps already taken under the existing Technical Instructions Acts, 1889–1891.

Its powers included the training of teachers, provision of scholarships and the paying of student fees in colleges or hostels. (In 1904, Training College Regulations encouraged LEAs to develop their own training colleges, for which they were to receive a building grant.)

The Bill was passed in the face of considerable opposition, particularly by those who regretted the passing of the old school boards and those Nonconformists who resented rate-support for voluntary schools.

In 1906, a new Parliament attempted to repeal the Act, but the new Bill was so drastically amended in the Lords that the government proceeded no further with it. It was described in the parish magazine for July as 'a time of much anxiety', for the church and its schools, for a principal clause had proposed the abolition of the voluntary schools by transferring them to the LEAs.

Other unsuccessful attempts were made later, one by Mr McKenna, the President of the Board of Education, in 1908. The parish magazine said of it:

> Mr. McKenna's Education Bill certainly works as if it was meant to strike at the Church of England's 11,377 schools ... our rural schools will be completely swept away, i.e., as church managed schools ... [there is] a tone of bitterness against the Church of England.

Education by Wadhurst to 1910

Until towards the end of the Nineteenth century, local affairs, both civic and church, had continued to be governed by the church vestry, the work of which was diverse. It included the appointment of such parish officers as churchwardens, salaried assistant overseers, assessors and collectors, constables, surveyors, etc and in 1856 a Nuisance Removal Committee was appointed. However, by an Act of 1894, its power, which steadily had been eroded over the past century, passed into the hands of a locally elected parish council. The last appointment of parish officers by the vestry was made on 27 March 1894. The vestry book ended on 7 February 1895, when a Poor Rate of 1s in the pound was levied.[45]

In 1894, the parish magazine commented: 'Much interest necessarily attaches to the coming of the Parish Council.'

A number of parish meetings took place, at which 'several gentlemen' assisted in the discussion of the Act's provisions. These 'gentlemen' included Mr Andrews, solicitor, church-warden and choirman, and also Mr Watson, a Harrow housemaster, lately retired to Wadhurst.

The first meeting of the new parish council was held in April 1898, when a subcommittee was appointed for such concerns as finance, footpaths, lighting and the parish bakehouse. The meeting also discussed the drainage at Sparrows Green and Durgates, additional lamps and the revision of the assistant overseer's salary. One parish councillor was appointed as representative-manager of the schools.

In reality, however, little changed in the village, for those who had led, still led, and with the assistance of the village teachers, ladies of leisure and others, continued to support, encourage and help the many and varied village activities.

Football, cricket and cycling clubs flourished and a 'long-standing' Cottagers' Flower Show had its annual competition at which the children, through the schools, were encouraged to show their work in writing, needlework and kindergarten activities.[46]

Many and varied lectures also took place, probably in the schoolrooms. According to the interests and availability of speakers, they included such subjects as Education, the Police Court Mission, Ashanti and the Iron Industry. In 1905, Miss Buxton gave a lecture, illustrated with photographs, on a journey to the Sudan which she had made with her father, chiefly for 'sporting purposes'. Later, in 1908, the new vicar, the Rev. L.S. Stevenson, gave a reading of 'Marley's Ghost', for which there was a 'good attendance'. The vicar also pleaded for 'more reading'. 'Nowadays,' he said, 'so many people read nothing but newspapers...' and urged his audience to 'read more Dickens'.

A reading room was established, where a subscription of 1s a year, gave access to 600 volumes and in 1904, with Mr Larcombe as treasurer and secretary, a Village Institute for Men was set up in the High Street, at Town Gate, which˙was bought for the purpose at a cost of £900.

An Act of 1889 had allowed the introduction of technical instruction, and classes for laundry and singing were started in the village. First aid classes, taken by Dr Fazan, and home nursing classes were also organised. There was a large attendance at the first aid classes and, in 1900, 22 certificates were awarded.

By his own initiative, Mr Arthur Watson, in 1898, opened a 'night school' at his home, Uplands, now the site of the Community College. Mr Watson intended his School for 'Those who wished to keep up with what they had learnt'. Over 20 young men and lads enrolled and their regular attendance was awarded at the end of the session with a supper provided by the Watsons.[47]

Mr Arthur Watson played a considerable part in village activities. On the receipt of a legacy in 1892 he retired to Wadhurst, where he became a member of the newly formed parish council, a Justice of the Peace, a manager of the church schools, a churchwarden, as well as secretary and/or treasurer of various organisations, including the town band and the flower show. One of his daughters said that he was not really interested in music, but just wanted to help the band.

In order to keep them open, Mr Watson also walked the footpaths. He died in 1916, his wife, the previous year, but for many years his daughters remained active in the village.

No night school provision appears to have been made for women and girls, but Mrs Boyd of Hill House, who also played a considerable part in the life of Wadhurst, opened a cookery class for them at her home. For the course, wives and daughters of labourers and general servants, paid 1s and domestic servants and wives and daughters of farmers paid 2s 6d.

In 1903, the parish magazine suggested that classes in horticulture, dress-cutting, as well as 'instruction in some of the more advanced branches of ordinary school subjects', should be held. But would there be sufficient regular attenders or teachers willing to do the work for the payment offered? A later parish magazine drew attention to the more advanced classes available at the Technical Institute in Tunbridge Wells, where maths, music, art, commerce, cookery, building trade subjects and economics were among the subjects offered.

At the turn of the century and for many years before and after, there was much music making in Wadhurst, first finding organisation in the church choir and band of a hundred years before and then continued, stimulated by the Foleys,[48] musical families, school staffs and, from 1908, by the Rev. L.S. Stevenson. Taking advantage of the Act of 1889, a vocal class was started in the village, but it was soon to lose its grant. Local enthusiasm, however, was sufficient to create a Choral Association,[49] under the direction of Mr Pearse, the church organist and assistant master in the boys' school. The Choral Association, too, appeared short-lived and until the coming of the new vicar in 1908 Choral singing was restricted to that performed by an augmented church choir, or by a special choir formed for the purpose.

In 1902, following a lecture on the *Pilgrim's Progress*, the augmented church choir, conducted by Mr Knight, sang excerpts from it, suitably set to music by Miss F. Wickens. Another such event took place in 1907, when the augmented church choir, conducted by Mr Mabbett, with Mr Knight as accompanist, performed Stainer's *The Crucifixion* in Holy Week and also on Good Friday, to a 'very full church.' Mr Mabbett also conducted a Special Choir of Ladies and Gentlemen in 1905, when they gave a performance of *Princess Zara* in the Market Hall. Mr Mabbett was a professional musician who lived in Tunbridge Wells. Later he became organist and choirmaster at Hexham Abbey. He retired back to Tunbridge Wells in the mid-fifties.

Soon after his coming, Mr Stevenson formed, trained and conducted a new Wadhurst Choral Society of 50 voices, which gave what was described as its 'first concert' in the Market Hall on Wednesday, 20 April 1910, with Mr Knight as accompanist. Choral items included Handel's *And the Glory of the Lord*, Mendelssohn's *He's watching over Israel*, and works by Morley, Wood, Pearsall, etc. This appears to have been the second First Concert, for an earlier one had been reported in the Parish Magazine of July, 1908, when Mrs Stevenson conducted and the Vicar accompanied.

The vicar believed that:

> to cultivate a love for the truly noble and beautiful in music is doing a good work that will influence the lives of the people in ways perhaps we never dream of ... it brings us into touch with great things ... to refine, elevate and purify the thoughts.

Mr Stevenson, together with Mrs A. Wace, also played a part in the formation of the North East Sussex and Tunbridge Wells Festival, which was to provide competitions for adults, schools and church choirs from the town and countryside around.

Its first festival took place on 29 and 30 April 1910, and was adjudicated by Dr William McNaught, who also conducted the concert which followed. Dr McNaught (1849–1918) was a musician, educationalist, conductor and Inspector of Music for Schools. He adjudicated at many festivals.

Eight adult and eight school choirs, together with one church choir, took part. Wadhurst Choral Society entered the eight available classes and gained four first prizes, three second, and one third place. It also gained a good deal of resentment from the other competitors for its high success rate.

Wadhurst Church Choir was the one entry in its class and

gained high praise. There were no entries from the Wadhurst schools.

An orchestra, perhaps a survival of the church band of earlier days, was, at least by the 1890s, known as the Orchestral Society and gave, or assisted at, many concerts and local functions and was frequently involved with other organisations to help them raise funds. A concert given in January, 1903, proved so long that it was carried over into the following night. The orchestral items were conducted by Mr Knight and included Sousa's *Stars and Stripes* and Elgar's *Salut d'Amour*. Violin solos, which included *Le Cynge* by Saint-Saens, were played by Miss Debenham. The second night included dramatic interludes, in which the Misses Watson appeared with Maurice Watts in *Scenes from Cranford*. The concert was given in the market hall, suitably lit by acetylene lamps. On Sunday afternoons, when the church was not in use, members of the orchestra would sometimes gather in the empty building, to play for their own pleasure – and that of the occasional passer-by who would slip in to listen. Members of the orchestra consisted of: 1st Violin: H. Newington, Miss E. Green, H.C. Corke. 2nd Violin: M. Watts. Viola: O. Newington. Double Bass: F. Boorman. Cornet: S.T. Wallis, Jnr. Drums: W. Wallis.[50]

In 1871, a brass band was formed which too, played at local functions. On Saturday nights it also played in the Square, when the shops and the pubs were open until late at night and the square was full of people, some rowdy and some drunk. Through lack of funds, the band broke up, but in 1896, it was reformed under the conductorship of Charles Piper, assisted by a monied committee, which included Mr Arthur Watson. The bandmaster was paid £5 a year and the band shared £3. Members were expected to be of exemplary behaviour: an appearance at Mark Cross Magistrates' Court would result in expulsion from the band.

In 1898, the Parish Magazine reported that the brass band had given an excellent concert in aid of the Football Club funds when it had made its first appearance in 'smart new uniforms'. In a later year, Mr A.G. Watson, honorary secretary and treasurer, reported that the band had had a successful year and for 24 of its engagements had played gratuitously.

A prospectus of 1898 gave the membership of the band as: Cornet – Charles Piper (Bandmaster), James Cane, William Bishop, Henry Saxby. Tenor – Edwin Watts, Edmund Toms. Baritone – George Elliott. Euphonium – Edward Pattenden. B^b Bass – Thomas Pattenden. Drums, etc. – William Piper.

Some years after the formation of the town band, a Salvation Army band, following the creation of a Wadhurst Corps in 1892, was also formed, with Mr Walter Fairbrother as bandmaster. Later, Mr Charles Piper took over. This band, too, gave frequent performances in public.

At the turn of the century, a minstrel troupe, formed by Mr Harry Newington and other members of his family, was also active, with Mr W.G. Foote on the piccolo and Mr Walter Wallis on the drums. The parish magazine reported a concert in which 'The Nigger Troupe delighted the ears and eyes of the audience'.

The Newington family also ran a dance band, with violin, piano, drums and clarinet. It played such dances as the Lancers and, with its coming, ragtime, which, Horace Newington said, 'Took some playing.' The band played at such places as the Castle and Carpenter's Restaurant and also for cricket and football dances and weekly dancing classes. Mr Horace Newington, who was born in 1889, attended Miss Waite's School of about 16 children, which was held on the top floor of the cottages, demolished in 1901, which lay to the west of Church Gate House. Later, Mr Newington went to the National School. At the beginning of the 1914–18 war he married Miss Lomas, who taught in the Infant School.

The church, too, ran its many activities, including the church choir, bell-ringers, temperance societies, Sunday schools, mothers' meetings and the Girls' Friendly Society, all of which had been active by the end of the nineteenth century. Later, in 1906, a branch of the Mothers' Union was formed; in 1907, a branch of the Church of England Men's Society; and in 1909, a company of the Church Lads' Brigade.

Many men, women and children, as well, still came under the influence of the church services, with their teaching by word, liturgy and music. Many were prepared for Confirmation, which, in these years, was frequently necessary for acceptance into good services. Numbers of those confirmed in Wadhurst Church included: 1897: 52. 1901: 55. 1903: 32. 1905: 104. 1909: 64. Services were not held every year and numbers sometimes included candidates from other churches in the deanery.

In 1909, the service was held on 15 March, a day of much wind and snow. The Bishop of Chichester was brought from Etchingham Station to Wadhurst, in a car lent by Mr Drew. During the service, which was being held on a weekday, the Bishop thanked those employers of men in the choir for allowing them to attend.

The Rev. G.G. MacLean, who had taken such a great deal of interest in the Wadhurst schools, retired at the end of 1907 on the grounds of ill health. In the following March, he was succeeded by the Rev. L. Stevenson, who, earlier, had been Mr Drew's chaplain at Wadhurst Hall. Mr Stevenson was born in Ashpark, Co. Derry, in 1878. He gained his M.A. at Trinity College, Dublin, was ordained Deacon in 1901 and Priested in 1902. His Induction into the living of Wadhurst was on 23 March 1908, for which, during the morning, the schools were closed. Mr Stevenson was married and, in 1909, a son, Patric, was born.

Mr Stevenson, by virtue of his position, was Chairman of the School Managers and, also, frequently took Scripture lessons at the school. Although he took a great deal of interest in the Sunday schools, the new vicar's main activity lay in music. He played the piano, had a good baritone voice, wrote music and trained and conducted the church choir, which, from the middle of the previous century, had been in the hands of masters from the church school.

Of the Harvest Festival of 1908, the vicar commented on the marked improvement in the choir's singing, which, in the setting of the *Magnificat* and *Nunc Dimittis* specially written by him for the occasion, was 'very effective'. The Easter music of 1909, too, was 'well rendered', with a 'marked improvement in the singing which was commented on by many'. The vicar considered that:

Reverence and Intelligence is what we want ... how much good music can do to accomplish these ends. To make the singing good, two things are necessary: punctuality and regular attendance on the part of every single man and boy and real hard work.[51]

In Holy Week and on Good Friday of the following year, 1910,[52] the choir sang Stainer's *The Crucifixion*: with a 'thoroughly reverent and impressive and finished interpretation of this solemn meditation at which there were magnificent congregations'.

By the end of his first year, the vicar turned his attention to the Sunday schools. In December 1908, he called a meeting of the teachers, which was held in the vicarage. After tea, he addressed them: he told them that their teaching should be brought up-to-date, for:

The old idea that anything would do to teach and anybody would do to teach it, would not answer now, when teaching in the Day schools was so thoroughly organised and carried out by highly trained teachers. Every effort must be made to make our teachers as efficient as possible.

A committee was formed, which then met to consider the matter further. As a result of its deliberations, a monthly meeting for teachers was organised at which their difficulties could be fully discussed.

The Sunday school teachers already belonged to an area association, which held a number of annual meetings, which included services, quiet days and an annual general meeting.

In 1903, the AGM was held in Wadhurst, when, before the meeting, the teachers were entertained to tea by Mrs Boyd in the gardens of Hill House, where they sat at table, 'in the shade of the trees'.

In the April of 1910, a 'successful' meeting of all the teachers in the deanery was held, under the auspices of the association, when a lecture, 'From the child's point of view', was given. Tea followed in Carpenter's Restaurant.

In the same year, the Sunday schools were reorganised to meet on Sunday morning only, but with a weekly service in the afternoon. The vicar was most anxious that mothers, too, would come, bringing their babies with them.

He wrote: 'So many never get to church [because of] leaving their young children, but all will be welcome at this service.' This family service continued on into the mid-Twentieth century for many years under the leadership of Mrs 'Maggie' Manktelow (née Linkstead).

Previously, from towards the end of the nineteenth century, Sunday schools were held both in the morning and in the afternoon, with a church service every third Sunday, increased to alternate Sundays in 1895. A yearly treat was given, at first in the church field, but by 1901, the children were being entertained in the grounds of the Castle. In a typical year, after a service in church, the children, 'with banners and flags', marched to the Castle, where they were entertained by the Watson Smyths to tea 'in the shade of the trees', while the teachers had their tea on the terrace. There were Maypole dances, coconut-shies, races and games and, at the end, a large bun was presented to each child. This was followed by 'hearty cheers' from the children, to express their thanks. About 150 children took part, including those from the Mission Church. The Sunday school children of Cousely Wood had a separate treat, given by Mr and Mrs Wilkin.

At the turn of the century, there appear to have been a number of Mothers' Meetings existing in the parish, including one in the station area, which was formed in 1898.[53]

Regular meetings, held in private houses and conducted by their affluent owners, were devotional in character, but with the addition of teas and entertainments, so often a feature of the various parish organisations.

95

In 1906, when the Wadhurst Meeting decided to affiliate to the Mothers' Union, a special gathering was held in the Market Hall, at which, after tea, provided by Mrs Boyd of Hill House, 56 of the 100 ladies present were admitted to membership. Subsequently, regular meetings, with towards 140 mothers on the roll, were held at the Castle. District services were sometimes held in the parish church. On one occasion, 'A very large congregation' heard a 'most correct and practical address' given by Canon Churton of Bexhill, who spoke on 'The Mother's Work in the Home' and her need for God's grace.[54]

In the following year, a Wadhurst branch of the Church of England Men's Society was formed, to 'embrace all men who are members of the Church of England, in a Union of prayer and work'. Unlike the women's meetings, which appeared, for the most part, to restrict their activities to worship, devotion, moral and religious teaching, with occasional teas, outings and entertainments, the Men's Society, in addition to its special church services, met for talks and discussions at the vicarage or school. The talks covered a very wide range of subjects, secular and sacred, to include Sunday Observance, Conscription, Evils of Smoking, The Prayer Book, Church Bells and Ringing, Heaven and Hell, and Vaccination, which were given by members or visiting speakers.[55]

Variety was provided, such as an entertainment by the Orchestral Society, lantern slides of a visit to Aix-les-Bains, shown by the vicar, and 'a very pleasant Social Evening' given by Mr Alfred Carpenter, in his 'just finished, smart new Restaurant'.

The Girls' Friendly Society, a branch of which appears to have existed in the village since the turn of the century, catered for young women. It frequently held its meetings at Uplands, the home of Mrs Watson, and its bi-annual festivals at Wadhurst Park, by the invitation of Mr and Mrs Drew. In 1904, however, the festival was held at Whiligh, where over a hundred members wandered round the lovely grounds, looked at the bookstall, had tea and games, and then 'in the shade of the trees' took part in a service. 'Earnest words' were addressed to them by a speaker from London and also by Miss Wetherell of Pashley Manor, Ticehurst, who was the Branch Secretary. Miss Wetherell trusted that 'hearts were stirred to think more of the great society to which we belong and to work more for it.' On another occasion, in July 1907, the Annual District Meeting, of Cousely Wood, Ticehurst, Stonegate and Mark Cross, was held at Uplands, with tea in the Wesleyan Schoolroom. An address was given by Mrs F.S. Parry, who was the Secretary of the West Marylebone Branch in London. She spoke of the work of the GFS in London, but said that the ends and aims of the society were alike for all.

There is little evidence of the form the regular meetings took, but it would seem that worship, religious and moral teaching were included, with some involvement in practical 'good works', such as the making of garments for the poor.

In 1909, the vicar, the Rev. Leslie Stevenson, was instrumental in the formation of a branch of the Church Lads' Brigade. At first, it met in the Vicarage Parish Room, with the vicar as chaplain and acting captain. Later, successive curates took over the work, with Mr Austen as lieutenant, and meetings were held in a room provided by Mrs Boyd in Hill House.

Although based on religious observance, its activities stretched far beyond. Weekly drills included musket and other training; football was played, camps held and a bugle band was formed. Skirmishes were held in the grounds of the Castle and of Whiligh and prizes were awarded for rifle-shooting, which was carried out on the rifle range, set up by the recently formed National Service League. It was significant, perhaps, that the parish magazine now, in 1909, featured a St George-like figure on its cover.

Further teaching and training came through the work of the temperance societies. During the nineteenth century, alcoholism was perceived as a growing problem and clergy were urged to preach sermons on the subject. The parish magazine commented:

It is difficult to say what can be accomplished by Legislation, though, no doubt, some greater restriction of the sale of intoxicants may be devised.

By the end of the nineteenth century, temperance societies had already been formed in Wadhurst, including the Band of Hope, for juniors, which put on 'varied and energetic entertainments'. One such took place on Wednesday, 19 June 1907, when a large audience listened to a long programme of songs, recitations, piano duets and a humorous cantata, in which 'the young performers were a credit to their trainers'.

The contents of the regular meetings appear to have had little reportage, but in 1908, the parish magazine contained the information that nine members had obtained certificates in a competitive examination organised by the Sussex Band of Hope Union.

A local branch of the Total Abstinence Society was also active in the village at this time, but, again, its regular meetings appear to have had little mention. Special events, however, included a social evening, over which Mr Bracket, the Honorary Secretary, presided. He also entertained the members with a lantern slide showing of 'Father Brown's Awakening'. A later social included Mr Bracket's performance of *A Touching Life* and songs sung by the vicar, his wife and Mrs Percy Smith.

A very wide range of charitable giving existed in Wadhurst, all of which was supported and encouraged by the church and much initiated by it. In 1898, a report of the Charity Commissioners listed seven 'charities' in Wadhurst, including the Kitchener Bequest of 1676 and the Barham Bequest of 1716. Some of the charities 'failed'. For many years, collections taken at the Communion services had been used, at the discretion of successive vicars and churchwardens, for the relief of the poor. Briefs, issued by Royal mandate, had also directed charitable giving to deserving causes, but to those foreign to the parish.

Briefs were an authorisation to collect for some worthy cause. They were read out by the minister during the service, to give details of the cause or use for which the collection was to be made. As the people left the church, it was taken up at the door by the parish clerk. The amount raised was handed to a travelling collector, appointed for the purpose. (In 1790–1, Wadhurst Records show that £4 18s 4½d was 'Paid in at Visitation at Lewes'.) Sometimes, there was little, if any, congregational response and sometimes the money did not reach its destination. In 1787, 3s 11½d was collected for a fire at Nether Wallop, but a house-to-house collection raised £1 for a fire at East Grinstead. From 1 April 1787 to 16 February 1794, 66 items raised £18 14s 10½d.

Briefs were at first papal and date from at least the thirteenth century. Abuse of the system led to its decline and to its eventual failure in the nineteenth century.

These two aspects of charitable giving, local and foreign, continued on into the nineteenth and twentieth centuries, but although the use and abuse of briefs died earlier, in the nineteenth century, more generous direct giving took its place. As early as 1819, a church collection had raised £10 for the Society for the Propagation of the Gospel and, by the end of the century, a branch of the society had been formed in Wadhurst, with Miss E. Watson of Uplands as its secretary. During this time and over into the next century, many other causes, supported by direct giving, church collections, collecting boxes, jumble sales and concerts, became the object of concern: the British and Foreign Bible Society, the Society for the Propagation of Christian Knowledge, Melanesian Mission, Mission to Central Africa, Indian Famine Relief, Mission to Seamen, The Police Court Mission, The Agriculture Benevolent Fund, The Tunbridge Wells Infirmary, St Luke's Hospital (for the Clergy), Chichester Board of Education, National Society for Schools, Church of England Temperance Society and The Church Pastoral Aid Society. In their aid, special sermons were preached, meetings held and societies set up in the parish, all of which led to many a person to become aware, not only of causes, but of people, places and concerns, at home and abroad, unknown to them before.[56]

In the parish, collections taken at Communion services continued to be for the support and relief of the poor, but, by 1908, the task was giving the vicar some concern. In the parish magazine he wrote that it was not easy to distribute the 'Poor Fund' in the best way and it was necessary to impress upon people that the church was not a great relieving agency. He felt that, very often, the poor valued a friend rather than alms. To help him in his task, the vicar reorganised the 'District Visitors', a committee which consisted of Mrs Watson, Mrs Boyd, Mrs Watson Smyth, Mrs Hicks, Mrs Morton, Mrs Apsley Smith, Mrs Bracket, Miss Milne and Miss Watson. This group of ladies, the vicar considered, had done a great deal of good work in the parish and had a most valuable knowledge of the people and neighbourhood.[57]

By the turn of the century, a Parochial Nursing Fund, supported by voluntary subscriptions, donations, church collections and concerts, had been set up to provide, in times of necessity, a nurse for the sick poor. A second nurse was appointed in 1905 to give special attention to maternity cases. By 1907, the parish magazine complained that the large cash balance of the previous years had been sadly reduced and that more subscribers were needed. It was also pointed out that the nurses made many visits to give help, but, in return, so little was given. Only 9s 7d had been received as voluntary offerings.

According to the parish magazine for September 1925, the association was founded in 1890 and Miss Cubbon, the first district nurse, was appointed the same year.

Miss Cubbon wrote:

When I arrived, snow had been lying for six weeks, and three miles or more each way was a common journey, even to see one person. There were journeys after dark.

There were no electric torches. I have walked fully twelve miles a day for three weeks together, Sundays included.

I do not remember the number of inhabitants, nothing like as many as at present: but naturally, often one patient was, say, at Church Settle, another at Cousely Wood or Woods Green. I tramped Wadhurst roads the best part of four years before I bought my first cycle. I can't tell you how kindly and grateful most of the sick folk and their friends were. Any tradesman would take anything he could for me in his cart, or offer me a lift, and glad enough I have been of the help.

Mutual self-help, which had existed in Wadhurst for many years, continued through the many benefit societies, national and local, which had grown up. Associated with them was the Annual Church Parade, but by the twentieth century it had been allowed to lapse. In 1906, it was revived in conjunction with 'Hospital Sunday', when collections for local hospitals were taken. The church was 'full to overflowing' and there were many spectators to watch the band-led parade. Collections were taken for the Tunbridge Wells Hospital and also the Ear and Eye Hospital, and amounted to £4 14s 9½d.

In the parish magazine for May 1907, it was explained that the friendly societies would have first call on any 'Orders of Admission' – sometimes called 'Hospital Letters' – which would be granted as a result of the collections. In this year, £21 12s 1d was raised, part of which was given to the Agriculture Benefit Society.

The rich abundance of activity to be found in the village – and in many others – helps to explain, perhaps, the overall wise, concerned and knowledgeable generation which these times appear to have produced: a generation, which, for the most part, had received a school education limited in both duration and scope.

Financial support provided by the education authorities for the schools was often meagre and that given by the Wadhurst parishioners, except on rare occasions and then only when stimulated by the vicar of the time, was never generous. This was reflected in the paucity of facilities and equipment and in the school conditions prevailing.

It would appear that the well-to-do of the parish were content, for the most part, to give effort and financial support to their personal interests and activities, but these, except in the earlier days and particularly in the person of George Campion Courthope, rarely embraced the schools.

In 1904, the vicar considered that £50 a year would have to be raised to maintain the Wadhurst schools and that several subscriptions had been promised or given.

By the end of 1909, the School Fund had an overdraft of £34 7s 6d.

10

The Wadhurst Schools, 1902 to 1910

The Boys' School

Frederick William Larcombe, in 1902, had been on the staff of Wadhurst Boys' School for 26 years, 12 of them as headmaster.

He had two assistants, his wife, Mary Ann (née Wallis), and Albert Knight, who was also the church organist. Mr Knight had come to the school in 1898, and Mary Ann the following year. As organist, Mr Knight received £25 p.a., raised to £30 in 1909. (The blower, H. Tester, received £6.)

The Wadhurst schools, by reason of the 1902 Education Act, were now to be controlled by the new Education Committee of the East Sussex County Council, centred at the county town of Lewes. Teachers were to be reappointed and paid by it.

Mr Larcombe was reappointed at a salary of £133 a year, which included £25 rent and coal allowance. The schoolhouse was rented from the managers, at £15 a year, inclusive of rates. Mr Knight was reappointed at £80, and Mrs Larcombe at £64, each inclusive of an allowance of £7. Salaries were to be paid monthly, although Mr Knight had to wait two months for his first payment: allowances were even longer delayed.

Education by the State

An order from the Board of Education had stipulated that the Wadhurst schools should have six managers. Four of them

104

were to be appointed by the existing foundation members, who, under the Schools' Trust Deed, had been appointed by the vicar (the sole ex officio member), and one each by the local education authority and the parish council.

All the existing managers became the new managers: the vicar (the Rev. G. MacLean), the curate (the Rev. W. Clough Hazeldine), J.C. Lane Andrews (chorister, churchwarden and solicitor) and Julius Drew of Wadhurst Hall; Alexander Courthope (born at Whiligh and uncle of Mr George Courthope and possessor of an estate at Horsmenden) represented the county council and Mr H.C. Corke (local shopkeeper, churchwarden and violinist) represented the parish council. Later, the Board of Education agreed that one manager could be elected by subscribing members to the School Fund. Mr Watson Smyth of the Castle was duly elected to replace the curate, who had resigned.[58]

Mr Julius Drew of Wadhurst Hall was born in 1856, the son of a clergyman. He entered the tea trade, later founded the Home and Colonial stores and by the age of 33, his fortune made, was able to retire from active participation in the firm. In 1899, shortly before his marriage, Mr Drew bought Wadhurst Hall, and over the next years had five children. He was patron of the living of Wadhurst and frequently entertained child and adult members of the church organisations.[58]

Governing Bodies
You have a right to vote for parent governors at your school, and to stand for election as a parent governor yourself. Parents have a strong voice on governing bodies.

Our Children's Education, DFE, 1994

The Boys' School, continued.

At this time, there were approximately 150 boys in the school, 50 of them in the smaller classroom and 100 in the schoolroom, where the boys were divided into two classes, separated by a curtain.

The work of the school appears to have been wide-ranging and varied: commercial geography, grammar, arithmetic and mensuration, together with nature knowledge, reading and laws of health are among those subjects mentioned in the school log-book.

Music continued to play an important part in the life of the school. On one occasion, when Mr Larcombe heard the upper division examined in singing, which had included 'Ear tests of Time and Tune', he found the result 'very gratifying'. Later, on New Year's Day, in 1906, with the temperature at freezing point, the boys listened to a 'selection' on the phonograph. On another, perhaps rare occasion, during playtime, one day in 1909, Mr Knight took some of the boys to sing to an old lady who was sick.

In 1903, Mr Larcombe attempted to form an after-school orchestral class. Twenty boys attended the first meeting, but no further mention of it is made.

Religious instruction, too, continued an important subject and was still examined by the Diocesan Inspector.

The headmaster, like Miss Page, frequently allowed circumstances to determine a lesson: a boy's dead mole provided a subject for the three classes; a pamphlet on the protection of birds led to a kestrel-orientated lesson; a Board of Agriculture leaflet became a conversation lesson for the upper classes, during which the boys discussed the uses of the spotted flycatcher and the lapwing; a book which the headmaster happened to be reading, led to a talk on 'Fresh Air', which continued into a second day.

It is not surprising that the inspector, when he visited, felt that 'More is possible in co-ordinating the studies as a whole'. Later, he also complained of the 'simultaneous repetition' which Mr Larcombe used and the boys' disorder as they left the room.

In 1902, Mr Larcombe had wished to introduce 'free-arm drawing' into the school, but the managers, fearing the cost, asked him to re-submit his requisition for the necessary materials when the new authority had taken over. The new authority apparently approved, for on 17 August 1903, Mr

106

Larcombe recorded: 'Second Division had Free-arm drawing for the first time. Holders having been fixed on Saturday'.

A few years later, in 1909, however, the inspectors felt that not enough handicraft work was being done and so encouraged the introduction of clay-modelling, cardboard-modelling and cartoon work, even into the extension class, which had just been formed for the most senior boys.

Drill and marching had long been a feature of school life. They were recognised by the Code of 1871 and still retained in some schools for another 80 years. Physical education came later, to which, in common with many other headmasters, Mr Larcombe had added organised games. These presented no problems until they were officially recognised by the Code of 1906.

On 10 October 1906, Mr Larcombe wrote in his log-book:

H.M.I. Gardiner, Esq., visited school, referred to him in regard to having 'organised games,' such as Cricket and Football. He advised that these should not take the place of Drill, but time be taken from that given to Geography.

The following month, the LEA Inspector, Mr Haig Brown, suggested that drill should be given each day, but for shorter periods of time, and games be arranged for Wednesdays and Thursdays.

On the following Wednesday, Mr Larcombe duly recorded that he had taken the 1st class to football in the church field, from 3.30 to 4.15 p.m.

Football clubs had begun to appear in London schools during the 1880s. Cricket, which did not appear on the timetable until 1909, had been played in Wadhurst for over 150 years. The present club was formed around 1870.

Out of school, games ranged wider: Mr Boys claimed that, during games of 'catch', the children would wander as far as Wadhurst Hall. Other games included leapfrog, tip-top-toe, rabbit home, puss-in-the-corner and marbles.

It was in the same year, 1906, that Mr Larcombe

introduced homework for the first time, in the form of general knowledge. On 7 December 1906, he recorded:

In several cases, parents have refused to allow the children to look up information at home or do anything there in connection with the questions on General Knowledge – having burnt the paper of questions. Others have, however, expressed their pleasure at the introduction of this work.

Weather, sickness, poor attendance and unsatisfactory conditions, in common with the other Wadhurst schools, were still a preoccupation for Mr Larcombe, but with his concern for both teacher and taught being more apparent.

On 9 October 1903, when the weather was very wet and stormy, he commented:

Many of the boys are from a distance of 2½ to 3 miles. Several of the boys are suffering from bad disorders of the skin.

Then, on 27 January 1904, when the weather was 'very stormy' and with but a 54 per cent attendance, he remarked:

Such an attendance as this, which is only too prevalent in a large parish like Wadhurst, seriously reduces the average attendance for the year and in consequence, the Head Teacher's salary is reduced under the Scale of the Salaries proposed by ... The East Sussex Education Authority...

And on the next day, followed with:

One can hardly expect parents to send children to school in such weather as today especially those living so far from the school.

In the same year, HMI Gardiner examined the Register of

Daily Temperature and expressed the opinion that 'The rooms could not be sufficiently warmed by the stoves in winter.'

There was some light in the darkness of 1904, for in that year George Barham, of Snape, the founder of the Express Dairy, celebrated his knighthood by treating the senior children to a trip to the London Zoo and the infants to tea and games.[59]

In the following January, the weather was so bitterly cold that the ink in some of the ink-wells froze and lamps were lit to assist in warming the rooms.

To the cold was added the discomfort of the smoking fire, particularly when the wind was in the west and south-west. On 14 March 1905, at times it was so bad that it was difficult to see the children on the other side of the room.

It seemed in the following November that, at last, something was going to be done: 'Mr. A. Courthope, Mr. Andrews and Mr. Corke visited with reference to the warming of the main room.'

And, later: '...visited by Mr. Corke and Mr. Luck [the local builder], to arrange about stoves.'

But, in February, 1906: 'No notice appears to have been taken with regard to the heating of the room.'

The fire continued to pour out volumes of smoke.

It was over a year later, in April 1907, that the managers at last came to the conclusion that the present warming of the school was insufficient and so discussed alternative forms of heating.

Estimates for water radiators were obtained, but proved too high; gas radiators were suggested – if gas could be laid on – but the LEA turned them down as being unsuitable.

At last, on 15 November 1907, following a discussion between the headmaster and the inspector, Mr Freeland, the managers agreed that the stove in the boys' room should be replaced by two tortoise stoves.

A fireless week at the beginning of December followed. The builder, Mr C.W. Ashby, was urged to expedite the new stoves, but unsuccessfully, it seems, for the remainder of the term was spent with borrowed oil stoves.

Mr. C.W. Ashby, born in 1849, was a lifelong member of the parish church, where he was a sidesman. He was a member of the Men's Meeting, at which he frequently spoke. He was also the Captain of the Fire Brigade. His uncle William, had been the miller at Riverhall Mill and cellist in the church band.

At last, two new stoves were installed during the Christmas holidays and, when the new term started on 2 January 1908, they were considered a 'great success'.

Both in winter and in summer, illness and epidemics of various kinds, together with their effect on attendance and on the work of the school were still constantly recorded.

In 1904 'much handicapped by sickness'. In 1905 'illness caused chiefly by the heat'. There were also cases of whooping cough and measles. Then, on 16 February 1906 '12 cases of mumps ... the school has been ordered to close'. After a closure of three weeks, there was no abatement of the epidemic – in fact, it had increased considerably, so that the medical officer gave instructions that the closure should continue, week by week, until it had abated, which was not until the following Easter, when, after a closure of nearly nine weeks, the school reopened on 23 April. In the August, there was still a great deal of sickness in the school and the attendance was lower than in any week in the year.

On 3 January in the following year, 1907, the headmaster reported that boys were absent owing to some form of fever, 'Two cases having been taken to the Isolation Hospital at Flimwell'. Then, on the 9th, he added, 'Three boys absent owing to Typhoid Fever.' By the 21st, 'three boys' had become 'several boys', joining those already suffering from mumps, measles and chickenpox. It was then decided to close the school. It remained closed for three months.

On 28 October 1907, the headmaster was absent 'to attend the funeral of little Jack Maryan, the victim of a Motor Accident'.

The following year, Mr Watson wrote to the managers advocating the erection of cautionary posts near Wadhurst and Cousely Wood schools. He said that the RAC would supply free posts.

The managers agreed to maintain them, but asked that they be erected by public subscription.

On 29 April, there were still 18 boys absent, most of them suffering from influenza, and of the boys present, the headmaster noted in his log-book that their coughing was 'distressing'.

A week later, Dr Stott, the Medical Officer of Health, together with Mr Mitchener, the Nuisance Inspector, visited the school. Following their visit, Mr Larcombe wrote: 'Dr. Stott requested me to write in the Log-Book that, "The schools should be washed and scrubbed, using some disinfectant ... at least once a month." '

In the parish magazine for June 1896, the vicar, Mr MacLean, had boasted of the new classrooms being 'large and airy and well-lighted', with 'sanitary arrangements made perfect' and of 'pure drinking water', but, in the early years of the twentieth century, there were almost constant reminders of the unhealthy and unsatisfactory conditions existing in the schools.

On 12 April 1904, the inspector wrote: 'a water supply should be laid on.'

On 18 July 1904, the headmaster recorded: 'Since Monday July 11 there has been no water for drinking purposes except what has been begged from neighbours'.

At this, the managers appear to have taken fright and action quickly followed. By 23 August, the Crowborough Water Company had laid on water to the school and school house.

In the same year, 1904, the inspector, Mr Gardiner, complained that the rooms were dirty and that the caretaker was not doing his work. The parish magazine for January 1905 tried to explain the reason for this:

The distance at which some of the children live from the school makes it necessary for them to bring their dinner with them and this renders it very difficult to keep the room perfectly clean and tidy for the afternoon.

111

At this time, the headmaster also drew attention to the shortage of desks and materials – even his request for a hearth brush had been turned down by the LEA.

Education by the State

In 1904, a year of so much distress in the Wadhurst schools, Robert Morant, Secretary to the Board of Education, issued his Elementary Code, which incorporated changes brought about by the Education Act of 1902.[60]

It contained an introduction, said to have been written by Robert Morant, which showed a new, fresh, lively conception of the aims of elementary education.

> The purpose of the Public Elementary School is to form and strengthen the character and to develop the intelligence of the children entrusted to it and to make the best use of the school years available in assisting both boys and girls, according to their different needs, to fit themselves, practically as well as intellectually, for the work of life...
>
> ...it will be the aim of the School to train the children carefully in habits of observation and clear reasoning, so that they may gain an intelligent acquaintance with some of the facts and laws of nature ... a living interest in the ideals and achievements of mankind ... familiarity with the literature and history of their own country ... power over language as an instrument of thought and expression ... good reading and thoughtful study ... to increase that knowledge in after years...
>
> ...encourage to the utmost the children's natural activities of hand and eye ... afford them every opportunity for the healthy development of their bodies ... appropriate physical exercises and ... organised games ... working of some of the simpler laws of health.
>
> ...Subsidiary object of the School to discover individuals who show promise of exceptional capacity to pass ... into Secondary Schools.

...the teachers can ... do much to lay the foundation of conduct ... by example and influence, aided by the sense of discipline, which should pervade the School, to implant in the children habits of industry, self-control, and courageous perseverance in the face of difficulties ... reverence what is noble, to be ready for self-sacrifice ... strive after purity and truth ... foster a strong respect for duty ... respect for others ... corporate life of the School, especially in the playground, should develop that instinct for fair-play ... loyalty to one another which is the germ of a wider sense of honour in later life.

...the Schools should enlist ... the interest and co-operation of the parents and the home ... to enable the children ... to reach their full development as individuals ... upright and useful members of the community ... and ... of the country to which they belong.

Education into the Next Century
Schools will have to concentrate more on preventing truancy, on stressing the difference between right and wrong, and on teaching their pupils how to behave responsibly and to be good citizens.

Parents too need to play their part. They need to set an example and take an active interest in their children's school work. Children learn best when the parents and the school work together.

Department of Education Pamphlet, 1992

Responsibility
Every day in Britain at least 480 couples are divorced, 170 babies are born to teenage mothers and 1470 babies are aborted.

A new crime is committed every six seconds in Britain – and a violent attack every two minutes.

Alpha Introduction, February 1997

In the following year, 1905, a *Handbook of Suggestions for Elementary School Teachers* was issued 'as an aid to reviewing their aims and practice, and as a challenge to independent thought on such matters.'

The preface included:

> The only uniformity of practice that the Board of Education desire to see in the teaching of Public Elementary Schools is that each teacher shall think for himself and work out for himself such methods of teaching as may use his powers to the best advantage and be best suited to the particular needs and conditions of the school. Uniformity in details of practice ... is not desirable even if it were attainable.

National Curriculum, 1991
The School must give you an annual report on your child's progress, showing how your child is progressing in the National Curriculum and other subjects. In the year when your child takes the national tests at 7, 11, 14 and 16, the report will give you the result.

The Boys' School, continued.

The inspector, Mr Freeland, continued to make complaints of over-crowded conditions and also of the unsatisfactory state of the desks.[61] To overcome the financial difficulties, he suggested that a set be requisitioned at the time. This was in 1908. In the May of the following year he reported: 'The lavatory accommodation is hardly worthy of the name and is quite inadequate for the number of boys.'

It took until the following November for the managers to decide that two handbasins should be fixed in the boys' lavatory. Previously, it would seem, the boys used the pump in the schoolyard.

In May 1909, the inspector still complained about the desks. He described the desk equipment in the main room as

114

being 'very old' and that it 'occupied spaces quite out of proportion to the accommodation'. He also drew attention to the large curtain which obscured the light. 'It was not improbable', he commented, 'that a glass partition may sooner or later be found to be necessary.'

A partition had first been recommended by an inspector in 1904, who thought that 'teaching conditions in the main room' must be 'trying'.

The Board of Education asked the LEA to provide such a partition: the LEA passed the responsibility to the managers, who refused to accept it. They maintained that, when the school was handed over to the LEA, all the work requested by the authority – which did not include a partition – had been carried out.

Poor conditions in the schools were compounded by those in the homes. The difficulty of nursing sick children in small, crowded cottages, some very remote, without running water and with but primitive forms of heating and lighting, is almost beyond belief.

The vicar's wife was particularly concerned about the scourge of tuberculosis. The parish magazine for April 1908 contained an article directing attention to the 'great crusade which now being waged by the National Society for the Prevention of Consumption and other forms of Tuberculosis ... tremendous stress is laid on the necessity of proper ventilation ... windows open day and night and all the light of sunshine ... a great preventative of consumption'.

Although there are few indications in the school records, poverty was wide-spread and met with a mixture of meanness and concern – the vicar himself had stated that the church 'was not a great relieving institution'.

Charlie Tompsett, one-time bandmaster of Wadhurst, said that one Christmas around the turn of the century, because of the snow, his father had been sent home with a wage of but 4s 6d, instead of his usual one of 12s. The farmer told him that he couldn't work properly with a sack round his shoulders. On the other hand, the Wilkins, of Cousely Wood, tried to help the poor by lending out clothes for the new babies and blankets for the winter. Charlie Tompsett remembered collecting and returning such blankets.

As a little boy, he also remembered saving up 5d in a year, by fetching and carrying sacks of bones, for which he was paid a halfpenny a sack. He started work on the land, at Yeoman's, at the age of ten. He was paid 6d a day. Lady Thompson, also of Cousely Wood, to help out, would have a pig killed and its meat distributed to those in need.

Mr C.W. Ashby's daughter Dorothy, later to become Mrs Fisher-Barham, remembered seeing children in rags passing their house on Wadhurst Hill, on their way to school. One particularly bad winter, Mr Ashby was moved to take into his house a little boy half-frozen with the cold, to get him warm.[62]

Education by the State

In 1906, following the election into power of a Liberal Government, together with the first 40 Labour Members of Parliament, an Education Act empowered local education authorities to provide school meals. In the following year, another Act empowered them:

> To make such arrangements as may be sanctioned by the Board of Education, for attending to the health and physical conditions of children in Public Elementary Schools.

Arising from this Act, a Medical Department was established, a Chief Medical Officer to the Board of Education appointed and a compulsory system of medical inspection set up.[63]

The Boys' School, continued.

Wadhurst's first inspection came in 1909 and Mr Larcombe wrote: 'Received notification for June 7 ... Received Sight

Testing Cards by post.' And on 28 May: 'Received Tin Box containing cards and measuring chart. Sent notices to parents of those to be examined by Medical Officer as 13 and over and also to those children thought necessary should be examined.'

And on 9 June the medical inspection commenced.

In spite of the overcrowded rooms, old desks, unsatisfactory sanitary conditions, closures through deep snow, measles, scarlet fever, influenza, whooping cough and with teachers and children sometimes 'really unfit to be present', 1909, which saw the introduction of School Medical Examinations and the Old Age Pension, also saw the introduction of local innovations into Wadhurst Boys' School.[64]

At this time, there were 172 boys on the roll: 111 in the lower division and 61 in the upper division. The boys in the lower division were housed in the large, curtained room, where they were divided into three classes, taught by the headmaster, his wife and an uncertificated mistress. The boys in the upper division were taught by Mr Knight in the small classroom.

Mr Larcombe decided to introduce prefects into the school, to be elected by the boys in the upper division. Mr Larcombe recorded in his log-book:

The following boys were elected by the Upper Division as Prefects:
F. Luck, G. Thorpe, J. Thorpe, G. Brooks, J. Wellman, W. Vidler.

Their main duty was to supervise the boys in the playground, but they were also to see that all was well in the 'offices'.

Later in the year, a Sports Day began to figure in the life of the school and then, mainly by the efforts of the headmaster, who personally invited donations, money was raised, at last, to buy cricket equipment.

HMI Freeland, at his inspection, said that organised games, taken in an excellent playing field, were encouraged and admirably supervised by the headmaster. Mr Freeland considered, too, that the physical training, as well, was 'thoroughly executed' by him.

A further innovation, at the instigation of the inspector, who did not approve of the existing teaching arrangements, was the formation of an extension class, to provide more advanced, independent work for the more competent boys.

Mr Freeland considered, too, that more instruction in hand and eye training should be given, and so clay and cardboard modelling and cartoon work were introduced into the timetable, for the boys to make such articles as wall-boxes, square boxes, cardboard trays and cups and saucers in clay.

Unpunctuality was no innovation: Mr Blight, the Diocesan Inspector, over 20 years before, had complained about it; at the turn of the century, the vicar, through the pages of the parish magazine, had voiced his concern, and now the inspector, Mr Freeland. Following the inspection in May 1909 he wrote:

The unpunctuality of a portion of the scholars, Boys, Girls and Infants, was ... a matter of comment ... serious steps should be taken.

It would appear that 'caning' had not proved effective.

At the Annual Prize Giving, held on a very hot day in August, with a temperature of 80°, both the vicar and the headmaster reminded the boys of the importance of regular and punctual attendance, without which prizes could not be won. Then medals for perfect attendance and certificates for good attendance were awarded to those who had reached the required standard.

With the help of Miss D. Courthope, 69 book prizes and £3 7s 3d in cash, as Flower Show awards, in writing and drawing, were also presented.

Two years earlier, in 1907, a Parish Magazine correspondent had complained that the County Council had provided too few medals and too little money which the teachers and managers had had to make good. In turn, the County Accountant complained that Cousely Wood School had overspent its prize money by 4d, and Wadhurst School had overspent by 19/6d.

In 1910, the year following the introduction of prefects, cricket equipment, the extension class and clay and cardboard modelling, the managers were faced with the very disturbing proposition that, on the forthcoming retirement in March of Miss Watson, the headmistress of the girls' school, the girls should be amalgamated with the boys.

Education by the State

The local education authority justified its recommendation of amalgamation on the strength of a Board of Education Regulation which required 10 square feet of floor space for each older child. This requirement could be met only by amalgamation, or by a building enlargement, for which the managers would be responsible. This was a most unacceptable idea, for, at the end of 1909, the school fund had an overdraft of £34 7s 6d.

The Boys' School, continued.

In a letter to the local education authority, the managers opposed such an amalgamation on the grounds that, apart from the questionable ability of the boys' headmaster to take charge of such an establishment, specialisation would become impossible, and more, they felt it undesirable for the girls and boys to mix: that, morally, girls should be separate, under a capable headmistress. In any case, they believed that the parishioners would not approve.

Later, after much discussion, the managers felt that the LEA had made up its mind that, sooner or later, it was determined to have a mixed school in Wadhurst: and so the managers bowed to the inevitable.

First, they visited a mixed school in Crowborough, where, after an hour of looking round, they expressed pleasure in all that they had seen. Then the local education authority was notified by the Chairman of the Governors of their acceptance decision, but with the provision that the top two classes of boys and girls should be taught separately, each under its own qualified master or mistress, the mistress to be paid a salary of £85 a year. The managers also suggested that the authority might like to help towards the cost of the new desks and partitions which would be needed.

On 24 March 1910, the school closed for the Easter holidays and as a boys' school, for ever.

1910 was the year of the Alice Comet. It appeared after dark, like a great orange, up over the fields beyond Ratcliffe's, the butcher's, which was on the south side of the High Street, opposite the vicarage.

For a week it was visible and, at nightfall, people came from all around to see it. Mr Larcombe and Colonel Ramsden were so impressed that they wrote to the newspapers about it, which soon brought a local reporter to investigate.

His investigations were only too thorough, to reveal that this was no comet, but the work of local boys, keen on kite-flying, who had made a great 6-foot kite, into which they had inserted a large, illuminated Chinese lantern.

Education by the State

Following the adoption of the 1902 Education Act, greater attention was given to the training of teachers. The Board of Education raised the minimum age for pupil-teachers to 16 (15 in rural areas) and reduced the normal period of apprenticeship to two years. Half of the pupil-teacher's time was to be spent in receiving instruction at a suitable centre, the rest of the time was to be spent in observation or teaching.

As an alternative, the board introduced a system whereby any secondary school pupil who had received instruction for two, or later three, years and wished to become a teacher, could either serve another year as a student teacher, or, after successfully completing its entrance examination, pass direct to a training college. This alternative scheme was adopted by many LEAs and after 1907 the number of pupil-teachers declined. Many pupil-teacher centres became secondary schools.

At a Wadhurst managers' meeting held in April 1908, it was decided that higher education classes at Wadhurst, as suggested by the Education Department were not feasible. At a subsequent meeting, held in the following month, Mr Larcombe reported that there were no boys in the school wishing to be trained as teachers.

The Girls' School

In 1902, Miss Watson had been headmistress of the Wadhurst Girls' School for 36 years. She was assisted by Miss Ellery and pupil-teacher Miss Measures, who in 1905 entered a training college.

Miss Watson, who lived with Miss Page in the School Cottage, received a salary of £77 a year, plus a rent and heating allowance of £10. Miss Ellery received a salary of £50, plus an allowance of £7. The friendship between Miss Watson and Miss Page created a special link between the two schools, which, sensibly, helped to bring them together. In her log-book, Miss Page recorded many incidents of co-operation between them, which included such as: 2 June 1902, 'Let the children go into the Girls' School and sing the National Anthem ... in honour of the Peace Proclamation.'

(The 'Peace Proclamation' followed the termination of the Boer War (1899–1902).[65])

On 26 March 1907, 'The Girls' Assistant, Miss Ellery, heard the little girls who are going into the Girls' School, read from an unseen Fairy Tale Reader and thought they read very nicely.'

4 February 1910, 'The 1st Class went into the Girls' School

and performed the historical scenes they had learnt.'

Miss Watson's log-books, sadly, have disappeared, perhaps destroyed, and other references to the school or its teachers are few.

Miss Watson herself referred to the earlier days of the school when she commented on the constant poor attendance and the problems it presented. She said it was not until the twentieth century had been reached that the average attendance warranted three teachers. Even then, the vicar regretted that there were so few girls on the books. In a parish magazine of 1901, he wrote that no doubt, the girls were 'useful at home', but

> it would be much to their advantage if their parents could send them regularly to school for rather a longer time than which is absolutely demanded by law ... it cannot be too strongly impressed upon parents that they can on no account be allowed to keep children under 13 at home ... unless in case of illness.

Membership of the church choir was one of Miss Watson's interests and, as did other members of the schools' staffs, she assisted with the various happenings of village life. When, in 1904, George Barham of Snape was knighted, and, as part of the celebrations, provided a tea party for the younger children, Miss Watson was among those who helped, for which, Sir George Barham 'returned well-earned thanks'.

In the same year, the school managers were rather less helpful, for when Miss Watson complained to them that the supply of rainwater to her school cottage had failed, and pointed out that main water had recently been laid on to the school and to Mr Larcombe's school house, Mr Corke, the treasurer, told her that, when water was laid on to a cottage, it resulted in a rent increase for the tenant of 3d a week.

Some other appeals made to the managers were perhaps even more disagreeable. One made in 1907 involved Miss Watson's assistant, Miss Ellery. Together, they complained of the insubordination of Frances Maryan, and also of the conduct of her mother, who, when she visited the school, used very violent language to the headmistress.

In December of the same year, Miss Watson was involved in dealing with Vivian Ellis, aged nearly 14, who had shown 'disgusting rudeness to some girls in the dinner interval'. The headmaster decided to expel him. A visit by the boy's father followed, when, together with the headmistress, Mr Larcombe went into the matter. The evidence of the girls was found to be rather contradictory, but, in spite of this, the expulsion was confirmed.

Miss Ellery, who had joined the school staff in 1901, resigned in this year, 1907. The parish magazine described her as 'a most conscientious and careful teacher', one who had given much efficient help to Miss Watson. Miss Ellery's work was also 'fully appreciated by the Managers' and the staff and pupils regretted her leaving.

Miss Ellery's place was taken by a Miss Burnett, but in 1909 she was asked to resign, as she was not capable of doing the work expected of her.

The parish magazine for April 1909, however, did congratulate Miss Watson when five girls gained prizes in a crochet competition, which had been organised by the North West School of Art. Then, in the following February, in the year of her retirement, it was reported that Miss Watson had organised a Christmas Tree and Concert for the infants' school.

The Education of Girls, 1909
In connection with the Flower Show, the Vicarage offers prizes for Cookery among elder school girls; to assist our girls to become capable and practical housekeepers and managers is for them worth all the pianoforte playing and so-called 'higher education' ever indulged in.

It is being felt everywhere that elementary schools should devote more time to practical subjects and consider local needs.

(From the Wadhurst parish magazine)

Miss Watson retired in March 1910, after serving as

headmistress for 42 ½ years. An appreciation appeared in the August parish magazine, which spoke of her 'many years of hard work and faithful service'. Her work in the church choir was also mentioned.

Mrs Boyd of Hill House, now a school manager, volunteered to collect for a presentation. The managers' own contribution, it was decided, should not exceed 10s 6d. It is not clear whether this was each, or between them.

In the following October, at a Prize Giving held in the now mixed school, the presentation was made by the vicar, the Rev. L.S. Stevenson, who 'in an interesting speech' dwelt on Miss Watson's 'painstaking and conscientious work'. Then, in the presence of a large gathering of local gentry, parents and scholars, Miss Watson was presented with a purse of 20 golden sovereigns, which was from the managers, residents and others, and also with a gold curb bracelet with a gold watch, together with a gold and pearl brooch, which were given by past and present scholars.

The parish magazine for June 1929 recorded the death of Miss Watson, at the age of 84, and also the blindness she had had to face in her retirement. Then, for the first time, it seems, her Christian name was mentioned – Hannah.

The Infants' School.

On 1 January 1902, Miss Charlotte Caroline Page, now Headmistress of the Wadhurst Infant School for 31 years, wrote in her log-book:

Recommenced school with 80 on the Books, having sent 20 boys into the Boys' School and 18 girls into the Girls' Room ... lessons as usual.

Miss Page was assisted by 22-year-old Miss Beatrice Fanny Green, an uncertificated teacher from Woodstock, Oxford-shire, and monitress Flora Bone, who was replaced a year later by Margaret Linkstead, born in 1886, who had been a pupil in the school.

Margaret Linkstead, in 1904, was accepted by the local education authority, with Board of Education approval, as an assistant teacher, at a salary of £35 p.a. The inspector advised her to present herself for examination, in order to gain the status of qualified uncertificated teacher. That prescribed, was the Senior Local Examination of Oxford and Cambridge. In her own time and at her own expense, Margaret went to classes in Tunbridge Wells. Later, the Wadhurst school managers decided to help her with a grant of £2, which was two-thirds of her expenses.

In the 39 foot by 18 foot schoolroom, Miss Page taught Class 1, the monitor, Class 2, and in the 19 foot by 16 foot classroom, Miss Green taught the babies, who, from the age of three, were received into the school throughout the year.

On 9 May 1903, Miss Page reported the first effects on the staff of the 1902 Education Act:

Teachers received their first payment from the Board of Education this morning, but for salaries only. No equivalent yet has been sent for furnished apartments and coals.

For her furnished apartment, which she shared with Miss Watson, Miss Page paid the managers a rental of £8 a year. Miss Page received an annual salary of £77, together with an allowance of £10; Miss Green, £57, plus £7, and the monitor, £14.

Charlotte Page continued to attract people's help and interest. The vicar, the Rev. George MacLean, particularly, was a frequent visitor to the school, bringing with him sweets and toys and practical help. On one occasion he 'kindly painted the heads of the King and Queen on the pincushions made by two little girls.'

Then, when geometrical drawing was introduced into the school, he entertained the children by doing some 'amusing drawings' in front of them, making use of geometrical figures.

The vicar's two daughters also visited the school and one of them 'kindly performed a Spanish Dance much to the pleasure and amusement of the children who greatly admired the pretty costume.'

On another occasion, the Misses MacLean brought along some ready-dressed dolls, which then figured in Charlotte's stories of Cinderella and Punch.

Former teachers, students from schools and colleges, visitors from abroad, as well as the ladies from the neighbourhood, came to see Miss Page's infants at work and play.

By now, Miss Page's teaching had been influenced by the kindergarten work of Froebel, in which children learnt through play and activity. Although the work became formalised by her (and by others) into specific periods for 'Kindergarten Games, Employments and Puzzles', its informal ideas did permeate the whole timetable.[66] A formal lesson was frequently linked to a game, or given a practical twist. During a gallery lesson on 'Tea', Miss Page made a pot of tea in front of the children, which all the children then tasted: a lesson on 'the Orange' involved a child planting pips in a pot mould, which had been brought, followed by the vicar giving an orange to each child, for it to test that 'It was, indeed, a refreshing fruit'. Live rabbits, dead badgers, bees in bottles, butterflies and slow-worms, dogs, frogs, leaves and buds of flowers, all were brought into the school by the staff or children, for observation, discussion and drawing, or to form the basis of a game or story.[67]

It was rarer, however, for the teacher to take the children from the class-room into the outside world, to see the plants in bloom. One such occasion was in March 1910, when Miss Page recorded an outing for the babies: she took them 'round the Boys' Playground for a walk and noticed the flowers in the School House garden'. Usually it was the heat, rather than educational considerations, which caused Miss Page to take the children from the classroom. On one very hot day in August 1909, each class took turns to have lessons in the playground and, two days later, when the room was still very hot, the babies were taken out into the fields, while other children had an oral lesson in the playground.

National Curriculum for nurseries
The nursery guidelines ... are part of a package of measures to improve standards for the under-fives. They set out broad targets which pupils should have attained by the time they enter mainstream education aged five...
Areas covered include language and literacy – pupils should be able to recognise letters of the alphabet and write their own names with the appropriate use of capital letters; simple mathematics – knowing what a circle is or what the term 'bigger' means; and creativity and imagination ... pupils will be expected to 'develop a sense of what is right and wrong and why.' They should also 'treat living things and property with care and concern...'

The *Sunday Telegraph*, 10 September 1995

The leaf was an object frequently used as a basis for the children's work:

26 July 1906	Took leaf-tracing instead of the usual games as it was very hot.
1 November 1909	1st Class commenced working a leaf they had pricked on a card.

It was when the children were drawing leaves that the inspector, Mr Gardiner, called. He showed them how to hold the chalk and also advised them on the 'cultivation of observation with respect to the object given to copy'. At this visit, the Inspector also recommended the use of brighter pictures, such as *Bubbles*, on the walls of the babies' room.

At an earlier inspection, in 1902, the Drawing Inspector, Mr Baker, had recommended that the children's work should be done in chalk, using a 'sheet of brown paper', rather than the books which were then in use.

Many types of handwork were in use: paper-folding and

cutting – on one occasion, paper daisies were made, modelled from a real daisy, which had been brought in – basketwork, orient work, lacing for the boys and knitting for both boys and girls. In 1904, Miss Page recorded that she had taken the 1st Class of boys for 'ring laying', while the girls made bead curtain-holders and, two years earlier, while the boys made scrapbooks, the girls made buttonhole rings. In that same year, the boys had worked embroidery, while the girls took 'string-work'.

Needlework, for some years, at least, played an important part in the work of the school and dolls, and the material to dress them, was still, as in times past, brought in by visiting ladies.

Stimulation for the needlework, knitting and kindergarten work was still provided by the Annual Cottagers' Flower Show, where the children's work was displayed and for which prizes were awarded.

The parish magazine for September 1902 recorded:

The Cottagers' Flower Show, which is always a red letter day in the annals of Wadhurst, was again held in the grounds of The Castle ... a ... tent was devoted to School Exhibits and the writing was as on previous occasions, deserving of much commendation, while the needlework and knitting might well challenge competition with other schools. The ingenuity of the teachers must be greatly taxed to find new methods of Kindergarten work which can be executed by very small fingers...

In 1904, Miss Page recorded that 10s had been allotted in prize money for needlework and 3s for knitting. There were 14 prize winners, including three boys, whose prizes ranged from 2s to 3d and were the subject of a little Prize Giving Ceremony at the school, conducted by Mrs and Miss Watson, the Misses MacLean and supported by the vicar. In the following year, Miss Page lamented that only three prizes had been taken at the Flower Show... 'as the time allotted on the Timetable for needlework, will not allow for any but small garments'.

A log-book entry for 17 January 1905 explains, perhaps, why needlework had lost a favoured place in the time-table:

Gave the 1st Class their first lesson in Clay modelling, each child forming a leaf. Great interest shown and, on the whole, good specimens produced.

Then, in the following year, for unknown reasons, the County Education Committee expressed a wish that needlework should not be exhibited at the Flower Show.

From the introduction of clay modelling in 1905, there were constant references to its use, frequently in association with other lessons:

23 May 1905	...Lesson on radishes. Each child being supplied with one. Some long radishes were then modelled in clay.
2 June	Several small tin pans supplied by the Vicar in readiness for colouring some clay models.
6 June	The Vicar very kindly gave the children their first lesson in colouring their clay models.

Castles, flowers, swans and frogs and weather vanes, all came up for discussion and subsequent modelling.

It was in the December of 1905 that the Vicar instructed Miss Page to admit no child under four.

Physical activity in the school was based on drill, which was first introduced into the schools in the Code of 1871, but modified by Miss Page in various ways. On 22 March 1902, she took flag drill in the babies' room and then flag and circle drill with the older children in the school room. On another occasion, weaving drill was performed for which the children learnt a song, 'White, blue and crimson stripes'. The children marched, learnt to form squares and when, with the coming of the new vicar, Empire Day became a feature in the school year, they marched into the boys' playground to salute the flag.

Physical exercises were first mentioned on 15 June 1903, when they were 'taken with singing', instead of the usual drill. At the end of the following year, Miss Page recorded that she had been supplied with a course of physical exercises, which she had begun to teach. Five years later, in 1910, physical activity took on another dimension, when, on 10 August, Miss Page taught the 1st Class to play battledore and shuttlecock.

When, in 1908, the new vicar, the Rev. Leslie Stevenson, introduced Empire Day to Wadhurst, Miss Page reported on 22 May that the children practised the Empire Hymn in the playground with the boys and girls and then, on 26 May, that the whole school had closed for the afternoon, in order to celebrate Empire Day with patriotic songs, speeches, processions and tea in the Market Hall.

Although music lessons were broken up with action songs and solos and sometimes a story, singing was taken seriously and Miss Page records giving the children breathing and singing exercises and mentions that 'new exercises were given to practise breathing at the proper time when singing', and on another occasion, that the children 'took their Scale Exercise very well'.

Songs were sung to entertain visitors and for the special occasion. In 1902 the National Anthem was not only sung to mark the Peace Proclamation on the cessation of the Boer War, but also in honour of the Coronation of Edward VII. Miss Page wrote:

| 20 June 1902 | Having learnt that it was the King's wish that all schools should have an extra week's holiday, I told the children we should not re-assemble until June 30 and having sung the National Anthem I then dismissed them. |

Tonic sol-fa was in use when Miss Page's new log-book

started in 1902 and continued progressively:

15 June 1904   The teachers taught some of the manual
                 signs in the Tonic Sol-fa lessons, which
                 much pleased the children.

The following month, she took manual signs for the chords
with the children and in December 1905, recorded a simple
lesson on the old notation and the tonic, for which simple
exercises were used. In the process, the production of good
tone was not forgotten, for, in the same year, Miss Page
wrote: 'The children sang their Tonic Sol-fa Exercises very
softly and sweetly.'

Then, on one occasion, on 1 January 1906, Miss Page took
the children into the girls' school to hear a selection of airs
on the gramophone.

Apart from an isolated mention of carols and a special tea
and entertainment given to the children in the Market Hall by
the vicar and his daughter in 1904, Christmas in the infants'
school for long appeared to have been a somewhat muted
affair. On 26 November 1908, however, Miss Page wrote:
'One of the children in the Babies' Room, presented us with a
very fine Christmas Tree, the gift of her grandfather.'

This gift seems to have stimulated Miss Page into further
action, for a few days later, came: 'Let the children make
paper chains for decorating the room.' Then, on 21
December:

Had the 'Christmas Tree' in the afternoon after the
children had given several Recitations and Action Songs.
Several parents and the following ladies were present:
Mrs. Stevenson, Mrs. and Miss W. Courthope, Mrs. and
the Misses Watson, Miss J. Courthope, the Misses Luck,
Misses Batchelor, The Vicar, Master Hugh Smyth, A.G.
Watson, Esq.

And the pattern was set for subsequent years.

With the help of parents and other members of the

community, treats for the children at other times of the year, were frequent. 9 June 1906: 'The babies had a K.G. tea-party as two of their parents sent milk and biscuits.'

In the following month Miss Page recorded:

> In the afternoon, I took 24 babies up to Mrs. Boyd's garden where all very much enjoyed themselves, having a nice tea, some Kindergarten Games and riding on a pony.

And, in their absence, the vicar brought sweets to the school for the children remaining there.

Apparently building on the idea of kindergarten parties, towards the beginning of August 1908, Mrs Boyd sent an enamelled soup and fish service for kindergarten activities and Miss W. Courthope sent six knives, forks and spoons in a pretty little plate basket, to encourage the children to lay the dinner table with care and neatness.

On another occasion, in April, 1907:

> One of the parents sent down milk, cakes, buns, etc., so that the Babies might have a Tea Party as a farewell for her two little children, Jackie and Winnie Baker, as they are leaving the Parish.

This tea party, too, appeared to have set a precedent, for other, similar parties took place in the same year. Another, rather more special party had taken place a few years earlier, in 1904, when George Barham gave a Knighthood Celebration Party for them, as well as providing a trip to the London Zoo for the senior schools.

Miss Page recorded another treat, in the form of an educational outing, on 26 November 1908, when she:

> Took 6 of the 1st Year Class children up to the Lodge at 3 pm., as Mrs. Courthope had kindly promised to show a collection of skins and curios from India. All were greatly interested and much enjoyed their visit.

Parents and others also gave their help during the more trying times of bad weather and sickness. In January 1908, with snow and measles prevalent, Miss Page wrote in her log-book:

> Received from Mrs. Tulley [of the Queen's Head], one of the parents, a large can of hot milk and biscuits which warmed the children before starting for their walk home and was greatly appreciated.

The next day, the kindness was repeated by Mrs Watson of Uplands, who sent a gallon of hot milk and, on another occasion, hot cocoa.

At a time of influenza, colds and snow and low attendance, Mrs Boorman, who at one time had taught in the school, also sent down a large can of hot cocoa.[68]

Over the years, Miss Page continued to record the devastating effect on her school of difficult weather conditions:

27 January 1904	A very rough, windy day ... 23 children came out of 85.
5 February 1906	The Stove smoked badly, causing the children who had bad colds to cough constantly and so interrupt the lesson.

In 1907, the thermometer stood at 34° in the babies' room, so that Miss Page 'had great difficulty in keeping them warm'.

But, at last, on 17 January 1908, following visits by the managers and Mr Ashby, and while the children were given a holiday, an extra tortoise stove was fixed, at a cost of £7 7s 10d. And, on 18 June, the children were told by the Headmaster that the school's Union Jack had been hoisted to commemorate the Battle of Waterloo, which had been fought on that day in 1815.

The following year saw weather extremes. On 9 March 1909, Miss Page recorded:

Much snow has fallen in the night and the roads are in a

bad condition and the Managers being consulted, consider it will be wiser ... to dismiss the children who have ventured here at once and tell them not to return until Monday next.

Then, on 7 July 1909, 'Weather very stormy, only 77 present.' And to distract the children from their fear of the storm, Miss Page gave them, not a story, as she had done as a young teacher way back in 1870 in the little hamlet school of Cousely Wood, but several kindergarten games.

Hardly a year went past without a closure through sickness. From 1903 to 1910 Miss Page recorded:

1903	Measles	:	Six weeks.
1904	Measles	:	August 23 to October 3, including Holidays.
1906	Mumps	:	Nine weeks, including Easter Holidays.
1907	Measles	:	Three weeks.
1908	Chicken Pox	:	Three weeks.
1909	Measles	:	Three weeks.
1910	Scarlet Fever	:	One month.

These illnesses usually coincided with others and even if, in 1905, there were no closures, whooping cough and diphtheria abounded.

On 9 April 1907, Miss Page recorded: 'Heard that one of our little scholars had passed away during the Easter week from diphtheria.'

The Act to place upon the local education authorities 'the duty to provide for the medical inspection of children' was certainly long overdue, but, at last, even although in some disarray, Miss Page was able to write:

27 May 1909   Heard this morning that a Medical Inspection would be held on Monday June 7th at 9.30 and as the holidays were to commence the next day and

	the time to send out notices was so short, the Managers tried to get it postponed for a week, but this could not be arranged.
28 May	School left in charge of the two Assistants as I was too unwell to be present. Closed for the Whitsun Holidays.
7 June	Just 52 children medically inspected by A. Beeley, Esq. Several of the mothers present, also Mrs. Boyd and Mrs. Stevenson for a short time...
8 June	The remainder of the children were inspected today making 82 out of 85 on the books. The parents seemed very pleased at the opportunity.

After the hop-picking holiday, the school reopened on 4 October with the staff and children finding 'The rooms beautifully fresh and clean, as the outer room had been fresh painted and the floor of each scrubbed.'

But the school was still to face another epidemic of whooping cough, to which, at the end of November, the headmistress also succumbed. The school was then left in the charge of Mrs Hunnisett, aided by the supplementary teacher, Mrs Rogers.

On 3 January 1910, the vicar wrote in the school log-book: 'Very glad to have Miss Page back again in School after her attack of whooping cough.'

And so, Miss Page was, at last, able to organise the School Christmas Party, which had been held over from the previous term.

Mrs Tulley, Mrs Hemsley, Mrs Hook, Mrs Edwards and others, sent toys, and a little boy's grandfather sent a Christmas tree. Class 1 sent out invitations to the local affluent and later the children were told that their parents could come as well.

Sadly, only 69 of the 91 children on the roll were able to be present, as whooping cough was still prevalent and several children had influenza colds.

The party was held on 18 January 1910, when Miss Page reported:

> Recitations and Action Songs were nicely given by the little ones which appeared to give great pleasure to several of the parents and other ladies and gentlemen who were present. The following kindly helped to distribute the gifts from the Tree: Mrs. Stevenson, Mrs. and Miss Boyd, Misses Luck, Mrs. Courthope, Mrs. and Miss Watson, Miss Crispin, Miss Wigmore, the Misses Watson Smyth, Miss Batchelor, Miss Gordon, Miss Ramsden and friend. The Vicar and Curate were also present, the former kindly proposing a vote of thanks to the little performers. Mrs. Boyd added to the pleasure by giving each child a large rock bun.

Following the party, Miss Page ventured into dramatic activity and, after play on 4 February the 1st Class went into the girls' school to perform the historical scene which it had learnt – *Caractacus Before the Roman Emperor*. This performance was repeated for the benefit of the vicar on 11 February, and, three days later, for several parents, *Puss in Boots* was also performed, together with songs and recitations. The parents 'expressed themselves very pleased with all they had seen and heard'.

More dramatic activity followed and, near the end of term, the vicar and his wife came to see the children perform, *King Alfred and the Cakes*, as well as *Puss in Boots*. A repeat performance to Mrs William Courthope followed, after which, perhaps as a thank-offering, she sent the children a white teddy bear.

The usual week's holiday followed, which was always given at Easter, as well as at Whitsun and Christmas. The summer hop-picking holiday still depended on the requirements of the farmers, which sometimes meant it started at the end of August, to finish, perhaps, in the middle of October.

In common with the senior schools, incidental closures included those for polling days, local sports, Sunday school treats of the various denominations, the Annual Flower Show and the Band of Hope outing to Hastings (to continue later, over the next 50 years, as a Sunday school outing).

Closures caused by Sunday school treats were frequent and became a source of annoyance to the managers, who, at a meeting in August 1906, decided that 'some arrangements should be made in the future to prevent treats interfering with children's attendance at school'.

At another meeting, in 1909, the correspondent was asked to write to the Baptists and the Salvation Army to say that the managers were prepared to give a half holiday on any of the first three weeks in August and that, if possible, treats should be arranged for one or another of these dates, due notice being given.

Local 'gentry' had no compunction in taking children out of school. The following log-book entry is typical of others:

23 December 1908   Four children absent to attend a party at Mrs Watson Smyth's.

The managers perhaps reserved a more sympathetic attitude for the affluent. In 1911, a holiday was given on the marriage of Miss Winnie Watson, because 'The Bride and her family were interested in the children'.

The new vicar, the Rev. Leslie Stevenson, created yet another at least part-day holiday when he introduced the Empire Movement to Wadhurst in 1908.

In the parish magazine for May of that year he wrote:

This great movement aims at the introduction into all schools of a moral form of training which lays the foundation of good citizenship, to teach the rising generation to subordinate the interest of the individual to the common interests of all.

137

On Empire Day, 26 May, at 3.00 p.m., and in successive years, children and teachers of the schools of Wadhurst, Cousely Wood, Tidebrook and Woods Green joined together in a 'loyal demonstration', which on this occasion, consisted of a 'most interesting' selection of patriotic and national songs, which was conducted by Mr Knight and accompanied by Mrs Stevenson on the harmonium, with Mr S.T. Wallis on the cornet. A 'splendid' tea in the Market Hall and games in the cricket field followed, where Mr Ashby had erected swings and seesaws.

The children were then gathered again in the Market Hall, where, after raising and saluting a large Union Jack and singing 'The Flag of Britain', they listened to a 'stirring address' on Patriotism and Duty, given by the Rev. F. Knott, Headmaster of the Skinner's School in Tunbridge Wells. After the singing of more songs and the National Anthem, a grand procession of teachers and children, led by the town band and supported in the centre by the Salvation Army band, marched through the village to the Castle, with banners and flags 'bravely waving'. At the Castle, massed bands and voices joined in yet another performance of 'God save the King'.

In the following year, 1909, 507 children took part: 380 from Wadhurst, 85 from Cousely Wood and 42 from a private school in Woods Green, a hamlet near Wadhurst.[69]

Inspections continued to punctuate the school year. His Majesty's Inspectors, the Local Authority Inspector, as well as the Diocesan Inspector, each came at least once a year to look at the work and physical conditions of the school and to make their reports, which, in these last few years of Miss Page's career, continued to be, in most cases, favourable ones.

H.E. Haig Brown, Esq., Inspector to the East Sussex County Council, visited in 1904, when Miss Page recorded: 'He expressed pleasure in all he saw and heard and encouraged us in our work by his kindly suggestions and manner'.

This was, perhaps, in reply to HMI Gardiner's remarks made earlier, when he described the infants as 'disposed to be rather fidgety'.

When the Diocesan Inspector came, it was to hold 'The Annual Scripture Examination'. Following such a visit, by the Rev. W. Walsh, in 1902, the parish magazine reported:

> The children who had evidently been taught with great care, showed much intelligence in the answers, some of them being especially commended and a number of certificates being left by Mr. Walsh.

Visits sometimes followed in close proximity, for on 4 November 1903 HMI Gardiner inspected the finished needlework garments and those in the course of completion as well as the chalk drawings of Class I, and then, just a week later, HMI C.H. Stevens visited and saw each lesson taken in the morning, when he made several suggestions regarding the writing lesson and also the teaching of letter sounds.

In March 1904, Inspector Haig Brown suggested that dual desks should replace the old ones and in July of the same year, Miss Page was able to write: 'Had the babies in the gallery to watch the older ones at drill, as the dual desks are being put together in the classroom'.

In the following October, Mr Gardiner expressed his approval that a start had been made on the replacement.

In May 1907, Inspectors Freeland and Garland measured the rooms, took class numbers and suggested a rearrangement of the desks – so that all the children could be in line with the blackboard. Shortly afterwards, Miss Page carried out this rearrangement.

Six months later, the inspectors again visited, measured the rooms, counted the desks and, again, suggested their rearrangement. Again Miss Page carried out a repositioning – in order that she 'might better see the working of the 2nd Class when engaged with the 1st'.

Back in 1905, HMI Garland had recommended that the gallery itself should be removed – 'as soon as possible'. By July 1908, the managers, with great reluctance , had agreed to pay the removal costs, as originally proposed by the Education Committee.

At last, on 5 October 1908, Miss Page was able to record in her log-book: 'Gallery removed'. And she marked the entry with a large red star. She added:

> Arranged the Babies in 36 little chairs sent with 12 oblong tables for the Babies Room by the County Council
> The Managers had the gallery removed and the room painted in the holidays.

> Maria Montessori (1870–1952), the Italian educationalist, advocated the use of this type of furniture in the teaching of children, for the greater freedom it could give them. Dr Montessori considered that children should be given freedom to develop through their own experience, as long as it did not interfere with others. The teacher was to be regarded as a 'source of guidance, direction and inspiration rather than an instructor'.
>
> (*History of Education in Great Britain*. Curtis, UTP.)

Visitors came in to admire the new furniture, the like of which was seen in very few schools for at least another 20 years. His Majesty's Inspector F.A.S. Freeland visited on 19 May 1909 and reported that:

> The equipment in the babies room is new and good and the furniture in the main room has been suitable arranged. The organisation is satisfactory and the children neat and orderly. The School has decidedly improved in the last two years. There is now a healthy atmosphere of infant training and the children are kindly managed, bright and interested. Due attention is given to hand and eye training and to suitable games, while the scholars are taught to observe what is beautiful in nature around them.
> A tendency to chronic unpunctuality in arriving at school should be corrected.

Then, at the end of the year, on 8 December, when the term

was drawing towards Christmas, the school was visited again by an inspector: Mr Garland had come to hear Miss Linkstead taking her recitation, singing and reading lessons.

11

The School at Cousely Wood, 1902–10, now Infants and Girls

In 1902 Mrs Ballard had been Headmistress of Cousely Wood School for 29 years. She was still assisted by Miss Mayne and her former monitresses, Frances Funge and Eva Easter, both of whom, in 1899, had been recognised as supplementary teachers. Within a few months, however, Eva left, to be replaced by monitress Alice Smith, a former pupil at the school.

> Frances Funge was born in Cousely Wood in 1882 and had first attended the school as a little girl of four. In her teens, she became a Monitress and stayed, to teach until she retired in 1947. For many years, she played the American organ for the church services which were held in the school. She gave up, at last, in 1966 and died two years later.

On the reappointment of the staff, following the 1902 Education Act and the establishment of the new local education Authorities, Mrs Ballard's salary was £77, plus an allowance of £21; Miss Mayne £50, plus £7; Miss Funge £23 and the new monitress, £7. The cleaner Mrs Paine received 3s 6d a week and was required 'to provide such brooms as may be required'.

Cousely Wood School was now for infants and girls; boys over seven were sent up to Wadhurst.

Each department still continued to receive reasonable reports from the inspector, although in 1903, he considered

142

that the girls needed more self-reliance and energy and that the infants had to work under great difficulties in an overcrowded room.

The local authorities at Lewes took this up and directed the managers to enlarge it. By the end of 1904, the work had been carried out by Mr Ashby, at a cost of £155 10s 8d, with a further £12 12s for architect's fees.

When the inspector visited in the next year, he noted that the infants' room had been enlarged, but now considered that half the gallery should be removed and replaced with more desks.

The inspector also commented that the mental arithmetic needed attention and that singing was not taught from notes. At the next inspection in 1906, he added: 'Infants should not be taught to read in a nasal unnatural tone ... too much simultaneous repetition after the teacher.'

To defray the costs of the enlarged infants room, the management made an appeal, to which a number of people from the area responded, by putting on an entertainment.

The entertainment was held in the schoolroom, when songs, dances and other musical items were performed. After 'considerable expenses' were met, only £2 12s was raised, and that was shared with the Parochial Nurses Fund.

Miss Mayne, who taught the babies, had not long to enjoy her enlarged room, for, on 30 April 1906, she resigned to get married and Eva Easter returned to the school to take her place. The parish magazine referred to Miss Mayne's long and faithful service to the school and drew attention to the long list of people who had subscribed to a 'handsome marble striking clock', which showed the very general 'esteem and affection in which she was held'.

During the year, Alice Smith also resigned. The managers had suggested that Alice, in order to be regarded as a supplementary teacher, should take part-time classes and the subsequent examination in Tunbridge Wells. Her parents were unwilling for her to do this and, in any case, Mrs Ballard felt that thereby she would be left short-staffed. Alice was replaced by her sister Kathleen, who, as she was still a pupil

143

at the school, first needed to pass the necessary examination in order to gain her 'labour certificate'.

The parish magazine for December 1906 said:

If parents wish to withdraw children from school they must have attained the age of 14 years or have attained a 'labour certificate' by passing an examination in Standard 5. Managers have no powers, but if there is any urgency, H.M.I.s will allow him to be examined on the occasion of his visit to a neighbouring school.

The penalty was: £1 parents, £2 employers.

Education by the Hamlet of Cousely Wood

By the turn of the century, the school had become the centre for a great deal of the hamlet's activity. Each Sunday, there was a church service, with its own choir, a Sunday school, of which Mrs Ballard was the superintendent, a Men's Bible Class and a Girls' Friendly Society meeting. During the week, there were horticultural and dressmaking classes. Entertainments, assisted by people from Wadhurst, were frequent.

In April 1905, the parish magazine reported:

The usual Tea to the members of the Cousely Wood Bible Class took place on Shrove Tuesday ... After justice had been done to the substantial tea provided by Mr. Carpenter, the seats were re-arranged for what proved a very successful entertainment. Several members of the Orchestral Society were good enough to assist and Mr. Larcombe kindly lent his piano.

(For the Harvest Festival Service held later in the year, Mr Carpenter also supplied a 'noble loaf' which 'was divided among large families to whom it must have been very acceptable'.) In addition to the items provided by the

Orchestral Society, there were songs and recitations, cornet solos by Mr S.T. Wallis, euphonium solos by Mr Message, and Messrs H. Newington, F. Hunnisett and S.T. Wallis played trios on two mandolins and the banjo. The greatest novelty of the evening, however, was the very graceful dancing of Miss Phyllis Talham and Miss T. Vaughan, which 'won much deserved applause'. The children of Cousely Wood School also took part and concluded the entertainment by providing, in costume, a bright chorus, 'Japanese Girls'. The accompanists were Mr Knight and Miss Funge.

The magazine concluded by thanking Mr and Mrs Ballard, Mrs W. Ballard and Mr Benge for decorating the room and making the arrangements. Mr Wilkin contributed a number of flowering plants, which his gardeners tastefully arranged.

The Bible Class Tea was an annual event. As early as 1900 the parish magazine reported a 'substantial tea' with entertainment, which included a 'capital concert' of vocal and instrumental music, with songs by the schoolchildren. There were also songs by such as Mr and Mrs Vaughan, Mr Benge, the Rev. C.C. Davies and recitations by Master J.S. Denyer and Miss Alice Smith.

The large membership of the Bible Class was put down to the great interest that Mr Hazeldine, the curate, had taken in it. In 1909, a membership of 50 was reported.

In August of the same year, 1905, the parish magazine also reported the Annual Sunday School Treat, which was held in the 'flag-bedecked field' adjoining Mr Wilkin's garden, to which, after a short service in the school, 80 children processed, carrying a 'brilliant array of flags'. The children were then entertained with games, including rounders, cricket, swings and coconut shies, followed by tea 'in the shade of the trees', where seats had been placed to include a large company of parents and friends.

Mrs Ballard and day and Sunday school teachers gave 'indefatigable' help, as did Mr and Mrs Wilkin's coachmen and gardeners.

The Wilkins, sometimes with the assistance of the cinematograph, gave frequent treats to the day and Sunday school children, and the church choir joined with that of the parish church to go on trips to London, Eastbourne and the like.

The School at Cousely Wood, Infant and Girls, 1902 to 1910, continued

At the end of 1907, the vicar, the Rev. George MacLean, retired from his parish. This was a bad year, of heavy colds, sore throats, chicken-pox, fever, mumps and other kinds of sickness, which was, perhaps, reflected in the Diocesan Inspector's Report, where he commented, that although there was some really good and conscientious work, it was not quite so satisfactory as the year before.

Visitors were few: Miss MacLean, the vicar's daughter, 'came to bid farewell to the children', Mr Ferris, the curate, attended to distribute the county council prizes and the Chairman of the County Education Committee, R. Laurence Thornton, paid a rare visit. In the log-book, he commented:

5 July Visited the School, very much regret that the Managers either do not take sufficient interest or are unable to find time to visit the school occasionally in order to give the teachers that help and sympathy that is due to them and to show the children that some one has interest in them.

At this time, the managers were: The vicar, who was the chairman and the correspondent, H.C. Corke, who was the treasurer, Mrs Boyd, Lane-Andrews, Drew and George Courthope.

In the following October, F.A.S. Freeland, HMI, made his first 'visit of inspection'. He wrote:

29 October The school has no fire in the main room no coal having arrived. It is a cold, wet day on which a fire is necessary. In the Infant

146

room a fire was lighted with coal provided by the Headmistress.

There are no means of drying the children's clothes.

The new year, 1908, opened with the entry:

Unable to mark the register today as few children came and they were so wet and miserable the time was taken up in trying to dry them.

The new vicar, the Rev. L. Stevenson, was inducted during the year, but, although he made occasional visits, once with his wife, and the children took part in the Empire Day festivities, there appears to have been no reawakened interest in the school. The Wilkins alone gave real support, with their treats, examination prizes and Christmas cards.

In 1909, Miss Easter gave up her duties again, on the appointment of Miss Mary McCraw. Unfortunately, Miss McCraw, at her school in Buckingham, had failed to carry out the conditions of the Board of Education that, within a year, she should qualify as an uncertificated teacher. Now, from her new school, she was required to resign.

Miss Easter, who by now had become Mrs Wilkinson-Cole, resumed as a supplementary teacher, until Miss Dorothy N. Saunders was appointed in October.

It was during this year that the children received their first medical examination and the school its first unsatisfactory Diocesan Report. In his report, the inspector said that he was:

rather disappointed with the work ... the results ... not commensurate with the work which has been done ... slow to answer ... supply of good pictures would be helpful...

Inspectors Freeland and Garland also visited and gave a detailed report, in which 'the scheme' was considered

147

'satisfactory', the supply of literary reading books 'sufficient', and the library of 50 books was 'freely used by the girls'. It was felt that with some 'slight modification' the timetable would form a 'good working arrangement'.

Although the composition was 'satisfactory', the physical exercises were 'irregularly performed', and the singing 'rather harsh and suffers from want of voice training'. It was considered that 'lengthy Mechanical work' figured 'too prominently' in the arithmetic.

In the infants' department, the new teacher (the unfortunate Miss McCraw) promised well.

The inspectors also felt that the school would 'do fairly well' if the general apathy and indifference of the elder girls and their unwillingness to take due part in the work could be removed.

The inspectors considered, too, that the sweeping and dusting was 'very inadequate'.

At the beginning of 1910, the infant class continued to suffer change. Within three months of her appointment, Miss Saunders was away sick, never to return. Yet again, Mrs Wilkinson-Cole filled in, until the appointment of Miss Nancy Spiers in April, for the commencement of the new term.

12

Education by Wadhurst, 1910–13

The death of Edward VII, on 6 May 1910, was announced to the people of Wadhurst in a parish magazine edged with black, and a memorial service, timed to coincide with the King's funeral, took place in a black-draped church. The service took the form of the Litany and Burial Service and 'in the presence of a huge congregation', Mr Knight played Chopin's *Funeral March*. There was a peal on the muffled bells and, in the Square, the town band played the National Anthem.

> George J. Courthope of Whiligh died in the September of this year. He was succeeded by his son, George L. Courthope.
> The parish magazine said of George J. Courthope that he was 'A Christian Gentleman' of 'strength and guidance to his son' and that, with 'manifold responsibilities' he was 'an example of Christian fortitude' with 'firm adherence to duty'.

The Coronation of George V and Mary, in the June of the following year, was celebrated in Wadhurst with a special service, consisting of the Litany and Ante-Communion, during which an augmented choir was accompanied by the organ, cornet (S.T. Wallis) and drums (W.J. Piper and Harry Newington), with 'most thrilling effect'. The choir sang Sir Frederick Bridge's *Homage Anthem*, with Master Jack Button as soloist, and the service concluded with the singing of the hymn, 'Now thank we all our God'. The whole service was considered by the parish magazine as 'worthy of the occasion', and many were 'impressed and stirred' by it.

There was also a secular celebration, preparation for which had gone on for many weeks before. In spite of unfavourable weather conditions, it was 'crowned with success', with sports, teas, bonfires and fireworks.

In this Coronation year, aeroplanes flew over Wadhurst for the first time, which caused the vicar to comment:

> I suppose there are still a few old people to be found who have never seen a train. Probably, before long, we shall have to hunt diligently to discover any one who has never seen an aeroplane 'on the way'.

In the following year, 1912, a 70-hp. biplane came down at Best Beech, to which there was a constant stream of people, motors, brakes, carriages and cycles, all rushing to see it.

The vicar also wrote that, both at home and abroad, 1911 had been a year of strikes, the effect of which had been felt in Wadhurst. He also complained that confetti, instead of rice, had been thrown in the churchyard; that children had played there and even stolen flower-holders from the graves. He remarked, too, that houses were springing up like mushrooms and that, when the fortnightly sewing class, which was working for the parish stall in the Grand Bazaar and Country Fair, met in the Long Room, in Mrs Carpenter's Restaurant:

> The noise of the traffic outside is amazing and the reading aloud has to wait for a lull. The fact that Wadhurst is growing and developing is vividly brought home to us.

In April 1912, the vicar again wrote of the

> dark cloud of trouble over-shadowing our country. The disastrous coal strike is still dragging itself along ... settlement appears to be further off than ever ... great

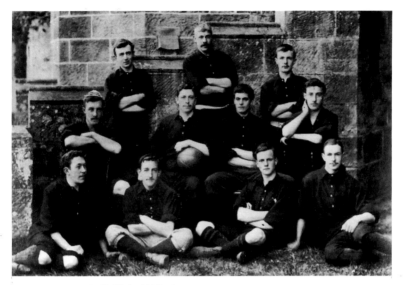

Wadhurst Football Club 1893–4

Wadhurst Town Band 1907

The Church

Lower High Street

The Castle

Pell Green

Cousley Wood

Boys of Wadhurst Church Choir, April 1962

waves of industrial unrest ... we hear of acute suffering and distress ... that such a condition of affairs should exist in a Christian Country ... shows that something is seriously wrong in our modern social and industrial life.

In this year, Adrian Drewe, of Wadhurst Hall, celebrated his twenty-first birthday. To mark the occasion, festivities of all kinds were held on the estate, which included fireworks by Brock, and tea in a large tent. Over 500 people attended from the surrounding district and Adrian was presented with a family portrait in oils, a 15-hp Napier car, a Bechstein piano, fishing rods and a gun. (In 1917, the death of Major Adrian Drewe by shellfire, was recorded in the parish magazine.)

Church services were so well attended that the Vicar felt the problem of insufficient room should be faced and so, in 1911, following a fire in the vestry, which was in the base of the tower, it was decided to open up that area. The screen was removed, together with the Ringer's Gallery, and bells were now to be rung from the ground floor. During the course of the work, two Norman windows were discovered and opened up. New vestries were built at the north-eastern corner of the church, and to enable this, on the evening of 15 August 1912, 30 graves were opened and the remains removed and reburied in another part of the churchyard. The cost of the building was estimated at £632 2s 6d, but Mr Drewe paid for a cloister to connect the chancel with the new vestries through a 2 foot 6 inch door in the north wall.

The vestries were dedicated by the Bishop of Chichester on 30 June 1913 at a 'very interesting and solemn service ... with music of an inspiring character'.

In the same year, as a gift from Sir George Barham, who died before their completion, new oak choir stalls, backed by panelling extending to the reredos, were put in hand. The organ console, too, was reversed and recased in oak – a gift from Mr C.C. Norbury of Buckland House, Cousely Wood, as a thank-offering for his recovery from illness.[70]

A gift of oak benches, carved by Rosier and constructed by Mr. C.W. Ashby, were installed in the porch, as a memorial to Annora Watson Smyth. In the following year, an alms box, carved in oak, also in memory of Annora, was given by her brother and sister. A brass to the memory of Mr Selby's son and a memorial window to Mr Whitty were also installed in the church.

> Annora, aged ten, was ill for one year and nine months, following a fall when playing on a boat at the seaside, before she died in April 1912. The parish magazine of June 1912 reported that she was 'called home on the evening of the 29th April'. It also spoke of her 'pain and weariness [but she was] unflinchingly brave and patient', and she bore 'several severe operations with marvellous courage and calmness. She would have liked to have lived ... but that she was quite happy and ready to go when the Good Shepherd came'.

Another useful innovation, as a gift to the church, was oak trestles, designed and worked by Mr Ashby.

Of greater significance to the general congregation, perhaps, was the replacement of the 30-year-old heating system by a new one, which was described as 'perfect'.

In 1913, His Majesty's Inspector for Schools reported that in the church schools the heating was inadequate, the wash-hand basin accommodation for the girls was also inadequate and the lighting was poor.

During these years, the church choir, frequently augmented, continued to be very active, including in Advent 1910, the singing of George Skinner's *The Captive of Babylon*, and, on Christmas Eve and at Matins on Christmas Day, the *Litany of the Incarnate Word*. At Matins, the choir also sang *Behold I Bring you Good Tidings*, by Norman Churchill, when the 'boys' voices rang out remarkably well and pleasingly in their passages'.

In Coronation year, in addition to the Special Service, Stainer's *The Crucifixion* was again sung in Holy Week. In May, 85 candidates and 9 from Tidebrook were confirmed by the Lord Bishop of Chichester, in the presence of an overflowing congregation. The choir and clergy, with a Church

Lads' Brigade guard of honour, met the Bishop at the Church Gate House entrance, and preceded him up the path to the singing of the hymn 'Soldiers of Christ Arise', in which the organ joined as the procession entered the church. The Bishop also preached at Evensong, when the choir sang Bunnett's *Service* and Stainer's 'God so loved the World'.

At Christmas, unaccompanied carols were sung by the choir and everybody sang 'The First Noel', in a manner which 'was a thing to be remembered'. There were also three hundred communicants.

In the following year, the vicar commented on the large crowds which attended the Harvest Festival services. He commented further: 'Why not always? ... we fear the family gatherings, tea parties, etc., are more the rule'.

And urged his readers to 'Turn over a new leaf ... come to Church regularly, at least once every Sunday'.

The Christmas of this year, 1912, was celebrated with the singing of some of Handel's music, of which the vicar wrote:

> This was an event in the annals of the Parish and after having Handel, we trust Wadhurst will not go back to the 'twaddle', (by comparison), of ordinary anthems.

The use of Handel's music was stimulated by a visit to Crystal Palace, the previous July, by men of the Parish and Mission Church choirs. They had been taken by the vicar to hear the rehearsal of the Triennial Handel Festival, at which a choir of 3,000 voices, accompanied by an orchestra of 1,000, was conducted by Sir Frederick Cowen, with Clara Butt and Ben. Davies among the soloists. The vicar thought that every choir and choir singer ought, if possible, be given the opportunity to sing Handel's music and was pleased that Mr Knight had introduced some of Handel's songs to the school.

In March, 1913, there were over 60 candidates confirmed, with 40 members of the choir present to sing the service. The vicar remarked on the female candidates in their white veils on one side of the nave and, on the other, the male candidates.

In Holy Week, *The Crucifixion* was again sung, by an augmented choir, for which there was a 'good attendance'. The Vicar commented:

> It would be difficult to find anything more suitable in the way of music for Holy Week for ordinary people who have not had the privilege of a good musical education ... The music is melodious and attractive without being cheap and vulgar. It is indeed devotional and reverent and is always impressive when well sung.

At Christmas, the Handel music was repeated, when Miss Mabel Watts sang the solo from the *Messiah* with 'singular purity of tone'.

During the year, the men of the two choirs had gone again to London, heard Matins at St Paul's Cathedral, the London County Council Band in the Embankment Gardens and also visited Westminster Abbey. For their outing, 25 choirboys were taken to Eastbourne by the curate. They went via Rotherfield Station, to which they had been driven in Mr Foote's brake.

In the autumn of 1910, following its successes at the Tunbridge Wells Festival in the earlier part of the year, the Wadhurst Choral Society, through the pages of the parish magazine, made an appeal for more members. Particulars of the music to be prepared, which included works by Palestrina and Benet, were also given. The vicar felt that 'we ought to be glad to be introduced to our old madrigal writers'.

The society, now with 53 members, entered nine classes in the ensuing festival and gained five prizes, as well as two cups and a presentation baton. Dr McNaught, the adjudicator, spoke of the 'discipline, good training and oneness of the Choir'.

The church choir also entered the festival and came first in its class.

In the following year, 1912, with 67 members in the Choral Society, more successes were recorded. The adjudicator commented: 'We have heard a quite extraordinary amount of good singing from the Wadhurst Choir.'

The *Courier* for 25 April 1913 reported a record number of entries for the Fourth Annual Music Festival, when 14 choirs entered in the senior section. The Wadhurst Choral Society came first in four classes, second in three, and tied in two. It also won a cup and a medallion.

For the first time, there was, also, a class for Scouts.

The Orchestral Society continued its activities, but appears to have had less mention in the parish magazine and no mention in the list of organisations printed in January 1912. Later in the year, however, it did assist at a concert organised by Miss D. Courthope, the proceeds of which were to help clear the debt incurred on the building of the rifle range. Mr Knight directed the orchestra, 12 members of the Girls' Friendly Society performed a cantata by F.H. Cowen and there were vocal quartets, solos and recitations, performed by the vicar, the curate, Mrs Ansell and Messrs S.T. Wallis, Mercer and Larcombe. Mr Larcombe also lent his piano. In the following year, the society again offered its services to the Annual Christmas Entertainment but, it would appear, they were not needed.

On 8 June 1910, the Whiligh Ladies String Band had made its first appearance. Under the conductorship of Mr Sutton, it gave a concert in the Market Hall, in order to raise funds for the Church Lads' Brigade, when the many items played were described as being 'very pretty'. Between them, the ladies played guitar, mandolin, banjo and harp and held their practices at Whiligh.

A year later, another new orchestral group made its appearance, when it played at an open air concert in the gardens of The Lodge. Mrs Stevenson conducted the orchestra in the *Toy Symphony* and among the players were Miss D. Courthope, Miss Ramsden, Miss Whitty, the Misses Gordon, Miss Gretton, Mrs P. Smith, Sam. Wallis and the curate (Mr Tomkins), with the vicar at the piano.

In January 1913, at the Annual Christmas Entertainment, held in the Market Hall, yet another 'band' made its first appearance in Wadhurst. This was the 'Wadhurst Hall Band', which consisted of members of the Drewe family. With Mrs Drewe seated at the piano and her three tall sons and eldest little girl grouped around her, playing on their various instruments, they made a 'pretty scene'. The items were 'very sweet' and 'greatly enjoyed'. Other contributions to the entertainment included a pageant play, *Empire Day*, in which Mrs Leslie Stevenson 'sustained the onerous part of Britannia with great dignity'. She was supported by 18 other performers, including 9 boys and girls. There were also humorous songs sung by Mr R.G. Gordon, recitations, a 'Nigger Sketch' given by the Church Lad's Brigade, a 'Comedy Sketch', as well as violin and piano pieces, played by Miss D. Ashby and Mr. H. Newington.

The Christmas Entertainment, organised by Miss D. Courthope, had become an 'annual'.

The entertainment of the previous year (1912), had included a cantata, with children trained by Mrs Percy Smith, in which 'pretty scenes' were enhanced by coloured lights thrown from Mr S.T. Wallis's lantern. Following this entertainment, the parish magazine complained of the great deal of whispering which had gone on at the back of the hall and suggested that a 'chucker-out' be instituted.

The town band continued its work. On 14 August 1910, together with The Foresters, The Star Benefit Society, the Wadhurst Branch of The Tunbridge Wells Equitable Society, The Cousely Wood Friendly Society, the Church Lad's Brigade, the Fire Brigade and the bands of the Wadhurst and Lamberhurst Salvation Army, it took part in the Annual Friendly Society Parade. The massed bands also played 'a few selections' at the Castle gates. The town band played, too, at the Grand Bazaar and Country Fair of 1911, the Sunday School Treat, held in Mr Carpenter's Town Meadow, and also at the Empire Day events of 1912.

The Hospital Parade of 1912, led by the town band, was held in the driving rain. Several hundred 'professing God-fearing men and women' took part in it, but, the vicar complained, 'not one half of them entered the House of God'.

The town band again took part in the Hospital Parade of 1913, but on this occasion it was 'assisted by a few friends'.

In these days before the First World War, musical and other activities continued in such abundance that even the vicar felt cause to ponder if there were not enough organisations in the parish and to suggest that, perhaps, those existing should be made 'really efficient and up-to-date'.

At this time, the population of Wadhurst was 3,033.

The Sunday schools appear to have been among those organisations that were 'really efficient and up-to-date', and in 1911 the vicar reported that 300 children attended them. He emphasised the enormous responsibility they presented to the teachers.

Monthly meetings for them continued, at one of which, Miss Gretton, 'a highly-trained teacher in the Wadhurst School', read a paper on 'How can the Day School teacher help the Sunday School?' At another meeting, 24 Sunday school teachers saw Miss Page, 'a born and highly-trained teacher', give a demonstration lesson. Better organisation of the Sunday schools was also discussed and it was decided to hold, following the major festivals, a combined service in the parish church, for the Sunday schools of Wadhurst, Cousely Wood and Faircrouch.

The children at the far reaches of the parish were not forgotten and so, in 1911, those attending Mr Drewe's Sunday school at Wadhurst Hall were invited to take part in the Sunday School Treat. After a service in church, all the children, with banners, processed to the Castle gates and then back to Mr Carpenter's meadow, where they played games, rode on seesaws and swings, listened to the band and had tea.

In order to cater for the children living on the borders of Wadhurst, Tidebrook and Mark Cross, in 1913, a new Sunday school was opened at Beechlands Oast, where 40 children were taught by Mr and Mrs Strutt and Miss Kirby.

1913 saw a further Sunday school innovation. Until that year, and for many years before, prizes had been awarded solely for attendance, but now it was decided to include the additional qualifications of good conduct, attention and answering. At the following Prize Giving, 70 prizes were presented, in the presence of a crowded audience. The audience was also entertained by a missionary play, especially written by the curate, Mr R.C. Johnson, in which 14 children took part, dressed in native costume lent by the Delphi Mission. The children had been helped with hints given by the Colonel and Mrs Ramsden from their experience in India. Help was also given by Mr C.W. Ashby, Mr H.C. Corke and Mr S.T. Wallis.

In 1911, three years after the founding of the Boy Scouts, a Wadhurst troop was formed, of which Mr Edward Courthope was the scoutmaster. By the following year, numbers had risen from 11 to 21. Meetings were first held at Hill House, or in the Carpenter's Long Room (part of Carpenter's Bakery and Restaurant at the corner of Washwell Lane),[71] but soon Mr Watson Smyth of the Castle gave a plot of land on which a permanent headquarters was built. Instruction was given in first aid, carpentry, shooting and lifesaving and within the first few months, together with other troops, the boys took part in a field day, in which they sent dispatches through the 'enemy lines'. On a later occasion, 27 boys were treated to a day in London, where they visited the Zoo and also saw a naval and military tournament.

The scoutmaster, however, complained that, after several months' training, no second-class Scout badges had been awarded and, following a camp near the hut, threatened that there would have to be 'some weeding out'.

In the summer of 1912, a camp was held at Camber, where, at last, six Scouts earned their second class badges. By the next camp, Mr Courthope had gone to India and Dr Wilkins had taken over. In the October of 1913, he said of the summer camp:

the boy who hasn't enjoyed his camp is a slacker ... I can't imagine a slacker having a good time at camp, more over, I can promise him my best endeavour to see that he doesn't get it.

The Church Lads' Brigade, run by a succession of curates, assisted by Lieutenant H.J. Austen and instructors, continued its efforts and, by 1911, had a band of five bugles, three side drums, a bass drum, given by Mr Drewe, and later, a pair of cymbals, a gift from Mrs Fazan. Mr Drewe also presented a 'magnificent' challenge shield.

Meetings were held in the vicarage, football played in Mr Carpenter's field, a night attack, with blank ammunition, was made on Mr Watson Smyth's Castle Farm and the company took part in a Battalion Day at Speldhurst.

In spite of inspections by General Wace and by Colonel Ramsden, a camp at Whiligh, with a church parade and drum service for parents and friends, and funds raised by concerts given by supporting parishioners, in the October magazine for 1913, the Captain in Charge wrote:

> a weeding out process has been carried out and some boys have left the company ... boys who did not come up to the required standard have to leave...

But, for all that, later, 'old boys' presented a 'Pace' stick to the brigade, a local football league was formed and a social held, at which the orchestra, under Mr Knight, played pending the late arrival of some entertainers.

The Church of England Men's Society, with Sam. Wallis as its secretary and treasurer, continued its fortnightly meetings, instituted a corporate communion for its members and on 20 February 1911, held a social evening in the Long Room, where the men enjoyed 'Games and Music ... a very delightful time ... excellent refreshments, mirth and good fellowship'.

At its regular meeting, held at the vicarage in the same month, the society held a debate on the subject of 'Gambling', for which there was a large attendance, with 'tongues loosened' and with men 'up on their feet'. Items at other meetings included 'White Slave Traffic', 'Should Sacred Subjects be Shown in Cinemas?', a talk by Mr C.W. Ashby on 'Old Wadhurst', 'Loyalty to the Prayer Book', by the curate, a lecture by Mr W.K. Hardman on 'Wireless Telegraphy', a discussion on 'Patronage', with 'lively views, for and against', talks on 'Poor Law Reform', and 'Church History', by John Courthope, and by Mr Carpenter on 'Church Finance'.

New Bible Classes for Men were opened at the Mission Church, Dewhurst and Fair Glen and, rather more rare, a Bible Class for Young Women, Married or Single, was announced, to be held at Hill House, at 6.15 p.m. on Wednesdays. Before long, it, too, was having social events, when songs and duets were sung and tea provided.

The Mothers' Union, with Mrs Watson Smyth as its secretary, continued with its regular meetings, for one of which Mrs Watson Smyth provided a 'sumptious tea', in the Racquet Court of Wadhurst Castle. She, herself, was unable to be present, owing to the grave illness of her daughter, Annora. By 1913, membership had grown to 170, but, sadly, only 70 of the mothers bothered to attend the Annual Service held in the parish church. The following year, Mrs Watson Smyth sent out a personal invitation to each member: 158 members answered the invitation by attending.

Mothers' Meetings also continued to flourish, including Mrs Boyd's at Hill House, which had a membership of 40. In addition to its regular meetings, it, too, had its frequent social events, together with its Annual Tea, which, in 1911, was preceded by a drive. Unfortunately, tea was marred by insects, but photographs were taken by Mr S.T. Wallis and games of cricket, croquet and beanbag played, with the addition of a 'tug of war' contest between the Mothers of Sparrows Green and the Rest. On occasions, the mothers were also entertained at Yeomans and Uplands.

As early as 1896, a Mothers' Meeting had been started in the station area. By 1908, it was being held at Dewhurst, the home of Mr and Mrs Whitty, where a room was specially fitted up for the purpose. The meetings were taken by Mrs and Miss Whitty.

In 1913, probably at the same time as the Sunday school, a Mothers' Meeting was formed at Beechlands Oast, to cater

160

for the mothers living on the borders of Wadhurst, Mayfield and Mark Cross. Very soon, the meeting was having its social events, which included a tea in the Mission Room, when the Misses Castellan entertained the mothers with a gramophone.

The Girls' Friendly Society continued active and, in 1912, held its Annual Festival at Faircrouch. The customary service was held in the Mission Church, which the parish magazine said, 'nestles under the hill in the corner of Faircrouch grounds'. On this occasion, the church was 'crammed to the doors'. Tea followed and then games, including croquet, and an address on the work of the GFS.

In 1913, an area garden party was held at Uplands, where 100 girls were entertained to tea, followed by games in the grounds of the Lodge. The girls were addressed by Mrs Spelman, who advised them to have nothing to do with 'low, vulgar and suggestive post cards, so freely exhibited all over the country'.

In the previous year, 1912, twelve of the girls took part in a concert which was given in aid of the rifle range. The girls, trained by Mrs Stevenson, sang, in costume, a cantata, *Village Scenes*, by F.H. Cowen. There were also items by the Orchestral Society and others.

The Total Abstinence Society, under its Secretary, Mr. F.H. Brackett, continued its work, as did the Band of Hope, with Miss Page as its leader. The special train to Hastings for the children and their parents was still an important event in the society's year.

A Band of Hope, under the leadership of Miss Whitty of Dewhurst, had been formed in the station area, and carried on its activities at the Mission Church. The society appears to have gone on frequent outings, including one to Hastings in 1910, when many, in a party of nearly 30, saw the sea for the first time.

By 1912, the Parish Poor Fund, yet again, had been reorganised by the vicar. The committee now consisted of the churchwardens (Colonel Ramsden and Mr J.C. Lane Andrews), Mr J. Williams as Honorary Secretary and Treasurer, and Messrs H.C. Corke, H. Edwards, A.G.

Watson, H.J. Whitty and the Rev. H.F. Tomkins. One woman alone remained – Mrs Boyd.

The Nursing Association reported that, during 1911, Nurse Milward had made 1,305 visits and Nurse Sidwell, 2,057. It again pointed that, although there was no charge for the services provided, more generous contributions were needed.

A Coal and Clothing Club was run by Miss Watson, the parish library continued at the Institute, with Miss Boyd as its librarian, and the Institute itself still had Mr Larcombe as its secretary. Evening classes at Uplands were no longer mentioned, but in June 1912, Miss Boyd and Miss Ramsden announced 'The Wadhurst Home Industry Classes', held at Hill House, where smocking, basket-making, crochet and other crafts were taught. In July 1914, the parish magazine reported that, at a London exhibition, one of its stools had been bought by Queen Alexandra.

In the same year, a 'Course of four lectures for Mothers' on 'The Care of Children', to be given by a trained nurse, was also announced, for which tickets could be obtained from Miss Amy Watson, at a cost of 6d.

The Work Guild, set up in 1904, continued to support St Thomas's Church, Bethnal Green, London, and in 1913 sent 127 garments and a cheque for £5. Earlier, the Vicar of St Thomas's gave a talk to the guild, boys from its Church Lads' Brigade played the Wadhurst Brigade at football, and Mrs Boyd invited poor working girls to spend the day at Hill House.

The church, also, continued to support a great number of societies, including the British and Foreign Bible Society, the Society for the Propagation of the Gospel, the Church Missionary Society, the United Mission to Central Africa, the Melanesian Mission and the Cambridge Mission to Delhi. In 1912, a British and Foreign Bible Society representative from Brazil spoke to a meeting held in the Market Hall, at which a special choir, trained by Mrs Stevenson, sang music by Mendelssohn and Gounod. Mendelssohn's 'How lovely are the Messengers' was among the items, with Mabel Watts, Mr S. Ansell and Mr F.K. Hardman as soloists.

In 1913, a junior branch of the SPG, the King's Messengers, was formed, with Miss D. Courthope as its secretary. The SPCK sent a preacher from the Assyrian Mission and the Rev. R. Harper, from the Mission to Seamen, when preaching at Matins and Evensong, held his crowded congregations 'spell-bound'.

Local needs were not forgotten: Dean Wace, son of the Rev. R.H. Wace, who had kept the preparatory school at Hill House, gave a site for a parish hall and also a Fire Brigade station.

The Wadhurst Fire Brigade was formed in 1904, with 44 members and with Mr C.W. Ashby as captain. It held its first meeting, for hose drill, on 15 June in the park at Durgates. Mr G.J. Courthope provided ten 50 feet lengths of hosing, one standpipe and two nozzle jet pipes, and the Crowborough Water Company, 14 hydrants. The hose was kept in a packing case at the Castle and delivered to where it was wanted, on a hand cart provided by Carpenter's.

The first fire attended was on a haystack at Hill House Farm, when it became apparent that more hosing and another nozzle were needed. These, together with a hose-cart, were provided by subscription. In 1910, 20 second-hand suits were bought, and in 1911, Mr J.C. Venables gave a fire station. An escape ladder and helmets were also bought at this time.

In order to raise funds for the erection of the Parish Hall, a Grand Bazaar and Country Fair was held in the Market Hall and in the field adjoining. There were many stalls and sideshows – including six pierrots, with Mr Knight at an American organ, hoop-la, run by Mr H. Boorman, and a shooting gallery, run by Mr M. Watts. There was also a coconut shy, a palmist and a donkey ride.

Over £300 was raised from an effort which had taken many months of preparation.

13

*The School at Cousely Wood, Girls and Infants,
1910–14*

Miss Nancy Spiers, the new teacher, took up her duties in
April 1910 and in the senior part of the school, Mrs Ballard
appears to have introduced subjects to extend and interest the
older girls. A housewifery course was included which dealt
with needlework, knitting, crochet, lace-making, darning,
mending and the making of garments, as well as health, food
and clothing, household management and expenses, and the
management of young children. In 1911, the girls also went
up to Wadhurst for cookery lessons. On one occasion, at
least, Mrs Wilkin visited to see the girls knitting, when she
gave them hints on 'heel-turning'.

Inspectors Freeland and Garland, with 62 pupils present,
visited the school on 3 August, when, because of, or in
spite of Mrs Ballard's efforts, they considered 'There are
... no facilities ... for a Senior Class' and suggested that
the managers confined the school to one for juniors and
infants.

The inspectors also felt that, although the singing was
better than in 1910, drawing was confined to the hard-point
and that the elder girls were 'reticent and inert in all oral
work, though they talk freely out of school. They appear to
have derived little benefit from their studies.'

A few months earlier the Diocesan Inspector, R.B.
Jameson, had found:

> The children of this little school are very well taught
> [with] care for their good ... and although the Infants

were rather timid ... the Upper Classes were attentive and reverent ... written work was very well done.

Her Majesty's Inspectors pointed out that there were six erasures in the register for 1911 and fifteen in those for 1910–11 and that the inspector's report for 1909 had not been signed by the correspondent.

Between the two inspections, the children had, at least, received a holiday to celebrate the Coronation of King George V and Queen Mary.

The defective registers proved a stimulation for the managers to visit the school, if only on a rota basis of once a term. Earlier in the year, the managers had decided that the school log-books should be presented by the head teachers at each of the managers' meetings.

At 12 noon, on Monday, 16 October 1911, the managers held a meeting at the school, when they interviewed Mrs Ballard and asked her how the proposed reorganisation of the school would work. She pointed out the difficulties that would arise from the playground size and from the 'office' facilities. No final decision was taken. The managers, however, did decide to have the creeper around the school house cut away, which, after warning, Mrs Ballard's husband had failed to do.

On 12 January 1912, Mrs Ballard recorded in her log-book: 'A very good attendance this week. Average 61.9'.

What Mrs Ballard considered a 'very good attendance' was not to last for very long, for within two months, heavy colds had taken their toll and then, soon, the school was closed by the medical officer through an outbreak of mumps. Another closure took place in the following month of April, but this time, in order that the teachers could attend the Musical Festival in Tunbridge Wells.

Towards the end of the year, a new HMI, Mr Boutflower, visited the school and again raised the question of the school's reorganisation. He felt that the 19 elder girls should be transferred to Wadhurst and replaced by the younger boys, aged between seven and nine, who now went to Wadhurst but lived in Cousely Wood.

165

At this time, but a world away from inspectors, Mr and Mrs Wilkin again gave their Annual Treat, preceded, as was the custom, by an examination in the three Rs, sewing and knitting and an essay on 'How can I help to make home happy?' The parish magazine commented:

The cosy little school was gay with burnished holly and ivy and when all the pretty curtsying and eager pocketing of the cash was over a splendid tea began ... after which a Conjuror from London gave a long and delightful programme.

At last, on 17 March 1913, with a school suffering from the effects of coughs and colds, flu and sickness, the vicar, the Rev. L. Stevenson, visited the school to tell the upper class girls that, from the beginning of the new year, on 31 March, they would be drafted to Wadhurst.

Education by the Hamlet of Cousely Wood

Organisations in Cousely Wood continued to flourish. The Men's Bible Class, run by the curate, Mr Tomkins, in 1911 had a membership of 63. Meetings continued to include socials and concerts, when local talent was assisted by that from Wadhurst. Songs, violin solos, recitations, handbells, mouth organs, plays and dances, were contributed by such as the vicar, the curate, Colonel Ramsden, Messrs Benge, Ansell, Newington, Watts and the Thorpe brothers. In June 1910, the parish magazine reported that 'the little Miss Watson Smyth took part in a Concert, before a crowded audience, for which Mr. and Mrs. Norbury lent their piano'. Then, in March, 1912:

little Miss Wilma Watson Smyth and Mr. Teddy Watson Smyth, took part in the Concert and the Misses Daphne and Beryl Courthope ... made their first appearance on a Wadhurst platform and received an encore for their well-executed dancing.

In the following year, again before a crowded audience, with 11 o'clock reached and with but part 1 of the concert completed, it was decided to leave part 2 for some future occasion.

The money raised at the concerts was used to defray the expenses of the Bible class outings. In 1910, the Bible class members went to Brighton, where dinner and tea were provided and some men saw the sea for the first time.

The Cousely Wood branch of the Girls' Friendly Society started its own Bible class at this time, which was held on Sunday afternoons. The branch also had a knitting evening, which was held at Collums. Socials, too, were numbered among its activities and in February 1911 its members were entertained to tea by the Wittersham branch of the society with games organised by Miss Watson. Later on in the year, the branch was entertained at Buckland House, where, as it was National Health Week, Mrs Stevenson spoke on 'Keep the windows open', which appeared to be one of her favourite topics.

In 1913, a Mothers' Meeting was started at Cousely Wood, which met on Saturday afternoons. In February 1914, around 50 mothers enjoyed a Winter's Tea Party, which also included duologues and songs by the vicar and his wife. There was, as well, a two-week-old baby present, of which the parish magazine recorded: 'It was a great joy to many to handle the little creature'.

The School at Cousely Wood, now Juniors and Infants

On 31 March 1913, Mrs Ballard wrote in her log-book: 'This school to consist of Junior Boys and Girls and Infants'.

Two months later, after chicken-pox in the school, the vicar visited the recently reorganised school and wrote in the log-book: 'A very good school and children hard at work and happy'.

Then, in August, HMI Boutflower, accompanied by the County Inspector, Mr Baines, also visited and reported:

167

Since the beginning of the year, a Junior School ...
Unfortunately, the Mistress has proved unequal to the
task of managing the boys and a serious want of
discipline prevails...

In 1914, Cousely Wood School started the school year late,
for there was diphtheria in the area. A little later, with the
children now ill with influenza, there was much rain and
those who did manage to get to school arrived 'dreadfully
wet'. On one day, the roads were in such a bad state only
20 children out of the 74 on the roll managed to get
there.

On 23 April the Diocesan Report arrived:

The new Syllabus has been ... taught with very good
results in each class ... everywhere happy and interested
in their lessons...

There was just one criticism: '...a little more attention to the
aspirates'.

On 24 April, HMI Boutflower arrived. His report, received
the following July, said:

...same unsatisfactory conditions as when last reported
on. In the Main Room, Classes I and II, the children are
grossly in-attentive and idle and a constant buzz of
conversation prevails ... control better in Class III where
the younger infants are taught...

As a natural consequence of the bad discipline in the
Main Room, the Upper Section of Class I was found to
be lamentably weak in R.R.R. ... neither here (Class I)
nor in Class II do the children make any attempt to
attend or keep the place. Writing actually deteriorates
through the classes. It was observed that four boys in the
Upper Division Class I took half an hour to write two
sentences in a Composition lesson and those were copied
from the end boy in the row. The Exercise Books are
imperfectly corrected in the class.

Observation Lesson ... the Mistress was scarcely audible at the back of the class...

The two sections of Class II:

commenced to change lessons at 11.45am., but it was not until 11.52am., that she was ready to take the Reading lesson of the lower section. As the bell for dismissal rang at 11.53, this Reading lesson lasted one minute...

The inspector said that he arrived at 9.55 a.m., but 'The Registers were found not closed and the Religious Instruction [which should have ended at 9.40 with the Registers closed at 9.45] was still proceeding.'

HMI Boutflower also complained that the managers' system of sending boys to Wadhurst as they reached the age of ten, all through the year, was 'distinctly objectionable'. He felt, too, that as there was no special training for two defective boys, there was no point in keeping them at the school above the age of ten,

The inspector, in addition, drew attention to the following:

Classes I and II : Schemes of Work were incomplete.
Class I   : No Record Book.
Class II   : Weekly Record incomplete.

Boys up to the age of 10 retained, but nothing done to the Offices or Urinal, which were very offensive on the day of Inspection.

Following the reception of the inspector's report, Mrs Ballard recorded in her log-book: 'The school was carried on by Miss Funge, assisted by Mrs. Wilkinson-Cole, myself too unwell to attend'.

The school had still very few visitors and its one unfailing supporter, Mrs Wilkin, had died in the Canary Islands earlier in the year.

Of her, 'cottagers' said, 'we have lost our best friend', to which the parish magazine added: 'A wise counsellor, a true friend, a liberal supporter of all good works, we shall not easily meet her like again'.

A brass plate to her memory was placed in Wadhurst Church on the north wall.

Both her death and the outbreak of war in August 1914 went unrecorded in Mrs Ballard's log-book.

14

The Wadhurst Schools 1910–14

The Infant School

A month into the summer term Miss Page was visited by H. Stott, Esq., MOH, 'with regard to the outbreak of scarlet fever, who suggested that the schools were to be closed until after the Whitsun Holidays'.

After a month's closure, the school reopened on 6 June with 63 out of 90 children present. The reopening coincided with some very hot weather, so some schoolwork was done out of doors, but before long, the weather changed and a fire had to be lit in the babies' room in order to dry the children's clothes.

The rhythm of the term was soon disturbed, first by a day's holiday when the senior children were treated to a visit to the London Zoo by Sir George Barham, and then by the annual medical examination, for which the babies were put into the main room, to leave their room free for the doctor. Miss Boyd and Miss Watson helped in the arrangements and Miss Page remarked that 'several mothers said that they would be present'.

Miss Watson, who had retired recently as head of the girls' school, also helped on a number of other occasions:

July 19 1910 Miss Watson kindly took the Babies for a walk round the field, which they much enjoyed.

July 20 1910 Miss Watson took the 1st Class for their morning lessons.

Miss Watson also helped out in the following year, when Miss Page was absent to attend her sister's funeral.

On 20 July 1910, HMI Freeland, together with HMI Garland, visited the school, heard the voice exercises and recommended the use of a certain singing book. Other visitors included Mrs Gretton 'who was pleased with the Babies' Room furniture', and Miss Whitty, who saw the various classes at work. Mrs Courthope came to present the Flower Show prizes, which amounted to 7s 9d, but she also gave a further 5s for a school toy, and Mr Tomkins, the curate, addressed 'a few, simple and encouraging words to the children'.

Meantime, the usual outings and treats took place, which included the Salvation Army Treat, the Band of Hope Outing to Hastings and the Mission Church Sunday School Treat.

After the hop-picking holidays, the vicar came in and 'very heartily' welcomed the children and staff back to school. Later in the month, the vicar looked at specimens of free-cutting and ruler-drawing, the work of the boys, which he thought 'Very Good'. Then, in October, supported by his wife, Mrs Boyd and several parents, he awarded the county council prizes for regularity, punctuality, progress and good conduct. Miss Page commented that the prize winners were 'very pleased with their prizes'.

For long, local encouragement had been given to the children, but, in 1904, to this was added an East Sussex County Council Grant for prizes, to be awarded annually for regular attendance, good conduct and progress. Later, cards for good attendance were also given.

Mr Freeland, accompanied by the County Inspector, Mr Baines, visited in November, looked at the equipment, saw leaves modelled by the 1st Class and also 'spoke a few words to each class'.

That the inspectors spoke a few words to each class appears to have impressed Miss Page. In the following year, she reported a similar incident, when, after Inspectors Freeland and Garland had seen the plasticine work, free-writing, and the making of paper flowers, they 'had a little talk with the

172

children'. It would appear that, at long last, some of the inspectorate at least, were becoming more human in their dealings with them.

During the term, the children were allowed to make a hop garden in plasticine and also to have a 'toy hour', when some of the children fitted up a Chinese junk, 'very nicely'. The 1st Class boys acted 'Guy Fawkes', Miss Page went through the dialogue 'Politeness' with the children, told them the story of the first Prince of Wales and promised that the 1st Class should act it, which, later, they did.

The vicar heard the children sing, a Canadian emigration agent was pleased with what he saw, the 1st Class made a model of a miners' cage and the assistant told the story of a mine accident.

Towards the end of the term, the 1st Class wrote invitations to those ladies who might be interested to come to the Christmas Tree Entertainment.

Thirty visitors attended who also helped to distribute the toys from the Christmas tree, which had been supplied by Mrs W. Courthope, Mrs Walker, Miss Linkstead and several of the parents. Sweets and buns were also supplied by various ladies. Mr Corke contributed seven dozen oranges, and 'Each child contributed their best to the programme'. This included the dialogue on 'Politeness', action songs by the babies, and the 1st Class 'represented in character, the "Presentation of the First Prince of Wales to the Welsh Chiefs".'

The following day, the programme was repeated for the benefit of those parents who came. Action songs, particularly with the babies, were in frequent use, both to instruct the children and to entertain the visitors.

On one occasion, when the children performed the 'Rabbit Song', which had been the subject of an oral lesson, Miss Page 'Let two boys shoot off their toy pistols ... much to the pleasure and interest of the children'.

The following year, 1911, was Miss Page's last complete year as headmistress. For the past ten years, she had been assisted by Miss Beatrice Green, who in 1907 had become Mrs

Hunnisett but had continued to teach. Now, on 31 January 1911, she took a 'kindly farewell of the children' and was presented with a travelling rug and a pair of reindeer gloves from some of the children she had taught and from the present staff of teachers.

To take her place, Miss Ethel Winchester, aged 20, was appointed uncertificated teacher, having passed the Cambridge Senior Local Examination.

Miss Page still used the occasion to shape the lesson and so, on 29 May 1911, when the weather was so hot that she took the children out into the playground, she sat them in the shade of a tree and there told them the story of 'Oak Apple Day' and of the future Charles II hiding in an oak tree before he escaped to France.

> Oak Apple Day: The Opies' *Language and Lore of School Children* records the observance of this day as being held in Wadhurst (among other places). In the late 1950s, Barry Gadd, a pupil at the then secondary school, carried on the tradition by wearing a sprig of oak apple in his buttonhole.

On another occasion, when a storm was very heavy and the children were frightened, as in earlier days, Miss Page calmed them by telling them a story, but now she used an extra ploy – by illustrating it on the blackboard as she did so.

The children themselves continued to do a lot of drawing and colouring and so, one day, when a rough gale was blowing, they were told to draw a picture of a windy day, from which a lesson about the wind was given.

On 5 April 1911, however, blizzards were so bad that only eight out of eighty-one children managed to reach school.

During another cold spell, the caretaker was asked to light the school fires early, but when the children arrived, the temperature was still down to freezing point and so the children were moved and marched to keep them warm. Some of them were sometimes poorly when they were in school, but still they had to face a long walk home through wet, muddy or snowy fields and lanes. It was no wonder that frequently

174

children failed to return the next day, through illness or through clothes too wet to dry.

Miss Page's last year appeared coloured not only by her dramatic activities, but also by her desire to help her new 'young and inexperienced' assistant. To do this, she left her other assistant, Miss Linkstead, to take Classes I and II in the schoolroom, while she herself stayed with Miss Winchester in the babies' room.

On 21 March 1911, Miss Page wrote in her log-book: 'an Oral lesson conducted by Miss Linkstead on the Rook, as the children have been told to observe them and it gives me time to advise Miss Winchester in a practical manner'.

Two weeks later, Miss Linkstead was absent in order to sit for the second part of her Preliminary Examination, so Miss Watson, the retired headmistress, came in to help. Soon, Miss Page was back in the babies' room 'while they had a number lesson, some children acting as sheep and some as drovers'.

And on 1 August 'Baby Room teacher took a Farmyard as a number lesson and very nicely carried out the aim of showing 3 sheep + 2 = 5 etc.'. Then, on 3 August 'Went in for two lessons in the Baby Room to help the Assistant adopt the elementary methods of teaching'. On another occasion, the headmistress heard Miss Winchester give a lesson on the letter 'A' in the form of an amusing little tale and helped her to give the sound of some of the letters to the babies.

Miss Page also found time to give a demonstration lesson to the 24 teachers of the 300-strong Sunday school and, as in past years, superintend the Band of Hope outing to Hastings, with 150 children and 400 parents, friends and helpers on the special train.

After her retirement, Miss Page took over as Superintendent of the Infant Sunday School, from which she retired in 1919.

Miss Page's last year was not unmarred. Her sister died in the January, on two occasions a little boy, Edwin Fillery, was found stealing food from other children's bags and then, perhaps because it was but a few months before her retirement, in July, the vicar, Mr J.C. Andrews, who was one

175

of the managers, and Mr Cooke, a secretary from Lewes, visited to take the dimensions of the two rooms, with a view to turn the babies' room into a cookery room for the elder girls. This would mean that the babies would have to be taught in the schoolroom. Miss Page commented:

> should this come to pass the presence of over 30 babies (now taught on Kindergarten lines), in this room, two days a week, for 18 weeks, will prove very detrimental to the teaching of the elder infants.

Then, to the managers' 'regret', the Board of Education, in spite of Miss Page's long and distinguished service, refused to grant a year's extension to her, and the local education authority in turn refused to retain her until a new headmistress took up her duties. They suggested that, instead, a teacher from the senior school should be used for the purpose.

Three days before she retired, Miss Page was still giving help to her young assistant, Miss Winchester:

> January 9 1912. Helped the Assistant teach the Babies a conversational realistic on Winter-bare trees, sleeping animals, etc.

In the same week, Miss Page 'allowed' two of the extension class girls to come in 'to play with the little ones as they intend becoming nursemaids'.

Miss Charlotte Caroline Page made her last log-book entry on 12 January 1912. She wrote:

> As my certificate expires tomorrow (13th), I relinquish my duties as Headmistress of the Wadhurst Infant School after 44 years service.
>
> Had in all the children who had passed into the Mixed Department this year and gave each a card.

Charlotte Caroline Page.

The following August, at a special ceremony in the Wadhurst schools, in the presence of a large number of gentry, parents and friends, Miss Page received from the hands of Mrs Boyd, 'who said a few kind words', a 'handsome Testimonial'. This took the form of a Russian leather bag, a shilling for luck and a cheque for £100 0s 6d to which 400 people had subscribed.

In giving thanks, Miss Page said that, when invested, this sum would add materially to her small pension. She went on to recall the day, way back in January 1868, when she first came to Wadhurst.

> The station was a gloomy place, with one waiting-room lighted by a dismal oil lamp and outside the snow lay deep all round. The scene was so depressing to a young person straight from home and college life, that I felt strongly inclined to return to my home in London, but a few words from the genial old Vicar, the Rev. John Foley, who had kindly come down to meet me, cheered me up and I have never regretted my coming.

Songs, conducted by Mr Knight, teacher in the senior school and organist at the parish church, were then sung by the elder children.

The parish magazine for September 1912 recorded that: 'Miss Page left full of gratitude ... to tell her good news to her old friend, Miss Watson, who was unable to be present'.

The Wadhurst Infant School – New Headmistress, Miss M.G. Allwood, ACP

Miss Lomas, from the mixed school, took over the running of the infant school until the arrival of the new headmistress, Miss Allwood, who had been headmistress of the infant council school in Newhaven, Sussex.

Miss Allwood took up her duties on 15 April 1912, when she reported that the number of children on roll was 80, with

70 present. This followed a school closure and an extension of the Easter holidays through an outbreak of mumps.

In the main room, Miss Allwood took the 31 children in Class 1, Miss Linkstead the 28 children in Class 2, and in the classroom, Miss Winchester taught the 4 children in Class 3 and the 17 children in Class 4. On the first day of term, however, in order that the new headmistress could work out a new trial timetable, Miss Linkstead took over both classes in the main room.

Very soon, Miss Allwood received the usual visitors, including Mr Corke, Mrs Stevenson, Mrs Boyd and Mrs Walker. More disturbing was the visit of Dr Finch and Nurse Farrant, for the annual medical inspection. The classroom was again used for the purpose and all the children were taught in the main room. To avoid disturbing the doctor, the playground, too, was put out of use for the two or three days of the inspection. Luckily, the weather was very hot and so part of the difficulty was overcome by taking the children on a nature ramble. Nature walks and rambles were becoming more frequent. On a later occasion, the children of Class I took drawing boards and chalks with them, to sketch various objects.

Closures for Sunday school treats, Band of Hope outings, sports and various other treats, continued and on 13 August, Miss Allwood wrote: 'Owing to the Presentation to Miss Page, the former Headmistress of this school, the Timetable was somewhat disarranged this afternoon'.

Interference with the school's work by bad weather and illness, also continued and in October the headmistress herself was absent, unwell. When it was suggested that a draughty room didn't help, Mr Corke suggested that a sandbag might be used to prevent it. In the following year, one of coughs, colds, chicken-pox and scarlet fever, Miss Allwood, suspecting that she had been exposed to scarlet fever, went home for disinfectant.

In November, the usual Prize Giving was held and the distribution made by Mrs Stevenson, the Misses Watsons, and Mrs Streitfield. Two parents were also present.

Very soon, Christmas preparations got under way and Standard 1 from the mixed school came in to see a dress rehearsal of the Christmas Tree Entertainment. On the next day, 17 December, at 2 o'clock, the entertainment was given to the 40 ladies who were present and toys, oranges and bonbons were distributed to the children. On the following day, the entertainment was repeated to the 40 parents who came.

Local ladies and gentlemen donated about 400 presents, the balance of which were distributed to the children by means of a 'bran pie' on the last day of term.

The new term started on 1 January 1913, with 85–101 children present. Miss Allwood complained that she had only 95 seats for these 101 children, which resulted in a visit by an assistant inspector. When she complained about the dirty state of the rooms, a visit by the vicar and Mrs Courthope, but not a lot of improvement, followed. A school inspector also made his complaints: lighting and ventilation were poor, the playground was too small and the offices too near the buildings. He also suggested that a partition was necessary.

A preoccupation of the headmistress was the supervision and the conditions of the children having meals at school. In February 1913, the managers decided that, for three days a week, a teacher should supervise and on the other two days, two or three elder girls from the mixed school should do so. The managers also provided a length of marble baize for a tablecloth and a kettle for making cocoa, and both the vicar and his wife called in to see how things were working. On the second day, following the introduction of the system, part of the stovepipe fell away. Later in the year, the headmistress recorded that the children contributed 1d a week for the cocoa and that 40 children bought it, including five from the upper school. By the January of the following year, the school log-book recorded that nearly 100 children, mostly from the mixed school, had cocoa.

Following the general election of 1906, local education authorities were empowered to provide school meals. The provision of cocoa at 1d a week, teacher-inspired, was, perhaps, a slight move in this direction.

Miss Allwood also proposed to the managers that a piano should be bought for the school, for which she would raise funds by putting on an entertainment. Mr Corke advanced £19 for the purchase of a second-hand instrument, which, he stipulated, should remain the property of the school managers and not be lent out without their permission. An entertainment was then organised, which raised £6 1s 6d.

At the end of July, with various treats taking place in the village, HMI Boutflower made his inspection.

His report was received at the beginning of the Christmas term. It praised Miss Allwood for her attempts to appeal to the interests of the children, mentioned a scheme of lessons based on *Alice in Wonderland* and considered that effective use was being made of paper-cutting, paper-folding and also of crayon-drawing for illustrating purposes. The inspector also noted that a piano had been obtained for the use of the school.

But:

> The teacher, however, does not entirely secure the ready obedience and active co-operation of the children and in consequence of this the progress made is not as rapid or as general as could be wished for ... younger children were reticent ... older ones ... call out simultaneously ... there is an evident desire to make the children's life a happy one and once it is realised that they are capable of a more sustained effort, these difficulties should tend to disappear.

During the period following the receipt of the report, Miss Allwood was away ill, which caused the vicar to write in the log-book that she was 'thoroughly run down'. Miss Winchester was also away, due to her mother's illness, but then, 15 days before Christmas, the school was closed through an epidemic of diphtheria, which continued into the holidays.

The Christmas entertainment was held over until the following March, when, in the presence of the vicar, Mrs Stevenson, Miss Boyd, Miss Griffiths, Mrs Wace and Miss Baker, together with about 30 parents, the children sang two songs, received toys, given by the ladies and gentlemen, and also oranges and sweets, given by Mr O.T. Corke and Mr Brissenden.

The beginning of the summer term brought with it the Diocesan Inspector, who commented that the children were 'Taught with much sympathy and kindness ... but I never find that arm-chairs for the Infants are very conducive to energetic answering'.

The answering of the elder children, however, was considered 'general and hearty'.

Mr Lane Andrews came in and heard some of the children in the 1st Class read and the vicar came in to say 'farewell' prior to a three-month visit to Australia. Even although it was now June, the headmistress reported severe coughs and colds and in July, 27 children were away, 20 of them with whooping cough.

Miss Allwood made no direct mention of the outbreak of war, but reported that, on 6 August, during the time devoted to religious instruction, the schools met in the playground for a service, which was taken by the Rev. J. Robinson.

From 21 August to 5 October, the schools were closed for hop-picking.

In the new term, Mr Andrews again called in, Mr Williams visited to examine the registers and also brought with him four Belgian refugees – two boys and two girls – who were given 'occupations' in the school. On his return from Australia, the vicar also came to see the children. Before long, Miss Allwood had staffing difficulties, for Miss Winchester was away with influenza and Miss Linkstead away to take a certificate examination. Mrs Rogers, however, came in to help.

At the end of the term, on 23 and 24 December 1914, in spite of the difficulties, the usual Christmas Tree Entertainment was held, with a large number of parents and friends present.

Margaret Linkstead successfully completed her Preliminary Examination in 1912, to then rank as an uncertificated teacher.

In May 1914, a salary increase for her was still being discussed. The LEA said that it required the recommendation of the managers before it could be raised. The managers then recommended that Miss Linkstead should be regarded as an uncertificated teacher, as from the date of her certification, and that her salary should be increased accordingly.

In 1929, Margaret married Harold Manktelow, but continued teaching in the school until her retirement after the 1939–45 War. She also continued as a member of the church choir and the leader of the family service, held in the church on Sunday afternoons. The Sunday School Outing train to Hastings became known as 'Maggie's Special'.

Mrs Manktelow died in 1962. A memorial inscription in the 'Children's Corner' describes her as 'The Children's Friend'.

The Wadhurst Mixed School

On 5 April 1910, Mr Larcombe wrote in his log-book:

> Re-opened after the Easter Vacation. The schools from this date were formed into a Mixed Department ... visited by Mrs. Boyd in the morning. In the afternoon ... the Vicar and Mrs. Stevenson, Mr. O.T. Corke and H.M.I. Freeland and Garland.

Mr Freeland visited again the next day, when he presented and explained to the headmaster, the vicar and Mr O.T. Corke, for the managers, his scheme for the new, mixed school. Not surprisingly, on 7 April, the headmaster commented:

> The lessons during this week have been worked from an Experimental Time-table. There has been a great deal of work to be gone through in arranging the books and apparatus to meet the requirements of the various classes.

It was providential, perhaps, that cases of scarlet fever began to occur in the school. The Medical Officer of Health,

Dr Stott, visited on 5 May, inspected the offices and complained of the waterless and dirty state of the pans. He also suggested that each of the six rooms should be scrubbed on a rota of one every six weeks, although he considered that even this was not really enough. The school was closed and remained closed until 6 June, when it was reopened with 229–287 pupils present.

A new, certificated mistress, 29-year-old Miss Ellen Gretton, had now joined the staff, to take the extension class for history, using a scheme which included 'Our Times', and also the upper group of boys and girls for singing. Later in the year, with the help of Miss N. Boyd, she also taught morris dancing to the senior girls.

Mr Knight was to take the extension class for geography and Miss Harris, who had joined the school the previous year from Cheriton, where she had been a pupil-teacher, the senior girls for drawing. Boys and girls were each to have nature study lessons, but to be taken separately.

During the course of the year, the inspector again visited and brought with him a new history–geography scheme. For the lower senior group, this included 'The World in Outline', and every three weeks, one lesson in 'Home Geography' and one lesson on the 'British Isles'. History was to deal with 'From Earliest Times to 1485'. The upper senior group was to study 'The World' in further detail, with special reference to the 'British Isles'. History was to be continued to the 'Present Day'.

The inspector also suggested that the special class, too, should deal with the 'British Isles' and the 'History of Modern Times'. Later in the year, Mr Freeland sent a scheme of work for this class, which included individual timetables for the boys. Mr Larcombe recorded in his log-book: 'Made Copies and returned originals the same day'.

Probably nearer to the headmaster's heart was the introduction of organised games, now to include the girls as well as the boys. He was also cheered by the arrival of nine new cricket bats, which, he wrote, were 'purchased by myself from subscriptions collected by myself'. Then Sir George

183

Barham visited the school, 'with a view to arrange for the children to visit the Zoo at his expense on similar lines to the visit of 5 years ago'. And the visit took place on 1 July 1910. In the same month, 50 dual desks were received.

> Sir George Barham's School Outing to London consisted of 205 children and adults from Wadhurst and 63 from Tidebrook.
>
> The party left Wadhurst by special train at 9.38 a.m., to arrive at Charing Cross at 11 a.m. Here each child was presented with a new sixpence before they all went by another special train to Regents Park Station. A walk through the park brought the children to the Zoo, where they were provided with lemonade.
>
> After dividing into parties and visiting the principal houses, the children were then free to look round for themselves.
>
> After a 'capital tea' at 3.15 p.m., the party was taken to see the lions and the sea-lions fed.
>
> At 5.15 p.m., the children left the gardens and were taken by charabancs through the principal thoroughfares (including Piccadilly, Trafalgar Square and Whitehall), to Victoria Station, where another special train brought them home to Wadhurst by 7.30 p.m.

Gardening continued to be the headmaster's other great interest and he reported that he had taken the extension class into his own garden, where he gave the boys a practical demonstration of the work entailed. Later, he submitted to Mr Corke a scheme of work for the subject.

The Annual Prize Giving took place in October and into it was incorporated the presentation to Miss Watson, for which 'there was a large attendance of the local gentry, parents and scholars'. The prizes were presented by Mrs Boyd and the vicar addressed the children on the importance of regularity, punctuality and good conduct. The headmaster also gave a brief report and explained the system for awarding prizes.

In December, the weather was so wet and stormy that 116

children were absent on the 16th of the month and the register not marked. The staff did what it could for the wet children present and 'Lessons were not quite in accordance with the Time-table'.

Over the year, the vicar and his curate had continued to visit the school and frequently took Scripture lessons. It would seem, however, that at least some of the managers were not happy with the content of the syllabus used, for on 31 January 1911, at a managers' meeting held in the vicarage, it was proposed by Mr Lane Andrews and seconded by Mrs Boyd that 'Following the provision of Section 7 of the Education Act, 1902, the Religious Instruction be in accordance with the Trust Deeds'.

Mr O.T. Corke opposed the motion, but Mr Drewe of Wadhurst Hall and Mr A. Courthope, who were absent from the meeting, sent word that they agreed with the motion, which was carried.

On 8 February Mr Larcombe wrote:

Rev. Leslie Stevenson and the Rev. H.F. Tomkins visited and took Scripture lessons. Commenced the teaching of the Church Catechism from the beginning by the instruction of the Managers.

Later in the year, the Diocesan Inspector visited the school and commented that the religious instruction

receives careful and reverent attention.
The two lower classes ... very creditable knowledge.
The Senior boys answered most readily and accurately.
... Thoroughly well taught ... interest was maintained to the last.
The Seniors were very well behaved and attentive ... devout teaching and care for the girls' welfare.

The inspector also remarked that, although the Apostles' Creed was not fully understood, the Commandments had been practically explained.

The headmaster's approach to the school gardening continued progressive.

[On 30 January] The boys taking Gardening lessons were taken to the Allotments this afternoon with the boys in the Extension Class. They were shown how to measure the Allotment and to measure it off into plots of 30' × 15' and stump out the paths between.

And then, a week later, on 6 February:

Commenced digging operations in the Allotment rented for the Boys' garden plots ... 14 boys [also] 5 boys of the Extension Class who are desirous of becoming Gardeners. Found the ground in a fearful condition ... not been cultivated for years ... bondweed, docks, etc.

Later, the gardening class boys were busy clearing up and wheeling 'road scrapings' (horse manure) on to the garden plot. Two apple trees, one plum and one raspberry cane were planted and sometimes, when bad weather had delayed the gardening, extra time was taken, at the expense of other subjects.

The year 1911 suffered from extremes of weather conditions. At the beginning of April, the headmaster reported snowstorms so severe that one-half of the children were away and the registers not marked. One girl's feet were so wet that Mrs Larcombe had to fit her out with stockings. In July, however, the heat was so intense that two girls fainted. Needlework was not taken and 'in spite of a large lump of ice and the sprinkling of the room with water', a temperature of 80° was reached. In August, an even higher temperature of 85° was reached and drill and gardening were not taken.

Mumps, chicken-pox and measles afflicted the school and the children, but they did receive the Barham trip to London, a week's holiday to celebrate the Coronation and various other treats and outings; even the headmaster was permitted to attend a National Union of Teachers' conference at Aberystwyth as a delegate.

In August, the inspection took place, carried out by Mr Freeland, who also had a long talk with the headmaster regarding the organisation and work of the extension and special classes.

It would appear that a drastic solution was to be applied, for on 15 August, Mr Larcombe recorded: 'Made arrangements for the re-organisation of the school after the Hop-picking.' Then, on the 18th: 'general clearance of cupboards ... moving of books and apparatus ... in view of the classes being moved after the holiday'.

At last, after the holidays, on 2 October:

> School re-organised in accordance with the instruction of H.M.I. Freeland. Senior Group of both boys and girls arranged in classes in what was the Girls' Department.

Mr Knight and Miss Gretton then took the senior and special classes in what had been the girls' room and Miss May Lomas took the lower seniors in the classroom adjoining. The junior boys and girls were now in the old Boys' School.

Miss Lomas, who was born in 1889, was appointed to the school in 1908, after serving as a pupil-teacher at Watton at Stone, Hertfordshire, then gaining her Oxford Senior Certificate. In 1910, she was 'approved as an uncertificated teacher for which she was qualified'. She resigned on 4 August 1914, to be reappointed in March 1915. In the meantime, she had married Mr Horace Newington.

Following the inspection, Mr Freeman's assistant, Mr Garland, had also recommended some changes. He felt that extra time should be given to writing and drawing and that a drawing scheme, progressive through the school, should be introduced. He also suggested that handicrafts should be used to illustrate other subjects.

There is no indication that, in the new term, these ideas were incorporated into the syllabus, but Mr Larcombe did record that cookery classes had, at last, been started, not in the infant school classroom, as Miss Page had feared, but in the Institute, under the direction of Miss Kitchen.

Extra to the curriculum, it was fitting that, in this Coronation year, 1911, Empire Day was celebrated with the singing of patriotic songs, the saluting of the flag and an address by the headmaster on 'Patriotism and One's Duty to the Country'. In addition, Mr Hallam spoke to the senior group on the 'Victorian League', when he strongly advocated the binding of the colonies to the motherland. The headmaster also gave a further address on the King and Queen's journey to India.

During this year, Mr Burbridge, Secretary of the Sussex Band of Hope, also spoke to the children, when he compared the food properties of half a pound of bread with an equivalent amount of beer.

The vicar, Mrs Boyd, Miss N. Boyd, Mrs and Miss Courthope and Miss Smyth were present at the Annual Prize Giving, when the senior group sang, in parts, 'I Know a Bank', John Button sang a solo and Kate Smith recited. Kate Smith was the daughter of the Attendance Officer. Later, Kate married into the Newington family, to run, eventually, the newsagent's shop in the High Street.

In December, several ladies and the vicar came to hear the children sing carols, and in the same month Mr Knight received a present 'on the occasion of his marriage'.

The headmaster also received the inspector's report, made on the visit of the previous August:

the Headmaster takes great interest in the organised games and gardening, but his influence on the general work of the School is not sufficiently apparent.

The scheme of work in the Upper Division and Special Class appears to have been drawn up by the Assistant teacher in charge [Mr Knight].

The organisation of these classes was described as 'not satisfactory'.

Arithmetic in the lower division had 'faulty preparation',

188

and a 'want of continuity with the good methods obtaining in the Infant School'.

There was no handwork for the girls and the school's drawing not only had no recognisable system, but the 'hard point' was used where 'blunt point' would be expected. (It would appear that Inspector Garland's suggestions had not been followed up.)

The physical exercises were satisfactory in the upper division but a complete failure in the lower. Games were considered well-supervised and the singing in the upper division 'Very well taught'.

The boys' special class received suitable work, but in the case of the girls, very little had been done.

Strangely, the extension class, which had been the subject of special attention by the inspector, appears to have received little or no comment and the gardening was dismissed with 'was commenced last month'.

In their general remarks, the inspectors considered that the school needed a 'broader curriculum, better methods and more vigorous control'. With the 'present efficient staff', the school could be 'established on a satisfactory basis'.

The report also commented: 'The instruction of backward children should not be conducted on the assumption that they are of normal proficiency'.

In January 1912, William Larcombe, now in his mid-fifties, had 308 children on roll – 123 girls and 185 boys.

He was assisted by his wife, Mary Ann, aged 50, Albert Knight, now in his mid-thirties and Miss Emily May Gretton, aged 31, all of whom were certificated teachers.

Miss Gretton was a niece of Dr Wace, one-time of Hill House, but now Dean of Canterbury. On her resignation, Miss Gretton was described as a 'very gifted and attractive teacher and a loss to the School'. She married a Mr Gadburn, then went to live in Hampshire.

Mr Larcombe was also assisted by three uncertificated teachers: Miss May Lomas; Miss Ethel Kate Parrott (born

1893), who, after three years as a pupil-teacher at Queens Park, Bedford, gained her Oxford Senior Certificate and, in 1911, joined the Wadhurst staff; and Miss Emily Hounsome (born 1892), who, as well, had gained her Oxford Senior Certificate, after serving three years as a pupil-teacher at St Nicholas' Girls School, Portslade, then in 1911 joined the Wadhurst staff. Each of these three teachers was paid a salary of £50 a year.

This staff, which, in his report, the inspector had described as 'efficient', did not remain intact for long, for at the instigation of the local education authority, on the retirement of Miss Page, Miss Lomas was sent to take charge of the infant school, pending the arrival of the new headmistress; Miss Gretton retired to get married, to be replaced by Miss Cecily Mary Tagg (born 1889), a qualified, uncertificated teacher from Newcastle, and Miss Ethel Parrott, after but one year in the school, 'ceased work'.

Mr Larcombe dealt with his immediate staff problems by making use of his daughter, Marjorie, who was a student at Brighton Training College, but mainly, it would seem, to give him more time for his gardening class. With still a teacher short, he also made use of his daughter Winnie to take some needlework and reading, but, again, his main objective appeared to be his availability to take more gardening.

On the arrival of the new infant headmistress, Miss Lomas rejoined the school, soon to be joined by 20-year-old Ruth Evelyn Sothcott, a qualified, uncertificated teacher from Bournemouth who was to receive £65 a year.

During 1913, the staff remained complete, but in the following year, Miss Tagg, Miss Hounsome and Miss Lomas all resigned. Miss Bertha Moon, a 21-year-old qualified, uncertificated teacher, replaced Miss Tagg, but as no application was received to replace Miss Hounsome, Mr Larcombe again had to call on members of his family: his 16-year-old daughter Gladys was appointed pupil-teacher, and his qualified, certificated daughter Marjorie was employed as a temporary assistant, at £75 a year, until the appointment of another teacher. An advertisement was placed in the *Schoolmaster* for two assistant, female teachers.

190

Later in the year, Miss Hounsome rejoined the staff, to replace Majorie Larcombe, but, complained the headmaster, he was 'Still a teacher short'.

In April 1912, the Diocesan Inspector, R.B. Jameson, visited, but was unable to give a formal examination as due notice had not been given. He did, however, report that 'The children were happy and in excellent order', and that they were 'trained in an interesting and reverent manner'. On the other hand, he felt that there was too much stress on Old Testament history and the teaching of the Catechism should be given as recommended in the syllabus, so that a better grasp of first Christian principles could be obtained.

Illness and weather continued to hamper the work of the school. Medical inspections had now been in operation for three years, but any necessary treatment was at the discretion of the parents, who, frequently, were too poor to pay for it and were unwilling to seek help to do so. Conditions in home and school were often still far from satisfactory and epidemics flourished.

On 5 February 1912, at 9.30 a.m., the headmaster reported a temperature of 28° and in the junior room the ink was frozen in the ink pots. To keep some of the older boys warm, they were sent out into the playground to clear the snow away, and the senior girls were given hot cocoa to drink.

On 9 March, following an outbreak of mumps, the school was closed for a month, but in August, nearly six months later, cases were still occurring and one boy, Charles Frederick Hemsley, died.

6 August   Have just received information of the death of Charles Fred. Hemsley who was present at school on July 29. He was then detained at home with Mumps. Saw his mother on Wednesday and advised her to take great care of the little fellow, but complications arose from which he succumbed.

In the same month, when the rain came down 'in torrents', by the time the children had reached school, they were wet through. Mrs Larcombe gave dry stockings to the worst cases, but when the rain abated, the children were sent home and the registers were not marked.

In the following year, 1913, coughs and colds abounded and many were absent through chicken-pox, influenza and ringworm.

On 7 June 1913, Mr Larcombe reported that he had re-admitted two Spooner boys from Cousely Wood:

> Albert was in a wretched condition about the feet. The soles of his boots were broken asunder and an attempt had been made to repair them with 2″ nails. One wonders how the poor boy could walk the 3½ miles to school in such boots. His stockings had no soles to them. Have fitted the boy out with some stockings and a pair of slippers until I can see the Vicar in order to find out if the boy can be supplied with a pair of boots from the Poor Fund.

Later, Mr Larcombe showed the boots to Mr Watson, who gave the boy a new pair.

On 11 February 1910, Mr Larcombe had already recorded: 'Inspector of the N.S.P.C.C. visited to see the boys Spooner whose parents had been reported for neglect and uncleanliness'.

In August 1913, with an epidemic of scarlet fever and diphtheria, the school was closed and not reopened until after the end of the hop-picking holidays.

On 29 July 1913, Inspectors Garland and Boutflower visited and inspected the school. Their report was received the following October.

> The Staff was diligent and painstaking but the results were not commensurate with their efforts ... More attention should be given to speech training ... the children are not sufficiently self-reliant, for the teachers do too much for them. There is not enough response...

The teachers prepare their work carefully and some good individual lessons were heard especially in the top two classes. The Assistant Master in the top class is a capable teacher who in a class of mixed attainment secures some quite good work ... it would be more effective if the children were more thoroughly grounded in the lower part of the school.

He deserves special praise for the Singing ... distinctly above average.

The Drawing and Handicraft is credibly carried out in the Upper Classes ... only seven of the older girls have been taught to use a sewing machine.

Over the years, the headmaster and inspectors had constantly pointed out the inadequacies of the school buildings, but neither local authority nor school managers appeared to have the money or imagination to deal with the problems. Although there was so much life and energy in the village, far too little of it was directed to the maintenance and support of the school.

At the end of 1909, the managers reported an overdraft of £34 7s 6d, and by the end of 1910, there were but eight subscribers to the School Fund. In this year, a balance of £10 6s 7½d was recorded, which included £3 3s from Mr Drewe, £2 from Mrs Boyd and 5s from Mr Corke.

A drive for more subscribers appears to have followed for, by the end of 1912, 41 were reported, giving between them a total of £38 10s 6d, which ranged from Mr Drewe's £3 3s to Colonel Ramsden's 5s. George L. Courthope, MP, and F.W. Courthope each gave a donation of £5 5s.

Expenses during this year had included general repairs to the roof and building, a new ventilator and the clearing out and the repair of the water tank, to which a new pump was fixed, for rain water.

All of this came to £32 14s 8d, which left little over for such items as the inspectors mentioned in 1913. At the end of the year, there was an adverse balance of £3 8s 8d.

In December 1912, Mr Larcombe wrote:

light very bad in all the rooms but more especially in the Main Room of the Senior School. This room is a difficult room to work in on account of the lighting arrangements.

In October 1913, the inspectors reported:

Lighting was poor.
Ventilation was ineffective.
Heating was inadequate.
Wash-hand basin accommodation for the girls and infants was insufficient.
Playground was too small.
Boys' and Infant Urinals were too near the School Buildings.
Dusting was not satisfactory.
Bad desks were still in use.
And, as had been pointed out seven years before:
Partitions were needed in the two big rooms.

However, on the following 1 December, the headmaster was still reporting:

so dark in the Main Room of the Old Girls' School this afternoon that for the greater part of the afternoon the ordinary lessons had to be changed.

For their part the Managers complained to the LEA that stoves were a necessity, not an improvement and so the LEA should pay for them. But, at least, on 16 January 1914, Mr Larcombe was able, at last, to record in his log-book: 'Received 30 new Dual Desks from the ESA'.

But, already, Mr Larcombe and the school managers were preoccupied with yet another epidemic of diphtheria. Dr Lakin was asked to visit the school and to enquire into these outbreaks which were occurring so constantly.

He visited on 5 December, took a number of swabs and reported that 'the children's throats were in a terrible condition'. He made a further visit on 10 December, when he advised that the school should be closed until 5 January 1914. He strongly advised that the schools should be damp-swept, using damp sawdust. He also complained about the state of the boys' offices.

At the next meeting of the managers, which was held on 29 December 1913, Mr Larcombe complained that not a quarter of the children had been examined, or had swabs taken, and asked what was being done about it.

On 6 January Mr Larcombe was able to report that Dr Lakin had examined 113 children and swabbed 41, plus 41 on a previous occasion.

On 19 January 1914, with 214–299 children present, the school reopened. On 23 February, 'Dr Dunstan swabbed 30 children who had been excluded for Diphtheria'. On 3 March, Mr Larcombe said that the School Medical Officer had inspected some more children, and had taken swabs, but had insufficient swabs to do them all. The managers felt that this state of affairs was far from satisfactory, and that it should be taken up with the Board of Education. Three weeks later, the managers did decide to ask the Board of Education to make representations to the county education authority and to the School Medical Officer.

Although some more swabbing was carried out and on 22 April Dr Robb attended to swab 26 children who had been excluded since December, it was not until a managers' meeting on 19 May that a long letter was received from the medical officer, explaining what steps he had taken to arrest the outbreak of diphtheria.

The diphtheria epidemic was still under way when Mr Larcombe reported an outbreak of whooping cough, which continued through into August, during a period when the classroom temperature reached 85°.

In spite of so much sickness over the years, with frequent epidemic closures, staff shortages and bad weather conditions, the work and life of the school still managed to carry on with, according to Mr Larcombe's log-book, games and gardening still receiving a great deal of special attention.

| 15 May 1912 | Gardening Class in the Morning. Organised games in the afternoon with the Senior Boys and Girls – Cricket and Rounders. |
| 19 June 1912 | Took 20 boys to Mr. Hicks of Yeomans in the afternoon. Mr. Hicks showed the boys round his garden ... methods of growing onions ... fruit, flowers and vegetables ... showed them a variety of foreign trees ... collection of curios collected in his travels in Egypt and Central South Africa. |

The boys were then entertained to tea by Mrs Hicks, after which, they explored the grounds and woods near the house and finished the evening with a game in the field.

Basic subjects, such as reading, do receive some mention in the log:

| 19 August 1913 | ... received from Mrs Ballard of Cousely Wood School: |

22 Copies of Robinson Crusoe
1 doz. of the Charings.
1 doz. John Halifax, Gentleman.
16 Ivanhoe.
1 doz. Household Magazines.

| 9 October | ...Examined children admitted from Infant Dept. in Reading. Of these only one could read words of more than 3 letters, some did not know all their letters. |

A month later, 12-year-old William Barrett was admitted from Pembury School, Tunbridge Wells. The headmaster reported that he, too, did not know his letters and could not add even small numbers. The headmaster considered, however, that the boy was not mentally deficient, but educationally 'sadly neglected'.

Singing still continued to play its part in the life of the school, with the upper division rendering several songs at the Prize Giving, at the presentation to Miss Page in 1912, as well as on the occasion when Mrs Boyd awarded the Flower Show prizes. Empire Day celebrations in 1913 called for some special songs, at the request of the vicar. Time was short, so Scripture lessons were used for their rehearsal.

The headmaster recorded that Miss Larcombe took the girls of the extension class for a spring walk and, at playtime one afternoon, 'the children had a splendid view of a Biplane which flew over Wadhurst and almost over the Playground'.

Children and staff were not necessarily more co-operative because of the bad conditions which so often prevailed. On 19 May 1914, Robert Dix refused to obey his teacher, Miss Sothcott, who sent him to the headmaster. Robert refused his punishment, but still was given several strokes across his back. The boy retaliated by kicking the headmaster in the leg, whereupon, the boy was ejected from the school. The managers were told, and decided to expel him. This did not prevent his mother from coming to the school, where she abused the headmaster and told him that her son was quite right to kick him.

Two months earlier, Miss Sothcott herself had been in trouble, when she was found to have destroyed her syllabus and her record book. In addition, Miss Tagg and Miss Lomas had destroyed their children's exercise books. They all pleaded that they thought none of these things would be needed for the new year's work, which started in April.

In the previous year, 1913, the headmaster himself had been involved in the accidental destruction of two registers. After dealing with them, he had laid them on top of the waste-paper basket, which stood beside his desk. Later, however, the caretaker's assistant, who was his daughter, took them away together with the waste paper and burnt them as part of the rubbish.

The headmaster wrote:

197

I at once notified the Vicar – the School Correspondent – and wrote to Mr. E. Young of Lewes giving full particulars. The matter is one of very deep regret and distress to me, especially as it can't be rectified.

Registers at that time were held sacrosanct – and for many years after, even when grants no longer depended on them.

Visitors to the school were still quite frequent, but now, except for the clergy, rarely gave help in the classroom. Mrs A.G. Watson of Uplands visited to present the special class with copies of the Empire Calendar and HMI Boutflower visited to confer with the vicar and Mr Corke about the provision of two tortoise-shell stoves; he then remained to confer with the headmaster about the special class. On another occasion, Mr Boutflower attended with Mr Baines, the County Inspector, regarding the retention of two girls in the School who were over 15 years of age. The headmaster was questioned 'minutely' on the subject, before the inspectors again took up the subject of the work of the special class. 'Both gentlemen [then] heard the singing of the Senior Group and were apparently very pleased.'

The two girls were Violet Warner and Gladys Larcombe, the headmaster's daughter. Their retention was not allowed and the headmaster was instructed to remove their names from the register. Later, Gladys returned as a pupil-teacher.

In the midst of the diphtheria swabbing, on 26 February 1914, the HMI for drawing, Mr Baker, paid an all day visit to the school. Before he left, he spoke to the teachers and advised them about methods. A few days later, Miss Williams, from the National Society, visited, to give a lecture on the Prevention of Consumption. She was followed very soon by the Attendance Officer, who had come about three summons which had been issued. A now rare event took place when Mrs Boyd visited and heard the reading of Standard 1, but many visits were made by Mr O.T. Corke to examine the registers. On one occasion, he came with Mr Lane Andrews, when he not only 'tested the registers' but also 'paid a visit to the school garden and saw the boys at work'.

Village events and outings still took the children out of school, but sometimes the headmaster was also absent, to deal with family matters or his other interests.

In November 1910, he asked the managers for permission for leave of absence and the loan of two blackboards for the Fat Stock Show, 'as in previous years'. The managers gave permission, but somewhat reluctantly, for they wrote to Mr Larcombe saying it 'must be clearly regarded as not establishing any precedent'.

At the same meeting, the managers also wrote to the headmaster empowering him to supervise the caretaker's cleaning – on their behalf.

In February 1913, the headmaster was absent in order to arrange for his son's passage to Canada. In 1910, the education authority had suggested that the headmaster's son Reginald should become a pupil-teacher at Wadhurst. The managers felt, however, that in the interest of the boy and the school, it would be better, generally, if he went elsewhere.

In April 1912, the parish magazine had advertised the Wadhurst Colonising Committee, which existed to aid emigrants with repayable loans. At a meeting held the following year, Reginald Larcombe gave a talk on British Columbia.

In 1913, Mr and Mrs Larcombe were both absent, in order to attend a relative's funeral at Gravesend. Miss Page helped out by taking Standard 1. Later in the year, in November, Mr Larcombe was again absent, to attend the funeral of Sir George Barham of Snape.

As 1914, with its diphtheria and whooping cough, moved on towards the hop-picking holidays, nothing in the life of the school was recorded to suggest that an outbreak of war was imminent. On 25 June the vicar visited the school to say 'Goodbye' to the children before he left to accompany Adrian Drewe on his long voyage to Australia. In the following month, on 10 July the headmaster had yet another funeral to attend, that of his nephew, at Lamberhurst.

On the same day, his daughter Marjorie commenced work in the school as a temporary assistant.

On 27 July, Mrs Boyd and Miss Alice Watson came to distribute the usual Flower Show prizes for writing and drawing: on 29 July the school closed for the Annual Band of Hope Outing to Hastings and 31 July, HMI Boutflower inspected the school garden. On 4 August Miss Lomas 'ceased work' at the school and Gladys Larcombe commenced work as pupil-teacher. On the following day, because of the rain, there were no games or gardening. But then, on 6 August:

Instead of the usual Scripture Lesson, a Special Service was held in the Playground, conducted by the Rev. J. Robinson, the Vicar's locum tenens. The hymns 'O God our help' and 'God bless our Native Land' and the National Anthem were sung. In his address, Mr. Robinson explained to the children the causes of the war with Germany and advised them as to their behaviour, etc., at this time...

In the afternoon, the School was visited by Mrs Stevenson with reference to the above entry.

15

Wadhurst – 1914

For many months in 1914, life in Wadhurst went on as in any year and change was of development rather than decay.

In January, the parish magazine reported: 'The old horse omnibus which has trundled quietly through our midst from the station for years and years had now vanished'.

An auto-car service between Ticehurst, Wadhurst and Tunbridge Wells had started up at the beginning of December 1913, much to the disquiet of Wadhurst tradespeople.

And if, in March 1914, the parish magazine asked:

Can the [Cricket] club continue? Lack of interest, few spectators, lack of regular playing members, can it be that the love of cricket is dying in Wadhurst?

and also reported that the Wadhurst Football Club had drawn one and lost nineteen of its thirty matches, the Choral Society was doing rather better, for, although it had entered fewer classes in the Tunbridge Wells Festival, it managed to gain three cups and a prize for sight singing. In addition, readers of the parish magazine were assured that Choral Society members were not 'mere Pot Hunters – we sing in Wadhurst because we love it'. Then, for the first time, the Annual Choral Society Concert included items contributed by the schoolchildren, conducted by Mr Knight. And in this year, a Wolf Cub pack was formed.

Although at the beginning of the year, the parish magazine commiserated with 'the cottage mothers who ... have the children all day on their hands ...' through the outbreak of diphtheria, for some, life continued as usual, and the Annual Christmas Entertainment produced a tableau, accompanied by the Orchestral Society, entitled *Scenes from the life of Mary, Queen of Scots*, which had been arranged by the Hon. Mrs Ramsden, and also an 'original Irish comedy', written by Mr Ernest Hall, Mrs Stevenson's brother. In the December magazine for 1913, 'hostesses' had been asked if they would:

> kindly remember they need plan no other attraction for their house parties on Wednesday, January 7, 1914, but bring along all their guests and send all their ... domestics to our Annual Christmas Entertainment.

Later in the year, at Whitsun, Mrs Boyd entertained, as was her custom, poor working girls from London. She also asked readers of the parish magazine to get in touch with the British Federation for the Emancipation of Sweated Working Women, for she was concerned about the 'sweat shops' which were then rife.

> Mrs Boyd died in 1934. She was said to be 'The very essence of simple unselfish goodness'.

The Church of England Men's Society continued with its talks and discussions, which included such subjects as 'Wireless Telegraphy' and 'Patronage', and the Mothers' Union had its usual annual service in the parish church. Mrs Watson Smyth was concerned that, when mothers moved away from the district, they should keep in touch with her, so that she could commend them to their new branch of the society.

> In June 1919, Mrs W.D. Watson Smyth herself moved away from the parish, to Edwins Hall, Woodham Ferrars, Essex, for in March 1918, her husband, 'who had shown a keen interest in all matters relating to the welfare of the Parish and of the Church', died aged 65. In the same year, her stepson, Captain Edwards Watson Smyth, was 'killed in action'. He was born on 27 October 1896, his mother,

Ethel Jeffery Watson Smyth, died on 4 November 1896. There is a commemorative mural in the church to the east of the south porch.

The Girls' Friendly Society, too, had its usual Summer Festival at Wadhurst Hall, to which 130 members, from six parishes, were taken in brakes, to enjoy motor-boat trips on the lake and to have tea in the riding school.

At Cousely Wood, the Men's Bible Society continued active and had a special gathering, in the form of a 'smoker', with refreshments, music and glees by Messrs Ansell, Knight, Mercer and Wallis.

New ventures, including the Mothers' Meeting at Cousely Wood and also at Beechlands, together with its Sunday school, continued to flourish and, in addition, a new Bible class for women and another for men, were started at Hill House.

This year, the Church Lads' Brigade got its new uniform, had a concert in the grounds of Hill House and a camp at Worthing, with a reveille at 5.00 a.m.

At the parish church, Lent 'Lantern Services' were introduced, at which anthems, such as 'God so loved the World', and 'Is it nothing to you?' were sung. On Good Friday evening, the lantern was used again and the 'Story of the Cross' sung. For this event, the church was full to overflowing and when the congregation sang the hymn, 'When I survey the wondrous Cross', the vicar said of it:

the volume of sound was magnificent ... people were less shy ... it moved me as few things have moved me, to look down the church from my seat at all those uplifted faces ... I have never heard anything like it in Wadhurst.

Earlier in the day, a three-hour service was also held, which too, was 'wonderfully attended'.

Choir outings were maintained: the men of the choir went to Brighton by auto-car and later, accompanied by

Mr S.T. Wallis, the boys also went to Brighton and on their way home, 'romped and sang'.

In this year, two retirements were announced – that of Mr J.C. Lane Andrews, churchwarden for nearly 20 years, and also that of Mr Martin, Wadhurst's stationmaster for nearly 17 years.

And in August 1914, the parish magazine reported that the vicar was enjoying a 'delightful voyage' to Australia.

Perhaps more in keeping with coming events were the Empire Day celebrations, held in June. Five hundred children took part and hundreds turned out to watch. The parish magazine said: 'Loyalty and patriotism are very much alive in Wadhurst today'.

During the proceedings, the flag was hoist, there was a service in church, a free tea for 570 people in the Market Hall and a concert, at which Major General Richard Wace, CB, RA, gave a patriotic address and children from the upper, infants and Wood's Green schools sang.

At the beginning of August, Wadhurst was practically deserted:

> holidays, parties, house-letting and journeying ... the Vicar in Australia, the Curate and the CLB in Camp at Worthing, Captain Courthope and our territorials in camp on Salisbury Plain. The Scoutmaster on Norfolk Broads, the Clerk and Sexton at Tenby. The Castle was let, Denstone was let, the Col. and Mrs. Ramsden were in Scotland, the Red Cross Society Quartermaster was in Switzerland ... by Wednesday, August 5, we were all feeling depressed, scared and miserable ... suddenly, it seems, has come now the most terrible conflict that Europe has ever seen, or will see ... the one great outstanding fact and consolation for us is the knowledge that we are embarked in a just and necessary war...

On that Wednesday, a special service was hurriedly called, for the Territorials, under Captain Courthope, were to leave for Dover that evening.

Mr. Knight was in attendance at the organ, quite a nice number of men and boys in their places in the Choir. The congregation ... got together ... at a moments notice [was] quite astounding in numbers.

The National Anthem and 'O God our help in ages past' were sung, Psalm 20 read as a lesson, special prayers said and a 'God Speed' given by the locum tenens, the Rev. John Robinson, for the vicar was away, accompanying Mr Drewe's son on his visit to Australia. 'At 7 p.m., Captain Courthope marched off from the Drill Hall at the head of his men, we cheered and waved flags'.

A writer in the parish magazine commented:

Wadhurst is still calmly slumbering on. Do our men not realise what a vital matter it is for the country – the coming forward of the men now? – not just this man, or that man, but all the men ... We begin to find ourselves looking askance on the many men who are still amongst us ... most of them could go and they ought to go...

On the 21st day of August, a Friday, at 7.30 p.m., a service was held in connection with a National Day of Prayer, when, in a crowded church, a special war version of 'God Save the King' was sung, the choir processed in to the Marseillaise, played on the organ, and 'Holy Father, cheer our way', was sung as a recessional.

In the parish magazine, a contributor commented: 'Wadhurst Church is always ready, on "active service" ... and thus we are enabled at a moment's notice, to organise a beautiful and helpful service'.

In September, following the Battle of Mons, the first wounded soldier of Wadhurst, Private Edward Tomsett, arrived back and the news that Mrs Boyd's son, Lieutenant Edward Boyd, had been killed in action, was announced. George Birmingham (Canon Hannay), gave a lecture on 'The War' and a small choir, accompanied by Mrs Stevenson, sang the National Anthems of Great Britain, Belgium, Russia and France.

In the schools, the hop-picking holiday had come and gone. Scouts were taken out of school to guard the main, continental telephone line, which went through Mark Cross and Mayfield; some old desks and forms were sent for the use of a school which was being set up for some Belgian refugees; a lady teacher from France heard the upper class of Wadhurst School sing the Marseillaise and other songs and, on the following day, eight young Belgian refugees joined in a game of football.

The November parish magazine reported that there were 214 men in the forces, and, by now, there were 20 wounded soldiers at Hill House. A Red Cross hospital had been set up at Tappington Grange and a number of refugees were now living in the village.

The magazine also advertised a lantern lecture on Palestine, organised by the British and Foreign Bible Society, at which the ladies were asked to be 'good enough' to 'select their smallest hats for this occasion, so that all may obtain a satisfactory view'.

Mr S.T. Wallis, on this occasion, kindly worked his magic lantern at a reduced fee.

At the end of term, the school celebrated Christmas with a 'post office', decorations and a concert, at which Belgian wounded soldiers from Hill House and Tappington Grange Red Cross Hospital and many Belgian refugees were entertained by some singing, 'which was very much appreciated'.

Illness was still in attendance, in a form of influenza with sickness and sore throat and the school was still in a 'dirty state'.

At the end of the year, in a letter home from the front line, Private William Ballard wrote that:

when coming up near the Germans, the General spoke to them, he told them that they were 'marching splendidly', but that in all probability, the whole of the 5th Division would have to be sacrificed – wiped out...

206

Private Ballard added: 'it will all come out when the war is over – what they suffered and why'. He also told of his feelings when the time came for them to make a bayonet charge: 'the fearful satisfaction of killing ... The mad moment, it is called'.

William Ballard saw a 'big mate [of his] raise his bayonet high up and shake his German victim on it in mid air, in a sort of frenzied ecstacy'.

In 1914, there were recorded in Wadhurst:

  40 Baptisms
  14 Marriages
  34 Burials
  The average age at death was 54

POSTSCRIPT

During the war years, Mr Larcombe continued to suffer staff shortages and replacement difficulty. Mrs Larcombe was frequently ill. In 1916, Mr Knight was appointed Headmaster of Wickham Church of England School, Hampshire, and several of the staff, in order to obtain higher salaries elsewhere, resigned. At this time, there were no national salary scales. Through the work of the Burnham Committee, constituted in 1919, such scales were established and came into effect in 1921.

In April 1920, following an inspection, Mr Larcombe was instructed to attend an enquiry at Lewes regarding his efficiency. At the enquiry, Mr Larcombe pointed out that, since 1916, he had suffered 16 changes of staff.

At the end of 1920, at a time when school funds were insufficient to pay the caretaker, Mr Larcombe asked for a year's leave of absence in order to look after his sick wife. It was not granted, but, at the end of the following year, after 45 years at the school, Mr Larcombe retired.

Mrs Ballard, Headmistress of Cousely Wood School for 53 years retired on 2 June 1916, but she was allowed to continue until the coming of a new headmistress, Mrs Heather Bloomfield, in August 1916. On her retirement, Mrs Ballard received as a present, a cheque for £83 6s 8d. She died in 1941.

Cousely Wood School was closed in 1949 and the children transferred to Wadhurst. Miss Marjorie Larcombe, who retired from teaching in 1952, was the last headmistress.

The Education Act of 1918, the Fisher, raised the school-leaving age to 14. This Act, together with the Hadlow Report of 1926, encouraged the provision of wider and more extensive education for all children and young people. It was felt that, for children aged 5 to 15, education should be provided in two stages: primary for the 5 to 11, secondary for the 11 to 15.

The Education Act of 1936 – which intended to raise the school-leaving age to 15 in 1939 – authorised grants of 75 per cent towards the building of church schools for the senior children of 11 to 15.

Wadhurst took advantage of the scheme, to then raise the balance required to build a senior church school (to serve the parishes of Wadhurst, Tidebrook, Ticehurst, Stonegate and Flimwell) on a 6½ acre site at Sparrows Green corner, at a cost of £1,000 for the land and £17,000 for the building. The school was planned and started, but, at the beginning of the 1939–45 War, was left unfinished. As far as possible, it was protected against the weather, but suffered as the result of enemy action.

In October 1941, the Vicar of Wadhurst, the Rev. E. Mannering, wrote in the parish magazine:

All we can do at present is to use our imagination and see it, we hope, prophetically filled with nearly 300 children over 11, meeting at their Assembly in the fine Hall and then moving off to the spacious and well-lighted classrooms and learning science and arts and crafts as well as the 3Rs ... organised games in the playground and in the playing fields ... May the dream come true ... of a better school for the boys and girls of Wadhurst and the neighbouring villages.

1944 Education Act:

it shall be the duty of the local educational authority ... to contribute towards the spiritual, moral, mental and physical development of the community by securing that efficient education ... shall be available.

In 1944, a new Education Act raised the school-leaving age to 15 (implemented in 1947) and formalised education into three stages, that of primary, secondary and further. In due course, many local authorities provided three types of secondary school, grammar, modern and technical, for which children at the age of 11, or sometimes 13, in the case of technical schools, were selected by aptitude and ability, with the 'modern' school as the main stream. Some authorities chose to deal with the three groups of children in one school, which was given the name 'comprehensive'.

After the 1939–45 War, the new school building at Sparrows Green, were repaired, completed and opened in 1949 as a county secondary modern school – now no longer a church school. The new secondary school occupied the buildings on a temporary basis until 1961, by which time new premises had been built for it on the site of Uplands, in the Lower High Street. The church primary school then moved into the vacated buildings in Sparrows Green and its old buildings in the Lower High Street became a home for the youth club.

In 1973, the school-leaving age, by now raised to 16, the Wadhurst County Secondary Modern School was redesignated a comprehensive school, to serve also as a community college – the Uplands Community College.

The college took its name from the house which had previously stood on the site, the house where Mr Arthur Watson, in 1898, opened a 'night school' for those young men 'who wished to keep up with what they had learnt' at school.

It was in 1973 that Miss Nesta Rhys Davids, granddaughter of the Rev. John Foley, Vicar of Wadhurst from 1846 to 1886, died in the little village of Amberley, Sussex. The local guidebook, *Dear Amberley*, records that she became a leading member of the community and of the Women's Institute. To her memory, a seat was placed at High Titten, a lane 'which skirts the east side of the chalk pits, where there is a fine view across the valley'.

210

Coda

'I believe in discipline, solid mental arithmetic, learning to read and write accurately, plenty of homework, increasing expectations and developing potential – all things which are anathema to many modern children.'

David Blunkett, Secretary of State for Education, 1997.

SOURCES

Church (Wadhurst)

Parish magazines, from 1893
Renovation of the Church File, 1839–1950

College of Arms

Courthope Papers, Vol. 26 (with map of Wadhurst village)

Collections

Sussex Archaeological Society Collections. Especially Vol. 2, 1849; Vol. 25, 1874; Vol. 60, 1915
Sussex Record Society, Vol. 57, 1958

Record Office, Lewes

Wadhurst:

Account book of Samuel Bush (Vicar of Wadhurst, 1743–83) from 1760. Also used by his successor, A. Litchfield (Vicar, 1783–1804) for sundry notes and comments
Burial in Wool Register, 1678–1749, subsequently used for other purposes, including a Register of Briefs, 1787–94, and the Sunday School Accounts, 1788–1802, and 1812–25
Calendars to Courthope Muniments
Choir papers including letters, papers, photos, etc.
Churchwarden and church accounts, 1812–1949
Courthope, William, manuscript book on Wadhurst church history
Diocesan reports, Wadhurst schools, 1872–92
Narratives of Samuel Bush, 1774
Notes made variously by Mrs Rhys Davids, née Foley, Mary Foley, Mr and Mrs A. Wace, together with enquiry-replies (church and parish)
Poor Law and other papers, 17th century onwards
School account book, 1826–61
School logbooks:

> Cousely Wood School, 1868–1937
> Wadhurst Boys' School, 1902–10
> Wadhurst Mixed, 1910–32

Wadhurst Infants, 1902–22
Managers' Meetings, 1902–22

Talbot, Henry, *Red Book of Wadhurst*, 1823
Vestry Book, 1855–95
Wadhurst People, interview c 1960

General:

Abstract Educational Enquiry, Vol. 8, 1835

Sussex Archaeological Society, Barbican House, Lewes

Collections, see above.
McDermott Papers (church music past), notes and interviews

Various

Correspondence with Walker and Sons, Organ Builders, re Wadhurst
    church organs
Deeds of Church House
Prayer Book of Frances Amelia Ashby (born 1843)

Books

18th Century

Burr, Thomas Benge, *History of Tunbridge Wells*, 1766, Shaw Joseph,
Parish law, Mid 18th century

19th Century

Bates, A. (comp.) *Directory of Stage Coach Services*, 1836, David and
    Charles, 1969
Bilby, T. and Ridgeway, R.B. *Infant Teachers' Asistant*, 10th Edition, 1846,
    Infant School Depot, London

20th Century

Barnard, H.C., *A Short History of English Education*, UL Press, 1958
Bettey, J.H., *Church and Parish*, Batsford, 1987
Chambers Encyclopaedia
Curtis, S.J., *History of Education in Great Britain*, UTP, 1967
Du Bouley, *Lordship of Canterbury*, Nelson, 1968
Edmonds, E.L., *The School Inspector*, Routledge and Kegan Paul, 1962
Fraser, Rebecca, *Charlotte Brontë*, Methuen
Maclure, J. Stuart, *Educational Documents, England and Wales*, 1816–1967,
    Chapman and Hall, 1968

Moorman, John R.H., *Church Life in England in the Thirteenth Century*, Cambridge, 1945
Musgrave, P.W. (Ed.), *Sociology, History and Education*, Methuen, 1970
O'Day, Rosemary, *Education and Society*
Savidge, A. and Mason, O., *Wadhurst*, Meresborough, 1988
Sutherland, Gillian (Ed.), *Arnold on Education*, Penguin, 1973
Tate, W.E., *The Parish Chest* Cambridge, 1946
Wace, A., *Story of Wadhurst*, 1924

Magazines and Pamphlets

Alpha Introduction, February 1997, Church Times Supplement
Express Dairy Story, 1964
Education Department pamphlets, 1991–94
National Trust Guide, Castle Drogo, Drewsteighton, Devon
Sussex County Magazine, 1935, 1940
Universal Magazine July, 1770

Newspapers

Church Times: February 1893, February 1993, September 1895, September 1995
Courier: Tunbridge Wells: February, April, May, October 1873, May 1910, April 1913
The *Sunday Telegraph*: September 1995, November 1996, February 1997

APPENDIX

1. Throughout the Middle Ages, schools were attached to cathedrals, collegiate churches and, in some cases, to monasteries. All gave an education in Latin. In 1215, the Lateran Council ordered that grammar schools should be appointed to those churches who could afford them.

   Although by the beginning of the sixteenth century, England had an estimated 400 grammar schools for a population of 2.25 million, little or no elementary education had yet been provided for the benefit of the poor.

2. As the clergy ranged from those with degrees to those who were barely literate, instruction from them, in all probability, was minimal and sermons rare.

   Congregational participation in the Services was slight and, set against the rigours of everyday life, seemingly, would have generated little spiritual or intellectual uplift.

   (See Church Life in England in the XIII Century. John R.H. Moorman, CUP.)

3. King Edward I was in Lamberhurst on 21 June 1299 and in Mayfield on the following day, that of St Alban, to whom the church was dedicated. In honour of the saint, the King gave an offering of 7s to the chantry chapel.

   He also levied fines for short weights and measures, including from Wadhurst:

   > Two sums of 10s each from the hands of William Wyly, paid in cash, and from William of Wadhurst, baker, 2s.
   >
   > (*Sussex Archaeological Society Year Book*, Vol. 2, 1849.)

4. By the time Nicholas Turke made his will, Greyfriars Priory had been dissolved by Henry VIII, its church

become a parish church and part of the priory buildings rebuilt and reopened as Christ's Hospital, to accommodate 400 'poor, fatherless children'. Christ's Hospital became known as the 'Blue Coat School'. (In 1902, it moved to Horsham and later in the century, its earlier contact with Wadhurst was renewed, when a master, George Harris, became its vicar, a vicar's son, Nicholas Plumley, became the school's archivist, and a Wadhurst choirboy, Robert Madge, a pupil.)

5. The education in these schools was based on religious instruction, stemming from the Prayer Book Catechism. To it, were added industrial occupations such as sewing, gardening etc. and sometimes writing and arithmetic. By around 1760, 30,000 children were being educated in them, but by the end of the century, educationalists, such as Mrs Trimmer, considered the teaching was defective, that the children learnt by rote and gained little knowledge of Christian principles or practices. There is no evidence that the work of the society reached Wadhurst.

6. Lucy Barham was described as 'a very subtle, ill-tempered woman who, when her husband was grieved by the death of his sixteen year old daughter on the eve of her marriage, used undue influence on him to devise his wealth to her, away from his own family'. She, in turn, left it to a relative, George Egles of Uckfield, who squandered it. Of later members of the Barham family, one died in the workhouse and another was a wheelwright in Sparrows Green.

7. Barhams had been connected with Wadhurst since the fifteenth century and had settled there by the sixteenth, where they were engaged in the iron industry and connected with most of the large houses in the parish, including Snape, Great Butts, Little Butts, Scragoak, and Shoesmiths. William Courthope, in his account of Wadhurst, written in the 1830s, said of Shoesmiths: 'There is supposed to be a subterranean passage from the cellar to somewhere south of the house, but it has never

been exactly ascertained.' Maurice Watts (born 1880) claimed that as a boy he found his way into it and believed it to go to Bayham Abbey. Suggestions have also been made that it connected with Riverhall, also associated with the iron industry. In 1960, the then owner of Riverhall said that a tunnel did exist, but it led from the drawing room to the mill house. It was said to have been in use during the eighteenth century, but blocked in more recent times. (Claims have also been made of tunnels from the vicarage to the Queen's Head, destroyed in 1956, and also to Hill House, in which house ghostly manifestations are said to have been experienced.) John Barham died seven years after his wife, in 1723. A large memorial on the south wall of the chancel, records the deaths and the charities.

8. As early as the first century, collections for the help of the needy were taken at similar services and, for long, the relief of the poor continued a bounden duty of the vicar. In 1597–8, the state authorised the appointment of overseers by the Justices of the Peace, to administer additional relief, at first from gifts of money, but then, by the poor law act of 1601, from the proceeds of a local tax.

At Wadhurst, at the turn of the 18th century, there were eight Communion services a year – Easter Day, Whitsunday, Trinity Sunday, Michaelmas, Christmas Day and, except for Trinity and Michaelmas, the Sunday following each of these. Distributions to the poor were made twice a year and, in 1791, included 6d for William Tomkins, described as a Methodist and, in 1795, 1s 6d for Smoker South and 6d for Old Goose.

For this period, records start on Easter Day 1784 and end in 1814, on the Sunday following Christmas. In that time, the lowest collection was 5s, which was on the first Sunday after Christmas 1788, and the highest, £3 3s, on the first Sunday after Christmas 1821. Attendance figures were sometimes given: the highest was 78, on the first Sunday after Christmas 1796, and the lowest, 18, on

Michaelmas Sunday 1799. There was also a 'home Communion' for Mrs Puxty, who was ill.

9. Even if the poor had been prone to contribute, wages were low and poverty rife. With the onset of the French Wars in 1793, prices began to rise, but wages were kept artificially low, eventually to be made up from the Poor Rate, which helped the employer, but not the employed. In 1783, the year of Bush's death, Wadhurst's rate was £850; at Litchfield's death, in 1804, it was £2,057. The poor became paupers and were so classed in the registers.

On 19 January 1795, the church accounts recorded that £3 17s 8d, collected at the Communion service, was: 'applied by the Consent of the Parish in Aid of a Public Subscription raised for purchasing wheat to assist the Poor – The present season being a very inclement one.'

10. In 1785, the Society for the Establishment and Support of Sunday Schools was founded. (At first, it had both Anglican and Nonconformist on its committee.) It advised: 'Be dilligent in teaching the children to read well ... Neither writing nor arithmetic is to be taught on Sunday.' Later, Sir James Kay-Shuttleworth, doctor and educationalist, said of the schools: 'The idea of education for the poor sprang from a religious impulse ... it regarded the school as a nursery for the church and congregation.'

11. The school accounts were kept on the unused pages of the Burial in Wool Register. The first account was headed 'A Sunday School instituted at Wadhurst, May 18, 1788', and carried on until 1802. The second, which began in 1818, was headed, 'Benefactions and Subscriptions towards the Establishment and Support of a Sunday School in the Parish of Wadhurst'. It ended in 1825. Other accounts in the register included 'Monies collected at the Sacrament.' (1784–1823) and 'Monies collected upon Briefs in the Parish of Wadhurst,' (1787–94). The register also contains entries re numbers at Confirmations.

Burial in Wool, under a penalty of £5, was required by

218

an Act of 1666 and of 1678. The Wadhurst Register was started on the 'First Day of August in the year of our Lord MDCLXXVIII (1678)'. At first, Affidavits were sworn and witnessed and the pages of the register signed by two magistrates, the vicar and churchwardens. From 1692, the vicar and churchwardens only have signed. After 1712, the pages go unsigned. The register ended in 1749. The Act gradually fell into disuse, but was not repealed until 1814.

12. Thomas Cooper, in 1812, took part in a Tenterden v Wadhurst cricket match, played on the green in the centre of Tenterden. The match started on a Wednesday and continued through until the following Saturday, after which, the team arrived back in Wadhurst at 10 p.m.

Other players included: Sam. Baldwin, Charley Baldwin, Ben. Baldwin, Silas Cooper (a very fine bowler who, in 1805, had played at Lord's), Jacob Pitt, Dick Vigor, Gideon Wisdom, John Newington of Towngate and Edward Blackman. As these two last players came from Tidebrook, they stayed overnight in Wadhurst and arrived back home on the Sunday, at 12 noon. (The story was told by Edward Blackman to his son William, who related it in the Parish Magazine of May 1914.)

13. Light is thrown on part of Thomas's church activities in the diary of William Courthope, who, at this time, was 19 years of age.

Sunday, 18th December, 1826.

... was much amused by the Clerk's having
to trudge every time they sang from his desk
to the pitch pipe loft where he headed the band.

William was on a visit from London, where he was a clerk at the College of Arms. He had come to Wadhurst to follow up the Courthope family tree. Later, he married Frances, the daughter of the Rev. Frederic Gardiner, who was the vicar's brother.

219

14. Henry Talbot wrote a very short history of Wadhurst, which he called *The Red Book of Wadhurst*. He described it as 'being a collection of the best information the author could obtain on the subject. 1823.' He added: 'To the/ Revd. Robt. B. Gardiner. M.A./ this manuscript/ is most respectfully dedicated/ and presented/ by his most humble servant/ and parishioner/ Henry Talbot./ Maplehurst/ Oct: 24. 1823.'

He described the situation of Wadhurst as: 'being very elevated, commanding extensive views, and the country around presents an undulating appearance, not unlike the romantic scenery in the West of England ... these beauties are counterbalanced by the uncivilized state of the inhabitants, and the overwhelming pressure of its taxation.'

15. In 1825, the church received an income of £393 16s 8d from the Church Rate of 2s in the pound, which was levied on land and property, basically for the repair of the church, but was also used for other incidental expenses. The rate was abolished in 1867–8, to be replaced by quarterly collections in 1870, and in the 1890s, by collections at morning and evening services. There was also an income from pew rents and, later in the century, from subscriptions. Collections at Communion services were still reserved for the needy.

16. The vestry, was a body of men, sometimes self-appointed, which met under the chairmanship of the vicar. It was so called because its deliberations often took place in the church room of that name. It was established in the fourteenth century, at first to help manage church affairs, but with the decay of the manorial system, gradually assumed responsibility for local, civil affairs. Its many, widespread duties included the appointment of parish officers and the setting, collecting and spending of local rates, including those of church and poor.

Churchwardens, of which there are usually two, are the chief lay officials of each parish church and are its legal guardians. They were, also, ex officio, senior lay members of the parish vestry, by which, as in Wadhurst, they were sometimes appointed, and from 1601, Overseers of the Poor. When, in 1538, Thomas Cromwell instituted parish registers, churchwardens were required to sign them.

17. *A Service at St Mark's College Chapel*
The Service was ordinary Mattins but was remarkable for one feature, the chanting of the psalms. These were sung to Gregorian chants and the effect was very fine ... here at St. Mark's you had a whole congregation singing the massive tones in unison and a congregation, moreover, that consisted of men who had been taught music ... There was one other fine effect, however, towards the end, in the hymn, "Jesu, lover of my soul", when every one joined in, and as each man sang his own part, bass, tenor, or alto, the result was something like that which one hears in a German Lutheran church when the congregation is singing a chorale of Bach's.

The Chapel at St Mark's College

As one waits for the service to commence the beauty of the Byzantine interior slowly forces itself on one. Outside, mark you, the building looks an unpretensious brick church ... once inside you are confronted with a reposeful, quiet, yet eminently helpful church ... as satisfactory as any in London.

The nave is plain, and is seated with oak benches, those on the south side being free to the public, while those on the north are occupied by the students. At the intersection of the nave and transept is a quasi-lantern, beneath which the choir stalls are placed, the lecturn and pulpit standing at the east end of these. In either transept are the galleries, the organ occupying the north ... The east wall of the nave is pierced by three arches, that in the centre opening into the sacrarium, while on either side are smaller ones leading into the ambulatory ... which goes right round the back of the sanctuary, being separated from it by massive columns. The altar is well-raised ... a cross and two candlesticks being placed on the retable...

From 'Typical Churches' – a late 19th century press cutting. Journal and author unknown.

18. Mr Barton also dealt in real estate. He bought the workhouse, which had closed down by 1836, demolished it and incorporated its site into the grounds of Clavers, which lay to the north, and which he had bought already. He demolished Clavers and in its place, built Prospect House, later to be improved and renamed The Lodge. The inmates of the old workhouse had been sent to the new 'Union' at Flimwell, for an Amending Act of 1834 had amalagamated groups of parishes to provide a joint workhouse. This was deplored by William Courthope, by now Somerset Herald and a Wadhurst historian, who wrote that Wadhurst's 'aged and worn out poor were no longer permitted to linger out their days in scenes familiar to them...'

19. Bilby and Ridgeway in their *Infant Teachers' Assistant* of 1846, pronounced that: 'The only text-book shall be the Bible, from which the Master shall select each lesson of the day.'

They then give a detailed description of such a lesson: Supposing in a School consisting of 80 children 15 were totally unacquainted with the letters of the alphabet, 15 perfectly knew them and were just entering upon monosyllables, 20 could manage to read the shorter monosyllables without having to spell them first, 20 reading monosyllables and dissyllables, and the remaining 10 competent to read the Scriptures, we should unite the first divisions in one and the classes would stand thus:

Class 1 consisting of 30 children, Class 2 of 20, Class 3 of 20 and Class 4 of 10.

The classes having been thus arranged, the manner of instruction is as follows:

Class 1. Form a circle and place in the hands of each

child who know his letters, a book, or some simple elementary lesson and by the side of that child, one who is unacquainted with the letters.

Having directed the class to the page, lesson and line, and ascertained by passing round, that every finger was directed to the right place, for example 'I cannot see God', etc ... the Master orders any child to commence, which he does as follows, every child simultaneously repeating after him:

Child: I. All: I. Child: c. All: c. Child: a. All: a. Child: n. All: n. etc. (Sentence given up to the word "God.")

...... the same child leads through the same line again, thus:

Child: I. All: I. Child: can. All: can. Child: not. All: not. etc., to be repeated through twice more in a similar manner. Each child then takes a turn.

Class 2. Read in a circle, as in class 1, only omitting the 1st gradation, and the lesson more advanced.

Class 3. Use the third gradation only, with this addition, supposing the sentence to be as follows:

"The Lord is my Shepherd, I shall not want."

Child: The Lord is my Shepherd.
All: The Lord is my Shepherd.
Child: I shall not want.
All: I shall not want.
Child: The Lord is my Shepherd, I shall not want.
All: Repeated.

Class 4. In this class the Master himself leads, by reading each verse slowly, distinctly, and with proper emphasis, previous to each boy's reading it.

Each class then shut their books and spell words from the lesson read. The fourth class to be questioned on the content of the lesson, as well.

20. The Nonconformists, in turn, resented the claims of the Anglican Church to control education. At the same time, most people, churchmen and Dissenters alike, agreed that religion was an essential part of education ... but the Established Church insisted on doctrinal teaching to which the Dissenters objected. Meantime, a growing number of securalists objected to any form of religious teaching and both Nonconformists and securalists objected to supporting church schools through the Poor Rate.

21. *The People of Wadhurst, 1844*

    Extract from a letter written in 1844 by Mr M.A. Waters to his cousin, also a Mr Waters, who held some property in Wadhurst:

    Wadhurst is a most horrid place to have property situated ... The people are very poor and some of them such desperate rogues that there is no such things as getting the rents.

22. In 1891, to commemorate members of the Gardiner family, a brass lectern was placed in the church.

23. The vicar's wife showed a particular interest in the church's music, which, according to A. Wace, in his *Story of Wadhurst*, she put on a 'good footing'. This appears to have included the exclusion of the church band and the intrusion of a barrel organ. This was the band in which William Ashby, miller of Riverhall, was the cellist. His nephew, Charles Ashby, who later became a builder and a staunch member of the church, was born at this time, in 1849. Alfred Wace published his book in 1924. He was the fourth son of the Rev. R.H. Wace of Hill House. Alfred Wace entered the Indian Civil Service and held a number of important posts until his retirement in 1895. He became a Sussex JP, and for a number of years again lived in Wadhurst. He died in 1931, aged 86.

24. Tidebrook School was built in 1859, but, without casualty, was destroyed by a flying bomb in 1944. The

children were transferred to Wadhurst and the school was not rebuilt.

Tidebrook church was built in 1856 and, in 1858 a new ecclesiastical parish was formed from parts of Wadhurst and Mayfield. From 1951, Tidebrook was again served by the Vicar of Wadhurst.

25. Mr Bocking, in all probability, was taught by Mrs Foley on the 'finger-organ' which was installed in the church in 1866. It came from a church in Buckhurst Hill, Essex, where, in 1859, it had been converted from a barrel organ with the replacement of the barrels by a keyboard. A pedal board was also added to the organ. On its installation in Wadhurst Church, further improvements were made. Expenses appear to have been met by the vicar, Mr Foley.

26. He made clear his attitudes in a pamphlet which he wrote in 1867:

> ...the lower classes ought to be educated to discharge the duties cast upon them ... that they may appreciate and defer to a higher cultivation when they meet it ... as ought to be found in the higher classes.

Kay-Shuttleworth viewed Education in a rather different way, which was:

> an inculcation of habits; a training of skills and a development of intelligence, with the school as a centre of social and cultural life.

27. Another side of Matthew Arnold is shown in Rebecca Fraser's *Charlotte Brontë*, where his is described as having formulated a scheme to separate pauper children from their parents on the grounds that the latter must be a bad example to them.

28. Herbert Ryle, later to become Dean of Westminster, was a pupil at the Waces' school, which he left in July 1868. In 1923, in response to a request from Mr Alfred Wace, he wrote of it:

My memory of those days is very vivid and for the most part, very happy ... I was ... two and a quarter years there [with] 9 or 10 other boys ... we were treated by Mr and Mrs Wace as if we were members of a large family ... the boys slept two in a room. We did our work in a large room to the left side of the entrance door ... garden ... a good stables and a playground ... with parallel bars and a climbing rope ... a big pond where we fished for roach ... we were allowed plenty of exercise ... taught to ride a pony ... Mr Wace himself rode a big brown horse...

[We were taught] on very old-fashioned lines ... elements of Latin and Greek ... well-coached in Arithmetic, Algebra and Euclid ... a small modicum of Ancient History ... never did examination papers. Mr Wace was drawing to the close of his career as a schoolmaster, but he made us work ... stern and occasionally ... lost his temper badly ... He was greatly assisted in the school work both by his daughters, Mary and Lucy and by his sons, Alfred, Walter and Ernest ... they assisted us both in our work and in our games ... we regarded them with affection.

Mr. Wace gave me some special private lessons ... by myself allowed to prepare ... Virgil or Horace or Homer ... very keen on my work and greatly enjoyed the opportunity of reading good, long, consecutive pieces by myself.

Mr. Wace [was] a devout strict, old-fashioned evangelical. His influence was good. Our Sundays were happy, peaceful days: church at 11.00 and 6.30 ... a good walk in the afternoon after the Sunday dinner ... [The] moral tone of the school was excellent ... devoid of cram and though when I went to Eton, I found myself in some respects, backwards ... I had learnt to work and read in my leisure by myself.

226

29. A model lesson, according to Bilby and Ridgeway, took the following form:

Teacher, (holding a small branch of tree):	*Child:*
What is this?	A bough, branch, etc.
Is it a whole tree?	No, only part.
What part of the tree does it grow on?	The upper part.
What is the lower part called?	The trunk, body, stem.
Is there any part below the trunk? etc.	The roots that grow under the ground.

'Questions should be put in a new point of view and every mode of question tried, that the little ones may exercise their understanding and not depend altogether on memory. We have to do with thinking beings, who should be exercised in every possible way, to call into action their moral and intellectual faculties.'

30. The Poor Law Amendment Act of 1834 had ended out-relief for the able-bodied poor, but medical help was to be available still. Many avoided it, for it was associated with the stigma of pauperism. Those who could afford it, turned to the benefit clubs, which increased in numbers and size; some, such as the Odd Fellows and the Ancient Order of Foresters became known country-wide.

Clubs had been in existence since the sixteenth century. In Wadhurst, there are early eighteenth-century references. In April 1729, a certain Henry Batchelor wrote from Maidstone to the churchwardens and overseers of Wadhurst, his parish of origin, to say that he was threatened with removal back to them. He asked for exemption because: 'I belong to a Club, which is allowed by the Society if I am sick seven shillings per week, and if I dye five pounds to Bury me'. He went on to say that he had 'no family but my Selfe and Wife', and that, 'I hope Gentlemen without any more trouble to a poor man. I hope you will grant me a Certificate'.

Later, in 1738, in the case of another Wadhurst parishioner, Elizabeth Eastland, widow, the Maidstone overseers wrote:

> [She] is in great want by reason of her being sick and can't possible subside without Reliefs. Therefore we desire you to Order her something to help her in her Illness, otherwise we must be obliged to Remove her and her three children to you by an Order...

The Overseers went on to describe Elizabeth as being 'Industerous when in health'.

31. *Standards for Seven-year-olds*
By the terms of the Code, children under six were not subject to examination. The remaining 12 in Standard 1 were:

To Read	from a story written in mono-syllables.
To Write	(form) capitals and small letters from Dictation on a slate or blackboard.
In Arithmetic	to form figures of up to 20 from Dictation on a slate or blackboard.

Name at sight figures up to 20.

Add and subtract figures up to 10, orally, from examples on the blackboard.

In 1992, the following requirements were expressed for a typical seven-year-old:

Reading and Writing: Read a range of material with some independence, fluency, accuracy and understanding.

Produce independent pieces of writing using complete sen-

228

tences, some of them with capital letters and full stops.

Mathematics   Read, write and order numbers to at least a 100.

Understand the meaning of a 'half' and a 'quarter'.

Know and use additions and subtractions up to 10.

Science: Ask questions and suggest ideas of the 'how' 'why' and 'what will happen if' variety.

Know that light passes through some materials and not others.

Technology: Develop their design proposals giving sample reasons why they have chosen to make their design.

Show that they can use simple hand tools, materials and components.

Use information technology for the storage of retrieval information.

(From an educational pamphlet from the Department of Science and Education, *How is your child doing at School?*)

In 1993, expressed as:

Reading and Writing: ...Produce, independently, pieces of writing using

229

	complete sentences. Spell correctly simple words they use regularly.
Mathematics:	... Solve simple additions and subtractions.
Science:	Know that plants and animals need certain conditions to sustain life. Know that magnets attract some materials and can repel each other.
Technology:	Unmentioned.

(From *Targets for your children – A Parent's Guide*, DES, 1993–94)

32. When Mr Boys left school, he became an apprentice at Greenhill's shop in the village. On most days he worked from 7.00 a.m. to 8.00 p.m. On Fridays, he worked to 9.00 p.m., and on Saturdays, to 11.00 p.m. On Wednesdays, he worked only until 5.00 p.m. One of his jobs was to walk to the station, take the train to Tunbridge Wells, go to the bank and pay in the takings of about £300.

Mr Boys left Wadhurst in 1896, finally to settle in Salisbury for 33 years.

His mother was Mary Smith, daughter of Jabez Smith, farmer, postmaster and saddler, who died in 1907, at the age of 88. Mr Boys' father took over the saddler's business, which, Mr Boys believed, had been established for 300 years and was housed in an eleventh-century building. This building was pulled down in 1888 and rebuilt as two shops, one to rehouse the saddler and the other, Jabez Smith's post office.

Jabez sold the land behind the shop to Mr Austen for

his market. Earlier, the land had been used for rope-making and later, it became a place where both boys and girls played and sometimes swung among the ash trees – for 'children had to make their own pleasure in those days'.

Jabez Smith had three other children: Naomi, Alfred and Rowland, who was a butcher and also farmed at Stone Cross.

Jabez farmed Round Oak, where Mary was born and from where, according to Mr Boys, in 1863, she was sent to fetch Mr Wace, the magistrate, from Hill House, for prize fighters and their followers had come off the London train and were setting up a fight behind Muddles, a farm near Sparrows Green.

Thomas King, Champion Prize Fighter of England, fought John Heenan, an American and after 24 rounds, won. King was brought before the Wadhurst magistrates, bound over to keep the peace and made to promise that he would fight no more in Sussex. (*Sussex County Magazine, 1935*).

Mr Boys's sister, 'a quiet patient woman', remained behind in Wadhurst, eventually to take over the saddler's shop. In later years, children pestered her for things which she didn't stock and time left her shop looking neglected and unoccupied, so that parcels and letters sent to her by her brother, were returned 'unknown'.

Around the middle of this century, Mr Boys returned to Wadhurst, to live with his sister. After her death, two years later, he passed to the church, through Mr Charles Bocking, the parish magazines which she had collected over the many years. They were now to help form an almost unbroken run of them from 1893, when the magazine had been founded by the Rev. W. Wace, a son of the Rev. R.H. Wace, of Hill House. The Rev. W. Wace, a missionary, was on furlough and acted as locum tenens for Dr Codrington (Vicar of Wadhurst from 1887 to 1893), who was revisiting the Melanesian Islands, where he had been a missionary.

231

33. Mr Charles Bocking, on his retirement as organist in 1886, continued work in the parish as Superintendent of the Sunday school, and also as organist on the harmonium at the Iron Church in Woods Green, where, occasionally, he also took the services.

In 1898, the Iron Church was re-erected on a site at Faircrouch, near the railway station, where it continued to be used for church services, (with its own choir), and also for other activities. It fell into disuse and was sold in 1958.

34. During his years of inspection at the Wadhurst Schools, almost invariably, Mr Blight showed himself as a wise and thoughtful person. At this time, although 'repetition' was used as a 'grade heading', Mr Blight appears very much opposed to 'dry, mechanical learning'. In 1873, he described the religious teaching in the girls' school as being 'too dry' and that the facts of the Bible were being taught as 'something quite apart from human nature'.

In the boys' school, Mr Blight appeared dismayed that 'facts seemed to be regarded as the only things necessary' and expressed the opinion that 'every narrative should be the basis of a living lesson'. On another occasion, he said, 'Facts should be clad with the living flesh of typical moral and practical teaching.'

Later, Mr Blight suggests that 'greater attention to fundamental Truths' should be given, 'rather than to suppose that children have an intuitive knowledge of them'.

In the infant school, when he expressed the opinion to Miss Page that a more systematic repetition of the Catechism was necessary, he qualified it immediately with the reason: it was to be 'for the help of the children when ... older'.

35. The church, too, was not neglected. In 1858, it was restored, re-pewed, redecorated and the old galleries removed. At Mr Foley's own expense, it would appear, organs had been installed: in about 1848, a barrel organ; in 1858, a replacement, with auxilliary keyboard and in

1866, a 'converted' barrel organ, with keyboard and pedals.

Earlier, in 1849, the church records show:

Two stoves were placed in Wadhurst Church by the Rev. John Foley, lighted for the first time on Sunday, Feb. 4th. This is the first time of stoves used in that church.

Nov. 15. The church was lighted for the first time.

In 1943, in a letter to the vicar, Mrs Craig, niece of Mr F. Austen of Cousely Wood, wrote that John Foley preached: 'Do as I say and not what I do.' And went on to say what she considered as his besetting problem.

Another intriguing glimpse of Mr Foley is to be found, perhaps, in the following:

During the lifetime of Mr Foley, Mr C.W. Ashby's daughter Marie, who married the headmaster's son, Henry Bocking, wrote the name 'Mr Foley' in her Prayer Book, against the entry 'Isaiah Chapter 48 verse 18.' This verse reads:

O that thou hadst hearkened to my commandment! then had thy peace been as a river, and thy righteousness as the waves of the sea.

The Prayer Book was once the property of her aunt, Frances Amelia Ashby, who was born in 1843 and was the sister of Charles.

36. *The Training of Teachers – St Mark's College, Chelsea*

Each candidate admitted to the College pays a fee of £17.10.0d . . .

He may and should remain at the College for two years, during which time his only expense will be for clothing, and books furnished at half-price.

The Freshman is assigned a dormitory, about nine feet long, by five broad.

233

It contains a chair, an iron bedstead with bedding, a wash-hand stand, and a looking glass. The lighting and heating of these rooms is done from the corridor.

The rooms are looked after by female servants during lecture hours.

The first year student rises in time to attend a divinity lecture at seven o'clock. At ten minutes to eight he goes to chapel, at a quarter-past eight he gets fifteen minutes for breakfast, at nine he has more divinity; at a quarter to ten he proceeds to geography. From eleven to one o'clock the student does private study. At one he dines; then he amuses himself as he chooses till three; at three he commences drawing; and at four he is offered Music. St. Mark's is a very musical college. At five tea comes, succeeded at six by grammar. From seven to nine, private study. Supper at nine; chapel at quarter-past nine; then study till half-past ten; and so to bed.

The lectures are informal and the kindly Professors succeed to no small intent in making every hour interesting and pleasant...

Besides having nearly the whole of Sunday to himself, each man has two complete half-holidays in the week...

The student should be able to pass the Government's annual inspection in reading, penmanship, school management, grammar and composition, geography and history, mathematics, economy, music and drawing, together with one language, nearly always French and one science subject.

Of all these subjects, the one that it should chiefly concern a Training College to teach should be school management ... but the many kinds of instruction the Code requires at its hands do not allow this instruction to be nearly sufficient.

(From *Schoolmasters at School* – an unsigned press commentary on the Annual 'Elementary Teachers of England and Wales Conference at Norwich in 1885)

Retraining of teachers

David Blunkett, the shadow education secretary, will this week announce plans for a drive to improve the reading levels of school-children, with a scheme to retrain primary teachers and set up summer schools for those pupils whose skills are falling behind.

The *Sunday Telegraph*, 23 February 1997

37. *The Pupil-teacher*

> For four weary years has the ordinary pupil-teacher to wait before he is allowed to enter ... college ... he apprentices himself to the craft at the age of fourteen, and begins to do double duty, as learner and as teacher, under the eye of some qualified elementary master. A dreary lot is his as a rule. He is like a pitcher from which and into which at the same time water is being poured. His immature brain often becomes muddled, his energies are over-taxed, the joy of living dies out of him ... before he is allowed to face the examination [to enter college] the candidate is put through the doctor's hands ... one out of every ten is rejected as unfit to go further.

From 'Schoolmasters at School', an unsigned press commentary on the Annual Elementary Teachers of England and Wales Conference at Norwich in 1885.

The Schoolmistress

> A good deal of cold water has been thrown upon the suggestion that ladies might adopt the profession of elementary school teachers ... there are women of

235

good birth who are compelled by circumstances to get their own living, and, supposing these to have gone through the necessary training, we cannot see why they, too, should not be eligible as teachers. Perhaps the least encouraging feature in the scholastic life is the isolation to which a rural schoolmistress is sometimes condemned. Her superior education places her somewhat aloof from the villagers, while the absence of a higher social element has kept the status of the teachers lower than it ought to be ranked. Given a vocation for teaching, and a readiness to take the rough with the smooth, we believe that "Our Daughters" could do very much worse for themselves.

From the *Church Times*, 27 September 1895. Reprinted 29 September 1995.

38. Tonic sol-fa is a system for singing music by sight by means of syllables applied to each degree of the eight-note scale: doh ray me fah soh la te doh. Devised by Miss Sarah Ann Glover of Norwich (1785–1867), it was later adapted and improved by the Rev. John Curwen. It gained acceptance into many schools and by the end of the nineteenth century, tonic sol-fa festivals were being held in the Crystal Palace and elsewhere.

In more recent years, singing has taken a far less central place in school music-making and tonic sol-fa, perhaps almost universally discarded. In 1992, however, its continued use in South Africa was reported in the journal of the Royal School of Church Music.

39. Mr H.G. Wallis was remembered for his squeaking boots and prolonged 'Amens', by which the Twitten, where he lived, became known as 'Amen Alley'. Mr Wallis built the wall round The Lodge and is reputed to have laid 1,000 bricks before breakfast. In 1894, he was succeeded by Mary Ann's brother, Sam. (baptised in October 1854), who also ran a choir, The Glee Singers, and until alcoholism overtook him, was a temperance worker.

In turn, Sam. Wallis was succeeded by his son, also called Sam. (S.T. Wallis), who was born in 1881, and worked as a monumental mason and part-time assessor. Sam. was a member of the church choir, the captain of the bell ringers, played the cornet, played in the Wadhurst cricket and football teams and was in constant demand as the magic lantern operator. His wife, Mabel, claimed that he was the first person in Wadhurst to build a wireless set. Mabel, also, was well-known as a singer and a member of the church choir and of the choral society.

Sam. Wallis died in 1934, shortly before he was due to move to Battle as a full-time assessor. He was remembered as having one of the finest of bass voices and his memorial inscription in the choir stalls records that 'His singing was an inspiration.' Mr Mabbett, a professional musician, who sometimes conducted and trained Wadhurst and other choirs, described it in these terms, when he re-visited Wadhurst some 20 years later.

40. Mr Harry Watts continued a lifelong member of the church and was still attending services when he was in his nineties. Mr Watts had been a bricklayer and worked for Lord Camden of Bayham, Sir George Barham of Snape and for Piper's, the builders, of Wadhurst. In 1973, Mr Watts entered Furze House, Flimwell, once the Union Workhouse, but then an old people's home. (This gracious building was pulled down in 1979, to provide room for a housing estate). Mr Watts said that his grandmother had nursed the Foley babies, who died in the 1850s, and that his mother had been cook to the Wace family at Hill House.

Mr Maurice Watts (1880–1958) was Harry's cousin and later, owned a gentlemen's outfitters in Wadhurst. He was active in several village organisations and a member of the church choir until his death. There is a memorial inscription in the choir stalls.

41. Mr Williams courted Miss Tully, who sang in the church choir and whose father kept the Queen's Head. Mr

Williams lodged with Mr Cropley, saddler to Mr Boys's father-in-law, at the house adjoining Twitten Cottage. The Queen's Head was destroyed by an RAF plane which crashed on the village in 1956.

42. On Wednesday, 8 April 1896, following the installation of the new organ, the church was almost filled for the dedication service, at which Mr Pearse played, with 'great taste', Mendelssohn's *War March of the Priests*, and *Andante Pastorale*, by W.H. Richmond.

It is possible that the choir was first robed at this time and moved to the chancel from the cross-aisle, where it had previously sat, dressed in ordinary clothes.

At the end of the nineteenth century, a refurbishment of the chancel occurred, which included a new reredos, Holy Table and a panelling of the ceiling. In 1905, the organ was divided and placed on the chancel walls, with a detached console below. In 1932, the organ was rebuilt by Norman and Beard, mainly at the expense of Colonel Cheale, and placed above the tower arch. The console remained detached, in the chancel.

Mr Pearse also gave an organ recital on Ascension Day 1896, at which he played 'with great taste and expression', Handel's *Largo*, Cowan's *Better Land* and Haydn's *Gloria in Excelsis*. The following month, July, the parish magazine recorded another recital, which included Handel's 'He shall feed', Rimbault's *Silver Trumpet*, and Sullivan's *Lost Chord*. Earlier in the year, a concert was given to raise money for the organ fund. Items included vocal and piano solos and glees by the choir. Mr Pearse was among the soloists.

43. The Reverend George Gavin MacLean was born in 1836 and educated at Wadham College, Oxford. In 1907, he retired from Wadhurst to live in Rusthall, Tunbridge Wells, and then to Heathfield. At each of these places, Mr MacLean helped with the Church services. He died in 1918 and was buried at Nutley, Sussex, where he had been Vicar from 1872 to 1883, and in which parish he had been married.

44. *Education into the Next Century: Education Department Pamphlet, 1992*

At present most schools are maintained by local authorities.

The Government strongly believes that grant-maintained or GM status is best for state schools.

GM schools remain within the state system and must provide a free education. But they govern themselves: They run their own affairs and decide how to spend the money available to them ... It can, of course, buy LEA services if it thinks they are of good value...

There will be a new national body – the Funding Agency for Schools.

As the number of GM schools in any LEA area grows, the Funding Agency for Schools will share with the LEA the duty to make sure that there are enough school places ... until 75% of pupils are in GM schools. From that point ... the whole duty will transfer to the Agency.

...LEAs will become mainly providers of services to schools...

All schools must teach all the subjects of the National Curriculum ... also ... develop their own interests ... the Government is keen to develop a network of Technical Schools...

45. 1. a) The last assistant overseer was Harry Pitt, son of Jabez Pitt, the previous assistant overseer.

b) The assessors and collectors had the duty of setting and collecting the various rates and taxes, including those of property, land, house and income, as well as those for the church and poor.

c) Constables: the last appointed, in 1872, included Barnes Usherwood, George Luck, Thomas Boorman, James Humphrey, William Ashby, Benjamin Boots, Thomas Rose, George Gallup,

239

Blacksmith of Best Beech. A professional force followed.

d) Nuisance Removal Committee: On 6 March 1856, a committee was 'duly elected'. It consisted of 12 members and included George Courthope, Esq., E. Watson Smyth, Esq., Mr Barton, Mr Joseph Newington, Mr James Benge, Mr H. Dixon, Mr Mercer, Mr Thomas Weiman, Rev. R.H. Wace, Mr MacDonald, Mr Brissenden and Mr I.G. Weiman. At a meeting on 15 March, the Rev. John Foley replaced Mr Newington and Mr Dixon and Mr Mercer were redesignated 'Esq.'

2. The gradual erosion of the powers of the Parish Vestry: The first of these was in the Poor Law Act of 1834, which set up commissioners and boards of guardians, to serve a union of parishes with its own workhouse to whom control of the Poor Rate passed.

46. The football club was founded in 1884. The parish magazine for January 1905 reported an entertainment given in aid of club funds, for there was a 'considerable sum' owing to the treasurer. 'Entertainments' of various kinds were frequently staged in aid of the funds of the various village activities.

Cricket was first mentioned in 1758, by the diarist, Walter Gale of Mayfield, when Wadhurst played Mayfield and won. When Wadhurst played Ticehurst 'away', according to Mr Boys, free fights broke out and it was a hard job to get home.

Cycles: were said to have been first supplied in Wadhurst, by Newington's the clock makers, but gradually Mr Gadd built up a business in the centre of the village, later to deal in cars and to be known for long as Gadd's Garage. In the early days, as many as 20 cyclists would be seen gathered together outside the shop. As early as 1893, a Cycling Sports Day was held. The parish magazine for 1897 recorded 'a most successful' event, although the day was windy and the programme so long that it was almost dark before it was finished. The

Wadhurst Band enlivened the proceedings with some 'very agreeable music'. By 1904, attendance had fallen, so that, in 1906, in order to draw the crowds, horse driving and jumping was introduced.

Flower Show: This was held at the Castle, or sometimes at South Park (now Wadhurst College), with games, town band and orchestra, when the village would be 'strangely emptied'. By 1904, however, attendance had fallen, money was owed to the treasurer and so it was decided to hold the show in the Market Hall, with sports and other activities in the neighbouring field. By 1907, an improved attendance was reported.

47. The parish magazine for April 1904 reported the 'end of session', when the Misses Watson, assisted by Mr and Mrs Williams and the Misses MacLean, provided a 'pleasant evening's entertainment'. The article expressed the hope that:

> Those who joined the Night School may not only have kept up with a good deal that they had previously learnt, but may have made advance in subjects beyond the ordinary range of school subjects.

48. It would appear that concerts consisting of vocal and instrumental music, penny readings and plays, timed to coincide with the full moon, were frequent. Caroline, Mary and Charles, the three surviving Foley children, took part in them.

Caroline married Dr Rhys Davids and had two daughters, Vivien and Nesta, and one son, Arthur, who was killed in the Great War. Nesta, in a letter to the writer, said of her mother, 'I remember her lovely playing from when I was a child.'

Vivien also wrote of the accomplished playing of both her mother and her Aunt Mary, and how her mother had told her that all three children took part in village concerts and would, for fun, perform music calculated to go above the heads of their audience.

Both Caroline and Mary were also organists, worked with the choir and were deeply interested in the music of their father's parish.

After her father's death, in 1886, Mary moved away from Wadhurst. She died in 1922 and her ashes were interred in her parents' grave in Wadhurst churchyard.

Caroline was interested in Wadhurst's history and her work survived to form the basis of Wace's *Story of Wadhurst*. By the time of her marriage, in 1894, Caroline had gained a Doctorate of Literature. Her husband was a professor of Buddhist and Pali literature, with whom Caroline collaborated in his work. She died in 1942, aged 84.

49. The Choral Association's first concert was given in the girls' schoolroom, where it was assisted by the Orchestral Society. The programme included a sacred oratorio, *Christ and his Soldiers*, by Farmer, in which the soloists were Miss E. Watson of Uplands and Miss Fanny Luck, and a play, *Freezing a Mother-in-law*. Another concert, but again referred to as 'the first', took place the following year, now under the direction of Marsh S. Goodall, who had succeeded Mr Pearse.

50. Mr Charlie Tomsett, Wadhurst's bandmaster just after the Great War, claimed that the orchestra was founded in the year 'dot' and years before the formation of the band. It was also claimed to have been formed by Mr Rigg, or by Mr Harry Newington. Mr Harry Newington, assisted in the family clockmaking business at the shop under the arch by the Old Vicarage. He also taught the violin and was a member of the Orchestral Society. He was one of eight children: three sisters played the piano and, between them, the boys played the violin, clarinet and the piccolo/flute.

51. The church choir also had its share of outings and treats. In 1893 an outing to Eastbourne for the adult members of the parish and Cousely Wood church choirs took place, with brilliant weather and much time spent in and out of the water.

In the following year, the parish magazine complained:

> The amount collected for the Choir Fund will not go
> far towards providing entertainment for the members
> of the Choir ... it is only reasonable that some
> return should be made by the congregation for the
> services of a voluntary choir...

Other outings, later with the Mission Church Choir,
included trips to such places as Brighton, Crystal Palace
and London. In 1906, 40 members of the two choirs
sailed up the River Thames on a steamer, visited the
Houses of Parliament, then went on to Earls Court, with
its Austrian Exhibition, bird display, water-chutes and
the like. One visit to Brighton included a cricket match,
when Kent played Essex.

The Mission Church at Faircrouch appears to have
had a good, energetic choir of men and boys at this time,
under the direction of Mrs Gordon, who died in 1914.
The Mission Church fell into disuse, was sold and
removed in c1958.

52. In 1910, the choir stalls were moved a little further back
in order to reveal more satisfactorily the iron ledgers
between them. The pulpit was also moved a few feet
nearer the north transept, to show more clearly the
chancel arch. Oak steps replaced the concrete ones to the
pulpit. In the same year, Mr G.J. Courthope presented a
printed list of vicars and two carved prayer desks for use
in the chancel.

53. This meeting was started by Mrs Selby, who came to live
at Dewhurst in 1895, and was held in her billiard room.
She was also instrumental in starting Sunday services in
this area near Wadhurst Station. Until the Mission
Church was moved from Woods Green, they were held in
a cottage near the station. Mrs Selby resigned through ill
health in 1910 and died in 1920, aged 59.

54. The Mothers' Union was founded by Mary Elizabeth
Sumner, in Old Alresford, Hampshire. It was to 'uphold

the sanctity of marriage' and also to unite mothers, to enable them not only to lead a Christian life themselves, but also to train their children to do likewise. Annual Festival Services were held on Lady Day, with Holy Communion at 8.00 a.m., and a special service, with Litany, at 2.30 p.m. In 1908, in spite of the bad weather, there was a large congregation to listen, 'with deep attention', to the vicar's address on 'The Influence of the Home'.

55. The Church of England Men's Society was founded in 1899, under the auspices of Bishops Lang and Winnington-Ingram, 'In the power of the Holy Spirit, to pray to God every day, to be a faithful communicant and by active witness, fellowship and service, to help forward the Kingdom of Christ'. The society's emphasis was on voluntary service in the church.

56. *Bible Society*: the Wadhurst branch received a visiting speaker from the society each year. In 1908, a new secretary, Miss Shepheard Walwyn, was appointed to the position at a drawing room meeting of the society, held at Dewhurst, the home of Mr and Mrs Whitty. A lantern lecture in the Market Hall soon followed. It was given by the Eastern Counties Organising Secretary of the parent society, to an audience of 300 people. In the following year, a concert was given by the 'Edgehill Girls' (a private school), in aid of the 'Funds of the Bible Society'.
Melanesian Mission: A previous vicar, the Rev. Dr Codrington, had been a missionary for this society. On 11 August 1907, he returned to preach to a large congregation, when 'his personal experiences gave exceptional weight to his advocation for the Mission'. £10 3s was collected. A previous collection, in October 1901, had raised £16 11s 7d.
Mission to Central Africa: in May 1901, an appeal raised £9.
Mission to Seamen: The response to appeals appears to have depended on the speaker sent. In 1904, £4 3s 6d was raised, but in 1908, £18 13s 2d.

National Society for Schools: In 1905, the organising secretary preached, but only £2 3s 9d was given. The parish magazine said that bad weather had kept people away, but, even so, it was a poor response to a society which had helped with a grant. In 1828, £7 18s 6d was given to the society. (In the same year, £10 16s 6d was given for the Relief of the Manufacturing Poor.)

57. During the early years of the twentieth century, collections at these services ranged from £2 to £14, with, perhaps, an average of £4 to £5 a month. In 1910, however, only £20 7s 9d was collected for the Poor Fund. Special Objects raised £135 11s 10d and General Expenses, £181 14s 9d.

On Christmas Day 1785, with 31 communicants, 15s 6d was collected. On Easter Day 1793, with 53 communicants, £1 7s.

In 1784, from four communions, £3 4s 6d was collected and distributed among 49 people.

58. The parish magazine for July 1908 records a Girls' Friendly Society festival held at Wadhurst Hall and tells of the long procession of brakes and waggonettes which brought the members: of the untiring efforts of Mrs Drew, the 'scrumptious tea' in the riding school and the walk and scramble through the gardens and fields to the shores of the lake.

In the perhaps mistaken idea that he was descended from the noble Norman family of Drogo, which settled in Devon, Mr Drew, in 1910, bought land in Drewsteignton, added 'e' to his name, to conform with local spelling, and with Edwin Lutyens as architect, began to build a great castle on the bluff overlooking the River Teign.

The 1914–18 War intervened, in which Mr Drewe's eldest son, Adrian, was killed, and the building, to a modified plan, was not completed until 1930. Mr Drewe died in the following year. The property is now National Trust and open to visitors.

Mr Drewe's furniture was removed from Wadhurst

245

Hall in 1927, the house sold in the following year, and demolished in 1948.

59. The old people of the village were remembered as well and given a 'substantial tea, a newly minted coin and a few kindly words.' Sir George Barham's 'few kindly words' included a reminder that, as well as memories, they had 'a future to look forward to, a better one than any earthly happiness could offer'.

George Barham, born in 1836, followed in his father's footsteps as a London dairyman, but with pasture-land fast disappearing into building-land, he organised fast train delivery of milk from more distant areas. To help with its transport, he devised the first conical milk churn and methods of chilling. With the growth of the business, the adoption of modern methods and a prime concern for hygiene, George Barham's advice on the industry was sought, not only in England, but also from other parts of the world.

At the end of the century, in order to cater for the ever-growing number of London office workers, his Express Dairy also set up a chain of teashops there. George Barham had five sons, three of whom died in infancy. Both the eldest son, Titus (who suffered from a congenital malformation of the spine), and the youngest son, Arthur, helped in the business and succeeded their father on his death in 1913.

(From *Express Story*, 1864–1964, published by the Express Dairy Company, 1964.)

60. Regulations for secondary schools were issued in the same year (1904). Earlier, in 1894–95, the Bryce Commission had met to 'consider what are the best methods of establishing a well organised system of Secondary Education in England'. The 1902 Education Act empowered LEAs to do this.

The regulations of 1904 defined a 'secondary school' as a

Day or Boarding School offering to each of its scholars, up to and beyond the age of 16, a general education, physical, mental and moral, giving through a complete graded course of instruction, of wider scope and more advanced degree than that given in Elementary Schools.

The course was to last not less than four years, to include English subjects, at least one language, other than English, mathematics, science and drawing. Provision was to be made for manual training and physical exercises. Music was not mentioned, but Latin could be included if it were not to the disadvantage of the school.

In 1907, a scholarship system for entry to these schools was adopted, in order to facilitate secondary education for children from elementary schools. All grant-aided schools were to admit not less than 25 per cent of its children who had been at least two years in an elementary school. The Scholarship Examination became a competitive rather than a qualifying examination and created divisions which, in some places, have continued to the present.

61. Mr Freeland first visited in 1907, when the parish magazine commented:

Mr. Freeland having come from the North of England, has necessarily become accustomed to children who in some respects differ a great deal from those in Sussex, so that he will be better able to form a judgement as to the work of the schools on future visits than on this first occasion.

62. Mr C.W. Ashby was married twice. His first wife was Miss Tomsett, of Scragoak. Marie Beatrice Ann, born in 1875, was a daughter of this marriage. Marie was the mother of Mr Charles Bocking, Manager of Watson's, the estate agents. Mr Ashby's second wife was Miss Cole. Dorothy, later to become Mrs D. Fisher-Barham, was a daughter of this marriage. Dorothy was thus Marie's

half-sister and, like her, was involved in musical activities. Dorothy's own first lessons were from Miss Howard (sister of Mr Howard, a local taylor), who had a small school in Church Street, but later she attended the Royal Academy of Music Centre in Tunbridge Wells. From 1919 to 1929, she taught the piano in Wadhurst. Some of her pupils, she felt, had lessons because their parents thought it was the correct thing to do.

63. Mr George Courthope of Whiligh, who was born in 1877, was elected MP for Rye at this election, which was the start of his political career. He was created a baronet in 1925 and a peer in 1945. On his death, in 1955, Whiligh passed to his daughters, Beryl and Daphne. In 1975, Miss Daphne Courthope paid for work to be done on the church organ as a memorial to members of her family. Miss Courthope died in 1980, after a lifetime of service to the community, particularly in the realm of education.

64. The Old Age Pension Act, passed in 1908, came into force in this year, 1909. The parish magazine for October 1908 published some of its provisions, which included:

> The payment of 5s a week to those 70 and over.
> But subject to:
> The deduction of 1s for each 1s received from other income over 8s.
>
> The loss of pension rights for those who had habitually failed to work and also those who
>
> Between the ages of 50 to 60, had failed to make provision for old age through membership of a Friendly Society, etc.,
>
> Or were in receipt of Poor Relief, or Insane.

65. In January 1902, the vicar wrote: 'The whole of the year [has] been overshadowed by the long protracted war in South Africa.'

In the following June, he was able to record:

good news has happily been received that the sad and wearisome struggle is at an end [let] bitterness and animosities be forgotten ... now live together in true Christian brotherhood.

On 8 June 1902, a Peace Service was held, for which the church was 'beautifully decorated'.

66. Froebel: (1782–1852), believed that a child's observation should be combined with free expression. He felt that the school should encourage a natural development of the children, where the teacher is as though the gardener and the children, the plants.

A Froebel Society was founded in 1874, with its influence spreading, first through the private sector, and then slowly into the public elementary schools. Charles Dickens was among those who recommended its ideas, but warned against the mechanical application of its methods.

Froebel's ideas stemmed from the work of Pestalozzi (1746–1827), a Swiss educationalist who believed that 'nature's march of development' should be encouraged: that education must develop the whole person, 'The head, the hand and the heart', through a guided self-activity and intuition.

67. Infants' Lessons

In 1902, Charlotte Page listed her topics as:

Things we	Eat including:	Apples, Coffee, etc.
	Wear	Pinafore, Straw Hat, Silk Scarf, etc.
	Use	Ink, Soap, etc.
Then:	Animals	Dog, Whale, etc.
	Insects	Wasps, etc.
	Fish	Salmon, etc.
	Birds	Sparrows, Ducks, etc.
	Reptiles	Frogs, Spiders, etc.
	Miscellaneous	Country Walk in Summer, Spring, Storms, Post Office, etc.

Later, the headings were changed to the seasons of the year – spring, summer, autumn, winter.

In 1904, she listed Conversation Lessons, which included:

Preparation for School	The Fire, the Kettle, etc.
Things seen on the way to school	Through the Town, the Fields and Woods.
Things used in School	For Writing, Needlework, etc.
The Dwellings of People	In our Country, Hot Countries, etc.
Miscellaneous	Helping Mother, Truthfulness, etc.

In 1907, Miss Page listed 'A Course of Oral lessons' for the year, which included: leaves, lambs, skylarks, etc.

Also another list of Conversation Lessons:

Events in the daily life at home and at school, Visits to other places, etc.

Other lessons included: Simple Historical Tales, Simple Talks about things that are conducive to good health, Fresh Air, etc. On 10 April 1907, Miss Page attended 'a Congress Meeting at Tunbridge Wells relative to the introduction of Temperance Teaching and Hygiene in School'.

On 3 March 1908, Miss Page 'Sent home Alice Bassett as I found her in a very dirty condition of vermin in her underclothing.' Six days later, this happened again, but on 19 March, Alice returned in a much cleaner condition.

68. Mrs Boorman had taught at the school as Miss Henge, and later married a dairy farmer, Mr H. Boorman. They had two sons in the school, one of whom was deaf. Miss Page resisted the inspector's suggestion that the boy should not be in the school, but later, an entry appears

in her log-book which records her visit to the Institution for the Deaf and Dumb, at Brighton, 'as a little scholar here will shortly enter there'. Later, Mr Boorman was gored to death by a bull and many years later, in 1958, his deaf and dumb son was killed by a tractor turning over on him.

69. Woods Green School was a private school run by a Plymouth Brethren, Mrs Thomas of Buckling Hill House. The headmaster, Mr Fred. Page, appointed in 1896, had two female assistants, one of whom was his daughter. Mr Page also conducted the Sunday services.

The children of the Thomas's own workmen could attend free, but other children, if found suitable, could attend on payment of 2s 6d a quarter.

An old pupil, Mr Thunder, who, after the 1939–45 War, kept the Cousely Wood Post Office adjoining the Baptist Church, said that it was a good, orderly school of about 50 children, who 'weren't allowed to be as wild as up at the national'.

Mr Thunder said that his house had been built at the time of the Napoleonic Wars by his maternal grandfather, Mr Kemp, a Baptist. The Baptists held their meetings in the carpenter's shop adjoining the house, but later, the shop was rebuilt as a church.

The Baptists in Wadhurst
This place was once inhabited by a great number of Baptists, who, in the reign of Charles the Second and successors of the Stuart race, were glad to fly to such wild and solitary places that they might un-noticed perform their religious duties according to the dictates of their own consciences...

From *The History of Tunbridge Wells* by Thomas Benge Burr, 1766.

70. Sir George Barham died in November 1913. The choir stalls were completed by the end of the following year. They were carved by Rosier of Frant, who 'signed' them with two caterpillars, one on the Vicar's stall, the other

on the Cantoris choir stalls. The joinery was carried out by Mr Bond (d.1968), who was also responsible for the work in the Children's Corner and on the Holy Table. The Holy Table, which was designed by Mr Bidlake, a church architect, resident in the parish, was also carved by Mr Rosier from Whiligh Oak, and was placed in the Sanctuary in 1926.

71. According to an advertisement in the parish magazine for 1908, the bakery had been established for over a century. During that time, it had provided bread for the Barham Charity and, more recently, had catered for church functions and sometimes provided a meeting place for them.

Mr Carpenter, the owner, had, in 1871, been one of Miss Page's first pupils at the Wadhurst Infant School. Mr Carpenter was described as 'a bit of a lad', and his name is to be found inscribed on a back pew of the church, where the lads of the village were accustomed to sit during services. He died in 1945.

Standards for Infants and Lower Juniors

1862

First Standard Arithmetic: To form figures up to 20 from dictation, on blackboard or slate; name at sight figures up to 20; add and subtract figures up to 10, orally, from examples on the blackboard.

Standard Two:

Reading: One of the narratives next in order after monosyllables in an elementary reading book in use in the School.

Writing: Copy in manuscript characters a line of print.

Arithmetic: A sum in simple addition or subtraction and the multiplication table.

Standard Three:

Reading: A short paragraph from an elementary reading book in use in the School.

Writing: A sentence from the same paragraph slowly read one and then dictated in single words.

Arithmetic: A sum in any simple rule as far as short division (inclusive).

1992 (Typical nine-year-old)

Reading and Writing: Read aloud from familiar stories fluently and with appropriate expression.
Produce independent pieces of writing using complete sentences, mainly with capital letters and full stops.

Mathematics: Read, write and order numbers to at least a 1,000. Know and use multiplication tables up to 5 × 5.

Science: Record experimental findings. Be able to describe the main stages in the human life cycle. Know that temperature is a measure of how hot (or cold), things are.

Technology: Apply knowledge and skills to select ideas for different parts of their design. Use a range of hand tools and equipment with some accuracy and quality. Collect information and enter it into a data-base.

(From Department of Education and Science pamphlet, 1992, *What is your child doing at School?*)

INDEX

256

257

258

260

261

262

263

270

272

273

INDEX, PEOPLE

Courthope, Mrs., 31, 32
Courthope, George John, d.1910, son of George Campion, 146, 149, 163
Courthope, George L., son of George John, 149, 193, 204, 205
Courthope, Miss Beryl, dau. of George L., 166, 248
Courthope, Miss Daphne, dau. of George L., 166, 248
Courthope, William, Somerset Herald, 18, 32, 216, 219, 222
Courthope, Mrs. W., 131, 136, 173, 188
Courthope, F.W., 193
Craig, Mrs., 232
Crispin, Miss, 136
Cromwell, Thomas, 16c., 221
Cropley, Mr., saddler, 238
Cross, Lord, Commission of 1886, 61, 67, 68, 69, 71
Cubborn, Miss, District Nurse, 101, 102
Curwen, Rev. John, Tonic Sol-fa, 236

Daniels, Mr., Scripture Reader, 42, 43, 55, 62
Dann, John, 10
Davies, Ben., singer, 153
Davies, Rev. C.C., Curate, 145
Debenham, Miss, 91
Dengate, Mr., teacher and organist, 75, 77, 78
Denyer, Master J.S., 145
Dickens, Charles, 249
Disraeli, 12
Dix, Robert, 197
Dixon, Mr., of Frankham, 31
Dixon, Mr. H., 240
Drew(e), Julius, of Wadhurst Hall, 85, 93, 96, 105, 146, 185, 193, 245
Drew(e), Mrs., wife, 96, 155, 156

Drew(e), Adrian, son of above, 151, 156, 199, 205, 245
Dunstan, Dr., 195

Easter, Miss Eva F., later, Mrs. Wilkinson-Cole, monitor, then teacher, 72, 142, 143, 147, 148, 169
Eastland, Elizabeth, 18th Cent., 228
Edward I, King, 1
Edwards, Mr. H., 161
Edwards, Mrs., 135
Egglestone, Mr., teacher, 26
Egles, George, 216
Ellery, Miss, teacher, 121–123
Elliot, George, brass baritone, 92
Ellis, Vivian, 123

Fairbrother, Walter, Bandmaster, 92
Farrant, Nurse, 178
Fazan, Dr., 88
Fazan, Mrs., 159
Fennell, Frederic and Elizabeth, teachers, 21–24
Ferris, Mr., Curate, 146
Fillery, Edwin, 175
Finch, Dr., 178
Fisher-Barham, Mrs. Dorothy, née Ashby, 116, 247–8
Foley, Rev. John, Vicar of Wadhurst, 1846–1886, 26, 31, 32, 40, 48, 50, 55, 56, 61, 62, 66, 67, 71, 177, 210, 225, 232, 240
Foley, Mrs. Caroline, wife, 40, 43, 55, 224, 225
Foley, Miss Caroline, dau., later, Mrs. Rhys Davids, 42, 43, 48, 241, 242
Foley, Miss Mary Celia, dau. of John Foley, 43, 66, 241, 242
Foley, Charles, son of John Foley, 43, 241
Fooks, Mrs., of Hill House, 13

277

Jeffery, Richard, 18th Cent. teacher, 9

Johnson, Rev. E.C., Curate, 158

Kay-Shuttleworth, Sir James, Educationalist, 23, 28, 29, 218, 225
Kekewich, Sir George, Secretary, Education Dept., 69
Kemp, Mr., Baptist, 251
Kemsett, Miss, teacher, 66
King, Miss Ellen Mary, (Mrs. Ballard, 1878), Headmistress, 62, 63, 64
  See also Mrs. Ballard
King, Thomas, prize-fighter, 231
Kirby, Miss, 157
Kirke, Rev. A., Curate, 73
Kitchen, Miss, 188
Kitchenham, William, 1676, 3
Knight, Mr. 'Wiggie', teacher and organist, 79, 80, 89–91, 104, 145, 149, 153, 155, 163, 177, 183, 187–189, 201, 203, 205, 208
Knott, Rev. F., Headmaster, 138

Lakin, Dr., 194, 195
Lancaster, Joseph, Quaker, Educationalist, 16
Lane Andrews, Mr. J.C., Churchwarden, Solicitor, 87, 109, 146, 161, 175, 181, 185, 198, 204
Larcombe, Frederick, Headmaster, 59, 75–78, 88, 104–108, 110, 111, 116, 117, 123, 144, 155, 162, 182, 183, 185–199, 208
Larcombe, Mrs. M.A., née Wallis, wife of above, teacher, 104–108, 117, 186, 189, 191, 192, 199, 208
Larcombe, Gladys, daughter, teacher, 77, 198, 200
Larcombe, Marjorie, daughter, teacher, 77, 190, 191, 199, 208

Larcombe, Winnie, daughter, teacher, 77, 190
Larcombe, Reginald, son, 77, 199
Legas, John, Ironmaster, 4
Legas, Anne, niece, 4
Legas, Paul, nephew, 8, 10
Linger, Lord, Permanent Secretary to Treasury, 68
Linkstead, Margaret (Maggie), later, Mrs. Manktelow, teacher 125, 141, 173, 175, 178, 181, 182
Litchfield, Rev. A., Vicar of Wadhurst, 1783–1804, 6–10
Lloyd George, Politician, 85
Lomas, Miss May, later, Mrs. Horace Newington, 92, 187, 189, 190, 200
Lowe, Robert (Code of 1862), 35–36
Luck, Fred, prefect, 117
Luck, George, 239
Luck, Mr., local builder, 109
Luck, The Misses, 131, 136
Luck, Miss Fanny, 242
Luck, Mrs., cleaner, 24
Lutyens, Sir Edwin L., architect, 245

Mabb, Mr. E., dealer, teacher, etc., 9, 10
MacDonald, Mr., draper, grocer, 22, 240
MacLean, Rev. George, Vicar of Wadhurst, 1893–1907, 74, 80–83, 93, 105, 125, 126, 128, 146, 238
MacLean, The Misses, daughters, 74, 126, 128, 146, 241
Mabbett, Mr. and Mrs., 89, 237
Madge, Robert, choirboy, 216
Makepeace, Miss Louisa, teacher, 66
Malin, Miss, 13
Mandy, Ann, servant, 5

278

Manktelow, Mr. Harold, 182
Manktelow, Mrs. Margaret, wife,
182
See also, Linkstead, Margaret
Manktelow, Nancy, monitor and
pupil-teacher, 63–66
Mannering, Rev. E., Vicar of
Wadhurst, 1935–1946, 209
Manser, Mary, 5
Markwicke, Gregory, 1638, 2
Martin, Mr., Stationmaster, 204
Maryan, Jack, car accident, 1907,
122
Mayne, Miss, teacher, 71, 72, 142,
143
McCraw, Miss Mary, teacher, 147,
148
McKenna, Mr., President, Board of
Education, 86
McNaught, Dr., musician, 90
McNess, Miss, teacher, 31
Measures, Miss, 121
Mercer, Mr., 155, 203, 240
Message, Mr., 145
Milne, Miss, 101
Milward, Nurse, 162
Mitchener, Mr., Nuisance Inspector,
111
Moncreiff, Mr., Inspector, 56
Montessori, Doctor and
Educationalist, 140
Moon, Miss Bertha, 190
Morant, Robert, Secretary, Board
of Education, 112, 113
Moren, Mr., farmer, 8
More, Hannah, authoress and
educationalist, 7, 8
Morton, Mrs., 101

Newcastle, Duke of, Commission
and Report, 1858–1861, 34–36
Newington, Harry, clockmaker,
brother of Horace and Owen,
92, 149, 242
Newington, Horace, 92, 187, also

Newington and H. Newington,
145, 156, 166
Newington, John, of Tidebrook, 8,
10
Newington, John, 13, 219
Newington, Joseph, 240
Newington, Mrs. Kate, née Smith,
newsagent, 188
Newington, Owen, 91
Norbury, Mr. C.G., 151, 166, (and
Mrs. Norbury)
Norman and Beard, organ builders,
238

Old Goose, 217

Page, Miss Charlotte, Headmistress,
40–49, 52–54, 58–61, 76, 81,
106, 121, 124–126, 128, 130,
133–140, 157, 161, 171–177,
188, 190, 199, 233, 249, 250,
252
Page, Fred., Headmaster, 251
Parkhurst, Mary, monitor, 64
Parnum, Mr., Teacher of Music, 72
Parrott, Miss Ethel Kate, 189
Parry, Mrs. F.S., 97
Patey, Thomas, Letter to, 3
Pattenden, Edward, euphonium, 92
Pattenden, Ruth, monitor, 31
Pattenden, Thomas, Bb Bass, 92
Pearse, Augustine, teacher and
organist, 79, 89, 238, 242
Penkivil, Mr., surgeon, 25
Pestalozzi, 249
Piper, Charles, bandmaster, 92
Piper, William, J., drums, 149
Piper's, builders, 237
Pitt, Harry, Assistant Overseer, 239
Pitt, Jabez, Assist. Overseer, 239
Pitt, Jacob, 219
Player, Alfred, 13
Plumley, Nicholas, 216
Pratt, George, 10
Preece, Mr., teacher, 27

279

Wace, Maj. Gen. Richard, 159, 204
Waite, Miss, Private School, 92
Wallis, Samuel, 18th Cent., 10
Wallis, George, Parish Clerk, 76
Wallis, H.G., Parish Clerk, 76, 236
Wallis, Mary Ann, dau. of above,
    later, wife of Frederick
    Larcombe, 76, 104; See also,
    Larcombe
Wallis, Samuel, son of H.G. Wallis,
    (bap. 1854), Parish Clerk, 236–7
Wallis, Samuel, T., son of Samuel
    Wallis, b. 1881, Parish Clerk,
    singer, sportsman, stonemason,
    assessor, 10, 91, 138, 145, 149,
    155, 156, 158–160, 203, 204,
    206, 236, 237
Wallis, Mable, née Watts, wife of
    above, singer, 154, 162, 237
Wallis, Walter, drums, 91, 92
Walker, Mrs., 173, 178
Walsh, Rev. Walter, Inspector, 75,
    76, 78, 139
Walters, Hester, pupil-teacher, 55, 63
Walwyn, Miss Shepheard, 244
Ward, Mr. T., 35
Warner, Violet, pupil, 198
Waters, Mr., letter, 1844, 224
Watson, Mr. A.G., J.P., 87, 88, 91,
    110, 161, 162, 192, 210, 241
Watson, Mrs., wife of above, 88,
    96, 101, 128, 131, 133, 136
    (with dau.), 198, 241
Watson, The Misses, 88, 91, 131,
    178, 241
Watson, Miss, 100, 101, 128, 136, 162
Watson, Miss Alice, 200
Watson, Miss Amy, 162
Watson, Miss E., 100, 248
Watson, Miss Winnie, 137
Watson, Miss Hannah,
    Headmistress, 31, 43, 52–54,
    58, 59, 75, 76, 81, 121–124,
    171, 172, 184
Watson, Smyth; See Smyth

Watts, Edwin, tenor brass, 92
Watts, Harry, 77–80, 237
Watts, Maurice, outfitter, chorister,
    etc., 77, 91, 163, 166, 217, 237
Weiman, Mr. I.G., 240
Weiman, Mr. Thomas, 240
Wellman, J., prefect, 117
Wesley, John, Methodist, 7
West, Mr., of Maplehurst, 18
Wetherell, Miss, of Pashley Manor,
    97
Wignore, Miss, 136
Whitbread, Samuel, M.P., 1807, 10,
    16
White, Mary, letter, 18th Cent., 3
Whitty, Mr. and Mrs. of Dewhurst,
    152, 160, 162, 244
Whitty, Miss, 160, 161, 172
Wickens, Miss F., 89
Wickham, Harry, servant, 5
Wilkin, Mr. and Mrs., of Cousely
    Wood, 66, 73, 95, 115, 145,
    147, 164, 166, 169, 170
Wilkins, Dr., 158
Wilkinson-Cole, Mrs. Eva, née
    Easter, 72, 142, 143, 147, 148
    See also Easter, Miss Eva, F.
William of Whiligh, 13th Cent., 1
Williams, Mr., teacher and organist,
    77, 78, 237, 238
Williams, Mr. and Mrs., 241
Williams, Miss, lecturer, 198
Williams, Mr. J., Secretary and
    Treasurer of Poor Fund, 161,
    181
Winchester, Miss Ethel, teacher,
    174–176, 178, 180, 181
Winnington-Ingram, Bishop, 244
Wisdom, Gideon, butcher, 18, 219
Wisdom, Mrs. Harriet, wife of
    Gideon, 17–19
Worth, James, teacher, 79
Wyly, William of, 13th Cent., 1

Young, Mr. F., of Lewes, 198

282

INDEX, PLACES

284

285